AQUINAS ON HUMAN ACTION

Ralph McInerny

AQUINAS ON HUMAN ACTION

A Theory of Practice

The Catholic University of America Press
Washington, D.C.

The paper used in this publication meets the minimum
requirements of American National Standards for Information
Science—Permanence of Paper for Printed Library materials.
ANSI Z39.48-1984.
∞

LIBRARY OF CONGRESS CATALOGING-IN-PUBLICATION DATA
McInerny, Ralph M.
    Aquinas on human action : a theory of practice / by Ralph
McInerny.
        p.   cm.
    Includes bibliographical references and index.
    1. Thomas, Aquinas, Saint, 1225?–1274.   2. Human
acts—History of doctrines—Middle Ages, 600–1500.   3. Act
(Philosophy)   1. Title.
BJ255.T5M35   1992
170—dc20
90-27754
ISBN 0-8132-0746-0
ISBN pbk 0-8132-0761-4

For Dave and Lou Solomon

In operationibus enim et
passionibus humanis, in quibus
experientia plurimum valet,
magis movent exempla quam
verba.

[*Prima secundae* 34. 1]

Contents

Preface

This book sets before the reader the theory of moral action found in the writings of St. Thomas Aquinas, particularly in the *Summa theologiae*. The human act is the primary vehicle of moral goodness and badness. In Part One, I think through the fundamental texts in order to display the coherence of Thomas's doctrine as well as its philosophical elegance. It is, I think, important to see that the theory of action is the link between the discussion of the human good or ultimate end, on the one hand, and of natural law, on the other. The effort to appropriate the Thomistic analysis in the first part of the book avoids alternative interpretations, lest controversy take the narrative down byways and obscure the presentation. Part Two consists of a series of considerations of relevant alternative or complementary discussions, so that the reader can place the interpretation provided in Part One in the ongoing philosophical discussion of Thomas's doctrine. The different purposes of the two parts are evident in their different styles, the first being expository and analytic, the second adopting the voice of dialectic and, sometimes, polemic. It would have been arrogant to present an interpretation of Thomas that ignored the views of others, but to mix interpretation with polemics runs the risk of obscuring the basic doctrine. The division of the book into two parts is done in the hope of having the best of two worlds: a clean line of presentation as well as the acknowledgment of the contributions and divergent views of others.

Notre Dame
October 1990

PART ONE

1. Human Acts Are What Humans Do

OUR FIRST task is to ponder the true but amphibolous statement that human acts are what human agents do. First, because the domain of human actions is identical with the domain of moral acts, yet not every feature of our lives, not everything we do, is subject to moral appraisal. Best then to seek a little initial clarity on the subject of human action.

It is first also because the human way is to move from broad and comprehensive ideas and statements through progressively narrower ones until we achieve such precision as a subject matter allows. At least that is how Aristotle, and Thomas after him, describe the natural procedure of human inquiry. But are they right? Does the sorter of apples need a preliminary notion of apple in general in order to keep the Jonathans away from the Macintoshes? Who ever sorted an apple in general?

The general apple is not another type to be sorted but that of which the types are types. Our experience is of sorts of apples, indeed, of singular apples. The sorter might at first proceed in a way indistinguishable from separating apples from oranges, or fruit from nuts, or edibles from inedibles. Nonetheless, since he is not a machine or hypnotized and knows what he is doing, he knows what an apple is, as well as what Jonathans and Macintoshes are.

Of course, when we ask him, he will simply point to the two piles. "Those are apples." Different sorts of apples? "That's right." What do they have in common? He needs something for contrast, so we bring out the orange. He, better than we, is in a position to say what Macintoshes and Jonathans have in common that distinguishes them from oranges.

So, although it is true enough that apple sorters do not commence their day's work or even their careers by recalling the general definition of apple, it can be said that they know that definition. They already have the wherewithal to express it, but it may well be that they haven't had the need or occasion to do so.

We are all sorters of human actions. We can identify acts of theft, adultery, cheating, ingratitude, and, on better days, of courage, nobility, generosity, and wisdom. And we can do all this without having asked what all these acts have in common. So why bother? There are times when we are not sure how to think of what someone has done. You have just seeded your lawn when a wild-eyed man rounds the corner of the house and goes trampling across your handiwork, ignoring the signs you have set out: Keep off the grass. You are outraged. But if a swarm of bees now comes around the same corner in pursuit of the man, your notion of what is going on changes. If subsequently you learn that he has been attempting to rob your hives, disturbed the bees, etc., your judgment alters again.

If what that man is doing is a human act, it is nonetheless obscure what he is doing. Indeed, in some versions, we might hesitate to say he is *doing* anything. In the back yard some evil children have devised a giant slingshot, stretching the inner tube from a tractor tire across the crotch of an apple tree. This poor fellow has been forcibly put in the pocket of the sling, then the rubber was pulled back and let go, and he was propelled across your newly seeded lawn.

These are not unusual cases. Questions of this sort arise all the time in discussing human acts. That is why there is an advantage in trying to state what any action must have in order to be a human act. Even with such clarity, we move on into the discussion of the vast variety of actions with many surprises before us. That is why Aristotle and St. Thomas thought of clarity about general features as a kind of confusion too, since the general account gathers together many things that, however alike they are, differ in many ways from one another. And it is those differences to which we want to proceed.

Human Acts Are What Humans Do

This statement seems to be a tautology, its subject and predicate the same. A is A—true enough, but so what? Where does it take us?

Consider a parallel. Dancing is what dancers do. If that is exemplified by the fact that Fred Astaire is a dancer and Fred is doing the samba, we might hazard the guess that to do the samba is to dance. But if Fred is doing time in prison and Fred is a dancer, it is true enough that doing time is what this dancer does, but Joel Grey is running around free, and he is arguably a dancer. The tautology is thus misleading—unless of course we mean to identify dancing with whatever any dancer does, in which case we would have a hopeless hodgepodge of characteristics, and radically conflicting ones. Think of all the things Fred Astaire does that no other dancer does and that may be the opposite of what other dancers do. Say he knits afghans, or golfs.

Fred Astaire is a dancer, and Fred Astaire golfs. Let us say that both of these are true. It is also true that dancing is what dancers do and golfing is what golfers do. Fred both dances and golfs, but we would not want to identify everything that dancers do with everything that golfers do. Hitting a nine-iron 110 yards is something the dancer Fred Astaire does. But we would not say that he does it insofar as he is a dancer. Dancing is what dancers do. If Fred golfs as well, the various activities that make up golfing are not said of him insofar as he is a dancer, but insofar as he is a golfer.

No surprises there; whether or not we have ever before explicitly thought this out, we already knew it. It is implicit in our ability to speak English. Dancing is what dancers do, but not everything dancers do is dancing. It is much the same with our original tautology. Human acts are what humans do.

As with the dancing example, we can begin in this way. Human acts are what humans do, Socrates is a man, so what Socrates does is a human act. Now Socrates may be no Fred Astaire, but he's no slouch either. Consider this partial list of the doings that can be truly attributed to him.

Socrates weighs 180 pounds.

Socrates has grown an inch this year.

Socrates won the Athenian lottery.

Socrates discourses in the agora.

Socrates is sleeping.

Socrates hears a jet go over.

The least imaginative of us could continue that list to a faretheewell. It is a list of the things that Socrates who is a man can truly be said to do. But human acts are what humans do. Are all the activities that we truly attribute to Socrates human acts? And remember that, for St. Thomas, every human act is a moral act. Of course we don't need much prompting to see that the activities on that list are very different from one another.

What kind of difference is it? Is it like the differences between Jonathans and Macintoshes, so that while they are all human acts, they are different sorts of human acts? Or do they differ as apples and oranges differ? Or are both kinds of difference involved?

We did not agree above that the truth of the statement that dancing is what dancers do commits us to the absurdity that any activity truly said of dancers is an instance of dancing. Can we make such a distinction here? Can we, despite the tautologous simplicity of "Human acts are what humans do," say that not all the things that humans do are human acts?

On the face of it, it does not seem possible. Fred Astaire as dancer is capable of a certain range of acts, as golfer of another range of acts, and that is why in his case it is true that the golfer dances and the dancer golfs, but being a golfer is not part of what we mean by dancer, and dancing is not one of the skills of golf except perhaps after a hole in one. Fred Astaire happens to be both, but real golfers don't dance, and most dancers would not be caught dead on a golf course.

In order for us to be able to distinguish human acts from the other things that humans do, we are going to have to come up with human doings that are not human, which seems an absurdity; but maybe not.

Consider the following contrast: Socrates' hair is graying, and Socrates is graying his hair. With reverse Grecian formula, of course; he will leave a little dark around the ears.

Or: Socrates is gaining weight, and Socrates is putting on weight. In the second instance, having been counseled by his physician, he goes on a diet to increase his weight.

Or: Fifi's hair is growing, and Fifi is letting her hair grow.

Fifi's hair grows whether she likes it or not, and by and large she likes it long, the better to give it a saucy toss in crucial situations. But wearing it long or short is something she does. If I say to her, "I like your hair that way," she takes it as a compliment. If I say to her, "Good idea, having hair on your head," her reaction is equivocal. The remark has the sound of either an absurdity or an insult.

These examples suggest that not every activity truly said of human agents is matter for praise or blame. "Shame on you for going bald"— only a huckster on cable television is likely to make such a remark, while flourishing a bottle of Emil's Capillary Elixir.

So it seems that among the activities truly ascribed to human agents we can distinguish those they do from others they don't do or, rather, the doing of which does not depend upon them. Who by taking thought can add one cubit to his stature? Not every activity that is truly ascribable to a human being is a human act.

Take a case. I stand at the window of a guest room in the Dominican House of Studies brooding over Washington, when what to my wondering eye should appear but a plummeting figure in white, Father Cesario. I call out, "Why are you falling?"

There are several printable replies that he might give.

"I'm not falling, you idiot, I jumped."

"Why am I falling? Gravity, you nincompoop."

"I was pushed."

"Don't lean too far out of *your* window."

And so on. Anyone conversant with falling Dominicans could rattle off a dozen or so possible answers.

When I am called to testify about this incident, I may be told to keep my answer to what I saw. "I saw a Dominican go by my window. Vertically. From top to bottom."

Would that tell anyone what happened? Of course not. The man either fell, jumped, or was pushed, and any of these in an infinite variety of ways. Physically, a Dominican may fall like a sack of wheat, and this could be expressed in a physical formula. Not even a court of law would consider that an adequate account of what happened.

Now in the case of the falling Dominican, of the three types of explanation we allow—he jumped, he fell, he was pushed—the last two, since they do not result from decisions of his, are not called human acts. He doesn't *do* them. Thomas calls such acts "acts of a man" rather than human acts. Acts of a man are those activities truly ascribable to a human agent but not as such, not as a human agent.

The first possible explanation—that he jumped—would very likely put us in the presence of a human action, but not necessarily. If he jumped because someone had given him a hot foot, he lost his balance, and he plummeted four stories to the ground, his going by my window would not be a human act.

A sign that we are dealing with a human act is that praise or blame is pertinent. We are praised or blamed for actions that we do, and that we do them is clear, because we must answer for them, answer, that is, the question: Why are you doing that? We are answerable or responsible for human acts, because we freely and knowingly bring them about.

Other sorts of answers are relevant when the activity the person is engaged in is not brought about by him. That he was pushed or fell are explanations, answers to the question why, and so in a way is gravity. These things might be said to be responsible for the activity. It seems that the Greek word for cause, *aitia,* first had the moral sense and then was extended to nonmoral causes. Of course if the descending Dominican was pushed, moral questions could arise in a way in which they could not if gravity were given as the reason for his fall.

Let us now look at the text of St. Thomas that these remarks are meant to paraphrase.

. . . actionum quae ab homine aguntur, illae solae proprie dicuntur humanae, quae sunt propriae hominis	. . . of the actions done by man those alone are properly called human which are proper to man insofar as he

inquantum est homo. Differt autem homo ab aliis irrationalibus creaturis in hoc, quod est suorum actuum dominus. Unde illae solae actiones vocantur propriae humanae, quarum homo est dominus. Est autem homo dominus suorum actuum per rationem et voluntatem: unde et liberum arbitrium esse dicitur facultas voluntatis et rationis. Illae ergo actiones proprie humanae dicuntur, quae ex voluntate deliberata procedunt. Si quae autem aliae actiones homini conveniant, possunt dici quidem hominis actiones; sed non proprie humanae, cum non sint hominis inquantum est homo. (IaIIae, q.1, a.1.)

is a man. Man differs from irrational creatures in this that he is master of his acts and only those acts will properly be called human of which man is the master. It is thanks to reason and will that man is master of his acts which is why free will is called a faculty of will and reason. Therefore only those acts which proceed from deliberate will are properly called human actions. If other actions belong to man they can be called acts of man but not properly human because they are not of man as man.

St. Thomas, as you can see, says it much more succinctly. That he makes this distinction between human actions and acts of man in the very first article of the moral part of the *Summa theologiae* is of the utmost importance, since human actions define the domain of morality. "Moral acts and human acts are the same" (ibid., q.1, a.3, c. in fine).

The Moral Life

Now that we have some idea of what counts as a human act and what does not, it is clear that all human acts are moral acts and all moral acts are human acts. A sign that an act is human or moral is that it is relevant to ask of the agent why he did it. He must answer for it. That is, we hold him responsible. If we cannot hold him responsible, if the question "Why" is inappropriate for one reason or another, we will not count the activity in question a human or moral act.

Our moral lives are made up of moral acts of this kind, and they have the character they do because of the character of the constitutive acts. We

Moral acts are Human acts.

Why did he do that?

speak of someone leading a good or bad life, and when we do, we have in mind more than a single act. Only human acts, not acts of a man, make up one's moral life.

It may seem that we can thus, once and for all, separate human acts from acts of man and, for purposes of morality, concentrate on the former. Matters are not quite that simple. For one thing, there is a continuing need to be careful that we are indeed speaking of a genuinely human act. For another thing, the story of our lives is scarcely the recounting of a suite of human acts, as if the acts of man, the activities which are truly ascribed to us but not as human or moral, were simply another story. They are part of the story of our life in the broad sense of the term—where by broad I mean the true tale from birth to now that includes our moral life but is not restricted to it.

There are a number of things we want to clarify here. First, we must face an obvious difficulty confronting the claim that human acts and moral acts are identical. That identification has the consequence that every human act is morally good or morally bad. What is the difficulty?

Consider such actions as these. Grover Capstan is a lab technician whose task is to fertilize human eggs with sperm in a dish in his lab. He does this with great skill and efficiency, as the awards on his wall attest. He is good at it; he does it well.

Willie Sutton robs banks because that's where the money is. Let us imagine he was so good at it, that he was never caught and his name remained unknown. But he himself and his immediate associates would consider him the best in the business. Willie is unsurpassed in the area of after-hour withdrawals. He does it well; he is a good thief.

Hazel plays duplicate bridge in a way that cannot be duplicated by anyone else in town. Playing the same hand as Hazel, the best anyone else got was four spades, whereas Hazel bid and made a small slam. She plays bridge well; she is a good bridge player.

Clarence is a sonneteer *sans pareil.* He is the best since Edna St. Vincent Millay. His octets are a marvel, his sestets grip the heart and mind. He writes sonnets well; he is a good poet.

The activities that Grover, Willie, Hazel, and Clarence perform are all human acts. It would be absurd to suggest that they are acts of a man but not human; they proceed from deliberate will, in St. Thomas's phrase. The activities are performed well or badly and, if well, we say the agent is good, if badly that he is bad. But are these moral appraisals? One who robs banks well is morally bad, just as a lab technician doing Grover's work is engaged in a morally questionable enterprise.

We did not really need these examples, since we already had those of golfing and dancing. Betsy King golfs well, and she is therefore a good golfer; Ann Miller dances well and is a good dancer. Previously we discussed such activities in order to arrive at clarity about what counts as a human act, but surely we did not want to suggest that golfing and dancing are not deeds done by human beings. The gorilla in the joke and the bear in the circus might golf and dance, respectively, but it is not at all the same thing. They do what they were trained to do and in any case are said to golf and dance only equivocally.

A good dancer is not as such a good person, a morally good person. But dancing is a human act, and all human acts were said to be just as such moral, that is, morally good or bad. Did Thomas move too quickly in making the identification?

Not at all. Most human actions can be appraised in several ways. When human actions are instances of skills or techniques, they will be judged in terms of the aims of the technique or skill. If robbing banks is accounted a skill, and it is, since it is not easy to do well, the good performance of it, accomplishing its aims with ease, stealth, and impunity, makes one a good bank robber—a good thief. Calling Willie a good thief indicates that regarding what he does as a skill and judging it as such can only give us a partial appraisal of his human act.

The Oldest Member sits on the porch of the club and sees Quincy Seagram on the eighteenth fairway. Quincy's drive has put him 220 yards from the flag. He addresses the ball, stands immobile for a moment while insects buzz, a far off jet roars, a car in the parking lot backfires. Quincy begins his backswing, deliberately, slowly, and the club is soon behind his head and parallel to the ground; a microsecond's pause, and then the carry through. Club meets ball, there is a fine arc described, the ball hits the green, bounces twice and drops into the cup. Quincy Seagram has just broken the club record for eighteen holes. The Oldest Member is in the group waiting to meet Quincy as he approaches the green. Cheering goes up when this final lucky shot is seen as one of only sixty-three strokes Quincy has taken in his round.

"What is that you're dragging?" the Oldest Member asks.

Quincy looks down uninterestedly at his burden. He lets it drop face down. "George Graphite. He took three strokes on the thirteenth and received one. I think he died as we were coming onto the seventeenth fairway."

The group falls back. One heavily insured doctor gets the toe of his loafer under the body's shoulder and turns it over. "By George," the Oldest Member says. "That's George." The doctor suggests calling the coroner. The Oldest Member returns to the porch where, over four gin and tonics, he ponders the question of how to characterize Quincy Seagram's record-setting round.

No one can take that score away from Quincy. His sixty-three goes into the club records, but what tends to be discussed in future years is Quincy's plaintive description of those final holes. "Shoot, drag George, shoot, drag George." This elicits little sympathy. On reflection the Oldest Member decides that Quincy is a good golfer, maybe the club's best, but an awful human being.

From this we can conclude the following. Although many human acts can be appraised technically, they can also be appraised morally. The identification of human acts and moral acts is not meant to suggest that human acts are not sorted out and assessed in nonmoral ways, only that any human act is subject to moral appraisal whether or not it is also subject to others kinds of appraisal. The technical appraisal can never be the ultimate appraisal of a human act.

Manifestum est autem quod omnes actiones quae procedunt ab aliqua potentia, causantur ab ea secundum rationem sui obiecti. Objectum autem	It is obvious that whatever actions proceed from a given power are caused by it under the formality of its object. But the object of will is the

voluntatis est finis et bonum. Unde oportet quod omnes actiones humanae propter finem sint. (IaIIae, q.1, a.1)

end and good. That is why all human acts are for the sake of an end.

This is the completion of the text we quoted earlier. Human acts proceed from deliberate will. Will is that faculty whereby we seek the end or good. Human acts, proceeding from deliberate will, are for the sake of an end.

By and large, when we ask someone or ourselves, "Why are you doing that?" it is the aim or purpose of the act we want to know—that for the sake of which something is done. The end is what the act aims to achieve, what will complete or fulfill it. Thomas maintains that an act is the kind or type of act it is because of the end for which it is undertaken.

Dictum est autem supra quod actus dicuntur humani inquantum procedunt a voluntate deliberata. Obiectum autem voluntatis est bonum et finis. Et ideo manifestum est quod principium humanorum actuum, inquantum sunt humani, est finis. Et similiter est terminus eorundem: nam id ad quod terminatur actus humanus, est id quod voluntas intendit tanquam finem. . . . Actus morales proprie speciem sortiuntur ex fine: nam idem sunt actus morales et actus humani.

It was said above that acts are called human insofar as they proceed from deliberate will. But the object of will is the good and end. It is obvious then that the starting point of human acts, insofar as they are human, is the end. So too it is their term, since that in which a human act terminates is what the will intended as the end. . . . It is from their end that moral acts are said to be of a given sort, for moral acts and human acts are one and the same.

The text is from IaIIae, q.1, a.3, c. It is the mark of the human act that it is undertaken for the sake of an end, with an eye to some good, to bring something about. An act of a man can also be for the sake of an end, but the end of such an act is not an end of deliberate will. The human act sets out to accomplish its intention, what is before the mind's eye as the end in view.

Human acts, as we have seen, can be appraised with respect to their end as technical or skillful as well as moral acts. That there is such a distinction is clear enough from our unwillingness to say that an agent is a good person on the basis of her being a good bridge player. In what precisely the distinction consists we will point out later in chapter 4 of Part One.

Voluntary, Involuntary, Nonvoluntary

Another way to characterize human or moral acts is to say that they are voluntary, that is, that they proceed from the reason and will of the agent. That the agent may be aware of those acts of man truly ascribable to himself does not turn them into human acts. They do not proceed from the knowledge he has of them. Of course modifications of them can be human acts, as we saw in the distinction between hair growing and Fifi allowing her hair to grow.

There are some acts which would be human acts, would be classified as voluntary, if they were not defective in one of the components of the human act. An act deficient in knowledge will be called involuntary; one must know what one is doing in order to be held responsible for it. So too force, whether physical or psychological, can cause us to say that what otherwise would be a voluntary act in this case is not. The human act is thus said to proceed from principles within the agent, within the agent's power, his mind and will. When violence is done to the human person, when one is forced to do something, the act does not proceed from that person's will but from outside.

Acting Unknowingly

Let us begin with a consideration of acts done in ignorance. One possible answer to the question, "Why are you doing that?" is "I didn't know I was."

Valence Quirk enters the building in which he lives and sees at his feet an envelope on which is printed in large letters: For Patricia Parlous. Valence picks it up, glances at the unmarked mail boxes in the lobby, then decides to slip the envelope under the door of Patricia's apartment as it has apparently been slipped under the entry door. He knocks on her door, hears the sound of a shower within, and does indeed complete the delivery, slipping the envelope under the door. He ascends whistling the whistle of the righteous to the floor above. Five minutes later a tremendous explosion rocks the building. Subsequent investigation discloses that Patricia Parlous, the *nom de guerre* of an IRA agent, was killed when a letter bomb slipped under her door went off. A horrified Valence Quirk thinks, "My God, I did that."

In what sense can Valence Quirk be said to have brought about the death of Patricia Parlous? That he did in some sense is clear enough. If he had not done what he did the letter bomb would have gone off in the lobby and whatever destruction it did or did not do would not have led him to say, "I did that." Our question is: does what Valence did count as a human act?

That Valence was engaged in a plurality of human acts in the little scenario is clear enough. He delivers to Patricia Parlous an envelope addressed to her and clearly intended for her. He means to do a good deed, to do a favor, to perform an act of kindness. That is the act he thinks he is performing. To that degree we are describing a human act. But in so doing, Valence delivers the bomb that ends the life of Patricia Parlous. That is a true statement. Is it a statement of a human act? It does not seem to describe an act of man.

It is clear enough that we must know how to identify the human act here in order to find out what Valence is answerable for and whether his action is morally good or not. The example is of someone who brought about what he did not intend but which would not have happened if he had not intentionally done what he did. A less charged, a happier, instance may make for easier analysis.

At a flea market I buy a copy of the Marietti edition of St. Thomas's *Quodlibetal Questions,* take it home, and put it on my shelf. Months pass. One winter evening, full of dinner and feeling philosophical, I take the book from the shelf. A stamp inside tells me it was cast out from a seminary library that shall be nameless. I am filled with a sense of the *lacrimae rerum.* The pages of course are uncut. In order to begin cutting them, I open the book on my lap. An envelope slides out. I open it. Inside are fifteen five hundred dollar bills. The stall in the flea market is empty, no one knows who occupied it at the time I can vaguely designate, the seminary that once owned the book is closed, I am richer by fifteen times five hundred dollars. What luck!

If you should have asked me in that flea market what I was doing, I would have told you I was buying the book mentioned. I could not of course have said I am about to come into possession of seventy-five hundred dollars. If I did not buy the book, I would not have found the money. Buying the book is the cause of my finding the money. What kind of a cause is it?

In the wake of this happy occurrence, I might become obsessed with flea markets, garage sales, and the like. Each night I might return home with a gunny sack full of books and shake them all vigorously, waiting for a bonanza which does not of course arrive. The connection between buying a used book—or at any rate a pre-owned book—and coming into some money is incidental and rare, however significant in this instance. We are not likely to attribute to luck what, though incidental and rare, is insignificant. It may happen that I am the 667th person with the initials R.M. to sit in a certain seat on the subway. So what? Only God and some angels know this. It doesn't matter.

Simply being rare does not suffice to establish that a connection is incidental. I have been golfing since I was fourteen years of age. Today, after forty-five years, I hit a hole in one. This is rare to the point of being unique. It is too much to say that I intended a hole in one on this occasion, but it is also too much to say that it was incidental to my intention. If I am called lucky here, it is because it is rare that a certain action achieves its intention in the best possible way.

In the case of something's being brought about by a human agent which is rare, significant, and unintended by that agent, we will say that it has come about incidentally, by chance, fortuitously. It attaches itself to what the agent does intend but is linked only incidentally to it. The agent as such brings about what he intends; he is the *per se* cause of it. Of that which attaches itself incidentally to what he *per se* intends, we will say that he is the incidental or *per accidens* cause.

St. Thomas learned the analysis of this fundamental fact about human doings from Aristotle. The human agent will be called the *per se* cause only of what he intends, and for that he is held morally responsible. The human or moral act consists only of what one intends, not of what in this instance is incidentally related to it. A person cannot be said to do what he does unknowingly, not in the full sense of "doing" involved in the notion of human action. After the fact, when he becomes aware of what he has done, he will be elated or appalled, depending.

Consider this text of St. Thomas (IaIIae, q.6, a.8, c.). He has noted that when the knowledge required for voluntary action is absent, we will not consider the act a human act. However, we must not think that just any sort of ignorance deprives the act of the knowledge requisite for voluntariness. Ignorance can attach to an act in three ways, Thomas says, namely, concomitantly, consequently, and antecedently.

Concomitanter quidem quando ignorantia est de eo quod agitur, tamen, etiam si sciretur, nihilominus ageretur. Tunc enim ignorantia non inducit ad volendum ut hoc fiat, sed accidit simul esse aliquid factum et ignoratum: sicut, in exemplo posito, cum aliquis vellet quidem occidere hostem, sed ignorans occidit eum, putans occidere cervum. Et talis ignorantia non facit involuntarium, ut Philosophus dicit, quia non causat aliquid quod sit repugnans voluntati: sed facit non voluntarium, quod non potest esse actu volitum quod ignoratum est.

Concomitantly indeed when there is ignorance of what is done, though, were it known, one would do it nonetheless. In this case ignorance does not lead one to will that this be done, but it happens that there is at once something done and something unknown as, in the example given, when someone kills his enemy thinking he is killing a deer. Ignorance of this sort does not make the deed involuntary, as Aristotle notes, because it does not cause anything repugnant to will, but makes it nonvoluntary, since that which is unknown cannot be actually willed.

If I do in ignorance what I would do knowingly, I cannot say that what happens is in conflict with my will. For this reason, Aristotle and Thomas decline to call such acting in ignorance involuntary, but simply nonvoluntary. The nonvoluntary act seems thus to coincide with good fortune. Good fortune obtains when in doing something or other I bring about something else which is a good for me, such that if I had known this would happen I would have done the deed for that reason. The ignorance in which I act negates the knowledge that is a necessary component of human action, but it does not cause me to do anything that goes against my grain.

How a person comports himself in the wake of such an occurrence will acquaint him with his true bent or desires. Indeed, we should want to appraise morally the reaction to such an event. The smirking, exultant hunter who has just done away with his chief rival quite accidentally, thinking he was bagging a deer, will scarcely be considered morally innocent, however true it is that he has not committed an act of murder. But it is of course his reaction to what has happened that is morally reprehensible.

Consequenter autem se habet ignorantia ad voluntatem, inquantum ipsa ignorantia est voluntaria. Et hoc contingit dupliciter, secundum duos modos voluntarii supra positos. Uno modo, quia actus voluntatis fertur in ignorantiam: sicut cum aliquis ignorare vult ut excusationem peccati habeat, vel ut non retrahatur a peccando secundum illud Iob 21,14: "Scientiam viarum tuarum nolumus." Et haec dicitur ignorantia affectata. Alio modo dicitur ignorantia voluntaria eius quod quis potest scire et debet: sic enim non agere et non velle voluntarium dicitur. . . . Hoc igitur modo dicitur ignorantia, sive cum aliquis actu non considerat quod considerare potest et debet, quae est ignorantia malae electionis, vel ex passione vel ex habitu proveniens: sive cum aliquis notitiam quam debet habere non curat acquirere: et secundum hunc

Ignorance relates consequently to will insofar as the ignorance itself is voluntary. This happens in two ways, according to the two modes of voluntary mentioned earlier. [1] When the act of will bears on the ignorance, as when one doesn't want to know in order to have an excuse for sinning or so as not to be held back from sin. "We did not want knowledge of your ways" (Job 21:14). This is called affected ignorance. [2] Ignorance of what one can and ought to know is called voluntary, just as not to act and not to will can be voluntary. . . . Ignorance of this sort occurs (a) when one does not actually consider what he can and ought to: this is the ignorance of bad choice, stemming from passion or habit, or (b) when one does not concern himself to acquire knowledge that he ought to have; ignorance of the universals of law, which every-

modum, ignorantia universalium iuris, quae quis scire tenetur, voluntaria dicitur, quasi per negligentiam proveniens. Cum autem ipsa ignorantia sit voluntaria aliquo istorum modorum, non potest causare simpliciter involuntarium. Causat tamen secundum quid involuntarium, inquantum praecedit motum voluntatis ad aliquid agendum, qui non esset scientia praesente. (Ibid.)

one is held to know, is voluntary in this sense as stemming from negligence. Since ignorance in either of these first two senses is voluntary, it cannot cause the involuntary simply speaking, but only in a secondary sense, insofar as it precedes the will's moving to do something, which it would not were knowledge present.

If we put our minds to not finding out things relevant to the circumstances in which we act, we may indeed act in ignorance, but this ignorance does not render our action involuntary in the full sense of the term. Affected or willed ignorance is morally more serious than what Thomas calls concomitant ignorance, and one would be held accountable for it. The ignorance itself is voluntary, much as we can say that not to do or not to will is voluntary. So what kind of ignorance is productive of involuntary action?

Antecedenter autem se habet ad voluntatem ignorantia, quando non est voluntaria, et tamen est causa volendi quod alias homo non vellet. Sicut cum homo ignorat aliquam circumstantiam actus quam non tenebatur scire, et ex hoc aliquid agit, quod non faceret si sciret: puta cum aliquis, diligentia adhibita, nesciens aliquem transire per viam, proiicit sagittam, qua interficit transeuntem. Et talis ignorantia causat involuntarium simpliciter. (Ibid.)

Ignorance attaches to will antecedently when it is not voluntary and yet is the cause of willing what a man otherwise would not will. As when a man ignores some circumstance of the act which he is not held to know and because of this does what he would not do knowingly. For example, when someone, exercising caution, not knowing that someone is on the road, shoots an arrow and kills him. Ignorance of this sort causes the involuntary in the full sense.

Bad luck and what Thomas calls antecedent ignorance seem to coincide. If one unwittingly does that which, when it becomes known, causes pain and anguish, since one would never have done it knowingly, then we speak of misfortune.

Forced Acts

On the face of it, the notion of a forced voluntary act is incoherent. By definition, a voluntary act is one which has its causes within the agent, since it follows on deliberate will. An act due to force or violence is explained by the external force and thus is the opposite of a voluntary one.

... duplex est actus voluntatis: unus quidem qui est eius immediate, velut ab ipsa elicitus, scilicet velle; alius autem est actus voluntatis a voluntate imperatus, et mediante alia potentia exercitus, ut ambulare et loqui, qui a voluntate imperantur mediante potentia motiva. Quantum igitur ad actus a voluntate imperatos, voluntas violentiam pati potest, inquantum per violentiam exteriora membra impediri possunt ne imperium voluntatis exequantur. Sed quantum ad ipsum proprium actum voluntatis, non potest ei violentia inferri.

There are two kinds of act of will: one which is its act immediately as elicited from itself, namely, willing; the other act of will is commanded by will and exercised by means of another power, for example, walking and talking, which are commanded by will through an intermediate moving power. With regard to the acts commanded by the will, the will can suffer violence insofar as the external members can be impeded by violence so they cannot carry out the will's command. But with regard to the will's own proper act, it cannot be affected by violence.

This text is taken from IaIIae, q.6, a.4, c. The distinction is basic. Force or violence cannot affect the will's own act, but insofar as the acts of other powers commanded by will can be interfered with, acts of will in this secondary sense, acts commanded by will, are subject to force or violence. Force or violence results in the very antithesis of the voluntary act.

There is no problem here, seemingly. If someone is tied up hand and foot and his mouth taped, we do not ask him why he does not walk or talk. That he might want to, desperately, is conveyed by the expression in his wildly rolling eyes, but he cannot perform these acts because of his bonds. His not talking and not walking are involuntary. In much the same way, we do not ask someone being forcibly hustled down a hallway why he is leaving. He is not leaving voluntarily. Obviously such acts will not be counted human or moral acts, and the one being forced will be neither praised nor blamed for the activity or inactivity. Or would they?

There may be room here for a nonvoluntary rather than an involuntary act. Sylvestro Fellini gets out of his car one night just in time to see his neighbor Elroy being mugged. Frozen in fear, Sylvestro stares at the incident, which engraves itself indelibly in his memory. Another car rounds the corner, the mugger turns away from the headlights and heads into the night with Elroy's wallet, watch, and rings. With the mugger gone, Sylvestro gains control of himself, comforts Elroy, and escorts him home. Some days later Elroy, poring over photographs at the precinct station, identifies his mugger as Razor Malone, Malone is arrested, and Sylvestro is called as a witness. Malone is quoted as saying that anyone involved in his conviction will hear from his friends. Sylvestro, in whom discretion drives out valor, trembles with fear. He does not want to testify. On the other hand, he cannot plausibly deny that he had a clear view of Elroy's assailant. At the trial, Sylvestro is asked if he can identify the defendant. He does not want to answer. In any case, at that moment a woman dashes to the witness stand, rubs Sylvestro's lips with epoxy glue, and presses them together, thus rendering him incapable of speech. Although he is prevented from speaking, this inability does not go contrary to his will, so in this case, we would not say that force rendered the act involuntary, only nonvoluntary. Of course, only Sylvestro can know for sure.

By and large, however, force or violence does not pose much of a problem so far as the identification of human or moral acts is concerned. Violence negates the voluntariness of the commanded act, removing it from the domain of the moral.

Acts done out of fear are harder to classify. On the one hand, we are unwilling to regard the act of a terrified person as his own; on the other hand, not just any kind of fear would seem to destroy the voluntariness of action. Thomas follows tradition in thinking acts done in fear are hybrids, mixtures of the voluntary and involuntary. Think of Elroy in the earlier example. He is confronted by a menacing mugger who demands his money and valuables. Elroy takes out his wallet, slips off his watch and rings, and hands them over. If Elroy were asked, "Is it your wish to give a stranger your money and valuables?" he would say no. The action he performs thus goes against his grain. Taken as such, it is not something he would voluntarily do. Nonetheless, confronted by the mugger he hands them over. The handing over proceeds from deliberate will. This leads Thomas to the initially surprising judgment that such an action is more voluntary than involuntary.

Sed si quis recte consideret, magis sunt huiusmodi voluntaria quam involuntaria: sunt enim voluntaria simpliciter, involuntaria autem secundum quid. Unumquodque enim simpliciter esse dicitur secundum quod est in actu: secundum autem quod est in sola apprehensione, non est simpliciter, sed secundum quid. Hoc autem quod per metum agitur, secundum hoc est in actu, secundum quod fit: cum enim actus in singularibus sint, singulare autem, inquantum huiusmodi, est hic et nunc; secundum hoc id quod fit est in actu, secundum quod est hic et nunc et sub aliis conditionibus individualibus. Sic autem hoc quod fit per metum, est voluntarium, inquantum scilicet est hic et nunc, prout scilicet in hoc casu est impedimentum maioris mali quod timebatur . . .

Rightly considered, such acts are more voluntary than involuntary: they are voluntary simply speaking, involuntary only in a certain respect. A thing is said to be simply insofar as it is actual, but as it is exists in knowledge alone it is only in a certain respect, not simply speaking. Now that which is done out of fear, is actual insofar as it is done: actions are singular, and the singular as such is here and now. Given this, that which comes to be actually is insofar as it is here and now and has other individual conditions. So it is that what is done out of fear is voluntary insofar as it is here and now, because in this case it is an impediment to a greater evil that is feared . . .

This text is from IaIIae, q.6, a.6, c. Abstractly considered, Elroy has no desire to rid himself of his money and valuables, but when he confronts the threatening mugger, he would rather hand them over than suffer bodily harm. Simply speaking, then, his handing over of his money and valuables is voluntary; it proceeds from within the agent. Taken apart from these circumstances, the deed is repugnant to will, but so taken it exists only for thought. And it is only as removed from the actual circumstances that the deed is involuntary.

A forced act is one to which no consent of the will is given, but in an act done out of fear, what is done is voluntary insofar as the will bears on it as something good in these circumstances, not in itself, but as a means of fending off bodily harm. That it is chosen for the sake of something else does not make it other than voluntary, since voluntary acts can bear on what is wanted for itself or on what is wanted for the sake of something else.

Acts done out of fear can thus be voluntary, that is, can be human and moral acts and thus appraisable as good or bad. A man who betrays his country under the threat that it will be revealed that he wears a toupee will not gain our sympathy as Elroy might. What Elroy does out of fear is not in itself evil, so the cases differ fundamentally. We can easily imagine situations where a person out of fear of great bodily harm does something morally wrong, say perjures himself, and we would be moved to pity. It would be instructive at this point to consider the fear and pity elicited in us by the tragic hero.

Needless to say, if the person out of fear does something in itself morally wrong, the action will be assessed differently depending on what is feared. If one acts out of fear for the safety of others, particularly when those others are innocent, pardon and pity would doubtless be accorded him, but variations would be introduced by the nature of the evil deed done. As in the case of the bashful bald man above, where there is a dramatic disproportion between the evil done and the evil feared, judgment will be harsh. Where the evil deed is done out of fear for one's own life, judgment will be mitigated. Where the fear is for others, other variations would be introduced.

This is not to say that pardon or excusing or pity deny that an evil has been done; rather they recognize the difference between an evil done under duress and one done willingly in a quite unequivocal sense.

Summary

The subject of moral philosophy is the human act, one that proceeds from deliberate will. Not every activity truly ascribed to a human agent is a human act. Every human act is as such moral and thus appraisable as morally good or bad. This is not altered by the fact that human acts can be appraised from the point of view of their particular aims or ends and said to be good or bad, and the agent thereby dubbed good or bad, in nonmoral senses of these terms. All such acts, since they are human acts, are also appraisable as morally good or bad.

The human act is voluntary. The voluntary act proceeds from within the agent, from his will and reason. Insofar as an act is defective either from the point of view of mind or from the point of view of will, it may be classified as involuntary, as not a human act, as outside the moral domain.

Acts done out of what Thomas calls antecedent ignorance will be involuntary. In such acts one unwittingly does what he would not knowingly do. In the case where one does unwittingly what he would do knowingly, the act is called nonvoluntary rather than involuntary. The ignorance Thomas says is consequent on will, far from causing an act to be involuntary, would seem to be a feature of morally bad action. There is a sense in which every evil act involves ignorance, but that is not exculpating so much as descriptive of it as evil.

Let this suffice as a presentation of the matters essential to identifying human or moral acts and to keeping them distinct from nonmoral activities.

2. What Does It All Mean?

THAT HUMAN acts are undertaken for the sake of an end is conceded even in the grim account Albert Camus gave of the typical day of a Parisian. Up at seven, coffee and croissant, through the rainy streets to work, four hours at the desk performing clerical tasks, lunch, a glass of wine, four more hours at the desk, then into the subway, and home again where, flaked out in front of the television, Pierre polishes off a bottle of cheap red and stumbles off to bed. Tomorrow and tomorrow and tomorrow creeps in its petty pace. . . .

Take any act Pierre does, ask him why he is doing it, and he has no trouble answering. So too with sequences of deeds at his desk, in the subway, in his apartment. But when we back off a bit and see the whole day and a life made up of such days, another and profounder Why? surges up in us. Some version of the question that serves as title for this chapter will occur to us.

When it does, we are in a position to understand what the Greeks meant when they asked what the good for man is. Thinking of Pierre can lead to talk of more meaningful work than that in which he is engaged, it can lead to proposals for improving the public transportation system, or to discussions of the triviality of television, and it can end with the suggestion that the city of Paris must mount a campaign—billboard ads, radio, and TV spots—against alcoholism. Would that answer to our sense of the futility of Pierre's life?

At almost any wake one hears remarks about how sad it is that the deceased never did this or that, saw here or there. "Poor Marge never did get to Tahiti." This lament conjures up, perhaps, a routine life like the one Pierre led in Paris. Marge never got to Paris either. When we ponder the lives of Pierre and Marge, we can of course mean to say that they were caught up in dehumanizing and trivial tasks, although romping in the South Seas may not be much of an improvement over what they did. Sometimes, perhaps in thinking over the lifespan of someone recently dead, we are gripped by the Romantic Agony because of the finitude that inevitably characterizes any life. If Marge had become a skydiver and plummeted from the clouds, if Pierre had joined the Foreign Legion, the scenes would have changed, but as human agents they would still have performed their deeds in a finite time, then died. What does it all mean?

The End and the Good

The big question is best approached somewhat obliquely. In setting it forth, in sketching lives that can seem absurd, we assumed that human acts taken one at a time are explainable in terms of their aims or ends. Running toward the Metro, Pierre is engaged in an activity aimed at catching the train. That Pierre sits next to a heavily made up Zsa Zsa Gabor wearing opaque sunglasses may be true enough, but he doesn't intend this and, in our story, is unaware of it. This is meant as a reminder that the full story of Pierre's life has to include all kinds of acts of a man as well as human acts. But the human acts are as such undertaken for the sake of some end, purpose, good. Good? Yes, since the good means that which is sought.

It is not simply that taken one by one, in isolation, human acts have goals; it is also true that they are linked insofar as some are undertaken not only for their immediate aim but also as ordered to the aim of another action, and indeed a whole suite of acts can have a common end or upshot. This can be seen in Pierre's case in that taking the Metro is meant to get him to the office where he will perform his tasks in order to be paid in order to have money with which to eat and drink. "Why are you working?" "A man has to eat."

Acts of different agents can be linked insofar as the deeds of each have ends which are subordinate to a common or shared aim. Over the course of three years, working diligently thirty minutes every morning, you produce a novel, *The Flame and the Fantasy*. Your agent peddles it to B. Smircher, Ltd., where your editor Dawn Dillon pores over the manuscript and suggests additional sordid scenes, which you dutifully write. Mia Opek, the copyeditor, goes over the manuscript to remove the grosser solecisms, and it goes on to the printer where A and B get it into type. You correct the proofs and send them back. Meanwhile, Noel Lafont has designed a cover that glows in the dark, the sales force has been briefed by Dawn and fans out over the nation. The PR people get you onto Geraldo and Morton Downey, etc., etc. Some months later, when the glitzy cover of *The Flame and the Fantasy* hurts the eyes of travelers in the airports of the nation and you and your publisher are swimming in money, a collective effort has achieved the end desired. Each of the acts involved has its particular end in view, but if the writer wrote the book and it was not published, his ultimate desire is thwarted. If the publisher brings it out and it does not sell, the book making process has achieved its end in a limited sense, but in another, ultimate sense has not.

Aristotle was fascinated by the fact that we can group a variety of activities under an ultimate, comprehensive end, as in the case of the project manager's orchestrating the activities of excavators, steelworkers, fireproofers, bricklayers, glaziers, etc., so that they come together to produce the building; or as in the case of the general who guides the various elements of his army, cavalry, infantry, artillery, so that victory is achieved. Is there such an end of the larger society of which we are all members? Is there an ultimate end of human agents to which all other ends are subordinate? Such an ultimate end would be the answer to, "What does it all mean?"

Is There an Ultimate End?

St. Thomas gives us a fairly abstract argument, not unlike Aristotle's, for the necessity of an ultimate end.

In finibus autem invenitur duplex ordo, scilicet ordo intentionis et ordo executionis: et in utroque ordine oportet esse aliquid primum. Id enim quod est primum in ordine intentionis, est quasi principium movens appetitum: unde, subtracto principio, appetitus a nullo moveretur. Id autem quod est principium in executione est unde incipit operatio: unde isto principio subtracto, nullus inciperet aliquid operari. Principium autem intentionis est ultimus finis: principium autem executionis est primum eorum quae sunt ad finem. Sic ergo ex neutra parte possibile est in infinitum procedere: quia si non esset ultimus finis, nihil appeteretur, nec aliqua actio terminaretur, nec etiam quiesceret intentio agentis; si autem non esset primum in his quae sunt ad finem, nullus inciperet aliquid operari, nec terminaretur consilium, sed in infinitum procederet. (IaIIae, q.1, a.4, c.)

A twofold order is found in ends, namely the order of intention and the order of execution, and in both there has to be something first. That which is first in the order of intention is like a moving principle so that, if the principle is absent, nothing would move the appetite. That which is first in the order of execution is where the operation begins, so if that principle were absent no one would begin to do anything. The ultimate end is the principle in intention whereas the principle of execution is the first among the things which are for the sake of the end. In neither order then is it possible to have an infinite regress, because if there were no ultimate end, nothing would be desired, no act would be terminated nor would the intention of the agent be fulfilled; if there were no first means to the end, no one could begin to do something, nor would counsel cease but would go on endlessly.

The argument has its appeal, yet can leave us uneasy, doubtless because of its abstractness. As such it does not establish that there is an ultimate end common to all men or even to some. St. Thomas doesn't take it even to establish that each agent has only one ultimate end, since he goes on to mount an argument against a plurality of ultimate ends. In the course of it, he tells us more of what he means by the ultimate end.

... cum unumquodque appetat suam perfectionem, illud appetit aliquis ut ultimum finem, quod appetit ut bonum perfectum et completivum sui ipsius. (IaIIae, q.1, a.5)

... since everyone seeks his perfection, one seeks as ultimate end what he seeks as the good which is perfective and fulfilling of himself.

Whatever anyone desires and pursues, he wants as fulfilling of himself, as providing what he does not have or as preserving it. The term *perfection* here may seem to introduce an exalted note, but it is not meant to. A process is perfect when it is complete or has achieved its end. An agent who wants his efforts to achieve their goal wants their perfection and derivatively his own. What, you may ask, has all this to do with ordering a Big Mac?

This: that whatever counts as a human act is done for the sake of an end may be easy to concede. That any human act thus aims at a good seems true enough. But to cite this as a basis for asserting that there is an ultimate end seems to overlook the fact that hamburgers, short naps, Beethoven's Fifth, a stroll in the country, and on and on and on are all aims and thus goods of human agents. If the agent can thus be said to seek the fulfillment or perfection of an act he has undertaken, this does not seem tantamount to saying he is seeking *his* fulfillment or perfection. And if this is just a roundabout way of saying he wants to accomplish what he sets out to do, and if, as surely is the case, he sets out to accomplish dozens of things each hour, surely it is Pickwickian to suggest that any or all of them amount to his perfection or fulfillment.

Choosing X as Good

We listed above a number of possible objects of choice—a hamburger, a nap, listening to music, a walk—and we can add that we choose and eat this quite singular hamburger, take a nap here and now, listen to this piece of music recorded by this orchestra on CD and so on. Needless to say, the walks we take are singular events not general occasions. But if actions are thus singular, the singular things we choose are chosen under formalities. X is chosen as a such-and-such—as tasty, relaxing, elevating, or diverting, say, thinking of our examples. Since these are the reasons they are chosen, we can say that things chosen as tasty or relaxing or elevating or diverting can all be said to be chosen as good. The good is that which is sought.

Such truisms turn up some interesting facts. A human being does not simply go for any desirable thing put in his vicinity. Desirable things trigger off desire in him, and probably whether he wants them to or not; but deliberate choice, human action, consists in what he does next. Let us say that he can either pursue or not pursue the attractive object. Let us say it is a chocolate sundae. No human being can be expected not to want a chocolate sundae when it is set before him. That it would taste good, etc., goes without saying. But the human choice is whether or not to choose that tasty good here and now. The thing that is good in the sense of tasty has to meet a further requirement. It has to be good in the sense of an appropriate object of deliberate will. Deliberate will involves an apprehension that goes beyond mere perception. Reason, as it guides our choices, is at least implicitly aware of our overall good and when something is deliberately chosen, the implication is that it serves our overall good.

That seems to be what St. Thomas means when he says things are objects of human choice *sub ratione boni.* A hamburger is chosen by the human agent, not simply because it is tasty, but because eating it here and now is thought to serve the overall good of the agent. Mind ranges over individuals and sees them as instances of kinds. Practical reason sees them as instances of good, that is, as what can fulfill desire, not simply the desire to eat, but the agent's presumed fundamental desire to make only choices that serve his overall good. To choose particular things, to choose things of a given sort, is also to choose them as good, under the aspect of fulfilling of the agent.

Any object of deliberate choice is a kind of sandwich of another sort. There is the particular kind of thing chosen—a hamburger—and its immediate aspect of desirability, say, tastiness. These are the underside of the sandwich, the matter of the object of deliberate will. The top half, the form, is the *ratio boni,* the formality of goodness—not partial goodness, but goodness as fulfilling and perfecting of the agent.

This *ratio boni* or reason for choosing any and everything we choose is what Thomas means by ultimate end. If it is the case that we choose foodstuffs as assuaging hunger, there is implicit in the choice that satisfying our hunger is good for us. And so too with other particular choices. The formality under which anything is chosen is the ultimate end, and of course then we can say that anything anyone chooses he chooses for the sake of the ultimate end.

Now it is not nothing to arrive at such a conclusion. Nor do I mean to suggest that the steps toward it are uncontroversial, commanding widespread even unanimous consent among philosophers. But such objections as I know seem answerable. Say they are. We are still left with an exceedingly abstract claim. We need more.

De ultimo fine possumus loqui dupliciter: uno modo, secundum rationem ultimi finis; alio modo, secundum id in quo finis ultimi ratio invenitur. Quantum igitur ad rationem ultimi finis, omnes conveniunt in appetitu finis ultimi: quia omnes appetunt suam perfectionem adimpleri, quae est ratio ultimi finis. . . . Sed quantum ad id in quo ista ratio invenitur, non omnes homines conveniunt in ultimo fine: nam quidam appetunt divitias tanquam consummatum bonum, quidam autem voluptatem, quidam vero quodcumque aliud. Sicut et omni gustui delectabile est dulce: sed quibusdam maxime delectabilis est dulcedo vini, quibusdam dulcedo mellis, aut alicuius talium. Illud tamen dulce oportet esse simpliciter melius delectabile, in quo maxime delectatur qui habet optimum gustum. Et similiter illud bonum oportet esse completissimum, quod tanquam ultimum finem appetit habens affectum bene dispositum. (IaIIae, q.1, a.7)

We can speak of ultimate end in two ways, either as the notion of ultimate end or as that in which the notion is realized. With regard to the notion of ultimate end, all agree in the desire of ultimate end, because all seek to fulfill their perfection, and that is the notion of ultimate end. . . . But with regard to that which realizes this notion, men do not agree about ultimate end, for some seek riches as the consummate good, others pleasure, others other things. Just as the sweet is delightful to taste but to some the sweetness of wine is most delightful, to others the sweetness of honey or something else. That sweet will be accounted most delightful in which those with the best taste delight. So too that good must be the most complete which those having well disposed appetite seek as the ultimate end.

In the *Nicomachean Ethics* Aristotle notes that men have a word for the ultimate end, and that word is happiness. That one does whatever he does for the sake of happiness is, verbal quibbling apart, the final word in motivation. But as Thomas points out with respect to ultimate end, this formal agreement covers a host of disagreements. In what does happiness consist? That question receives a cacophony of answers. We are not surprised, given the role Aristotle plays in Thomas's philosophy and thus in his theology, to see him devote the second question of the *Prima secundae* to happiness. The term is defined in the final line of Question One: "beatitudo nominat adeptionem ultimi finis: 'happiness' names the attainment of the ultimate end." Besides Sacred Scripture, Thomas's main sources for the discussion of the makeup of human happiness are Aristotle, Boethius and, toward the end of Question Two, Augustine.

The question can be put like this: Is any good or end such that it can function as the dominating and superordinating end of human life? Aristotle's answer to this is that the human good consists of a plurality of goods, hierarchically arranged, so that the best good is the superordinating good, but it cannot function as the sole constituent of human happiness in this life. Thomas holds the same so far as earthly life goes.

The candidates for dominant end of human life are familiar: wealth, honors, fame, power. Thomas gives four reasons why none of these can meet the demands of the notion of ultimate end. First, each has evils mixed with it; second, none of them alone can suffice for human happiness; third, having any of these can have evil consequences; fourth, these depend on factors beyond our control. That is why they are called goods of fortune (IaIIae, q.2, a.4).

Turning to internal goods, Thomas asks whether the goods of the body, survival or pleasure, could function as ultimate end, but argues that goods of the body are for the sake of the soul and thus cannot serve as ultimate ends.

Question Two ends by removing the remaining candidates, goods of the soul, and then universalizes this as meaning that no created good can serve as man's ultimate end.

Obiectum autem voluntatis, quae est appetitus humanus, est universale bonum; sicut obiectum intellectus est universale verum. Ex quo patet quod	The object of will, the human appetite, is universal good, just as the universal truth is the object of intellect. From which it follows that only the

nihil potest quietare voluntatem hominis, nisi bonum universale. Quod non
invenitur in aliquo creato, sed solum
in Deo: quia omnis creatura habet
bonitatem participatam. Unde solus
Deus voluntatem hominis implere potest. (IaIIae, q.2, a.8)

universal good can give rest to the
will of man. But this can be found in
no creature, only in God, because the
creature only shares in goodness.
Hence God alone can satisfy the human will.

Thomas does not mean that we want the good in general as something vague and indeterminate. What we want is an object which will realize completely the formality of goodness. No created good can do this, since any created good shares in and is not identical with goodness itself. But if there is some being which is not just good, sharing in goodness, but goodness itself, that being satisfies the notion of ultimate end. God is goodness itself, not just another good thing. God, then, is man's ultimate end.

Imperfect and Perfect Happiness

Man's ultimate end is that good which is better than all the others, because it satisfies the notion of ultimate end as the consummate perfective good, which fulfills completely the will's desire.

A first objection to this is that it pretty well defines away the possibility that anything can function as the ultimate end. Thomas concludes that God, who is goodness, the fullness of perfection, is that being which alone can satisfy the notion of ultimate end. This puts us in mind of those haunting words of St. Augustine, "Thou hast made us for yourself, O Lord, and our hearts are restless until they rest in thee." Or Chesterton's earthier expression of the same truth: The young man knocking on the brothel door is looking for God. But doesn't this suggest that happiness is unattainable in this life?

Thomas proceeds in these first five questions of *Prima secundae* on the assumption that his reader knows the *Nicomachean Ethics*. A mark of that work is Aristotle's rejection of an Idea of the Good, of a transcendent entity, as the human good. Aristotle says almost contemptuously that he is seeking a good attainable by human action, a quality of our doings, not a reference to a presumed far-off self-subsistent Idea. Thomas distinguishes between that which is the ultimate end and our attainment of it, and it is the latter he calls happiness or felicity or beatitude. And he takes Aristotle to be putting the emphasis on the pursuit of the end and on the means of attaining it. Let us reflect a bit on the difficulties which attend Aristotle's discussion of happiness.

Finis dicitur dupliciter. Uno modo, ipsa res quam cupimus adipisci: sicut avaro est finis pecunia. Alio modo, ipsa adeptio vel possessio, seu usus aut fruitio eius rei quae desideratur: sicut si dicatur quod possessio pecuniae est finis avari, et frui re voluptuosa est finis intemperati. Primo ergo modo, ultimus hominis finis est bonum increatum, scilicet Deus, qui solus sua infinita bonitate potest voluntatem hominis perfecte implere. Secundo autem modo ultimus finis hominis est aliquid creatum in ipso existens, quod nihil est aliud quam adeptio vel fruitio finis ultimi. (IaIIae, q.3, a.1)

There are two senses of end, first, the thing itself we seek to have, as money is the end of the miser; second, the having, possession, use, or enjoyment of the thing that is desired, as if it were said that the possession of money is the end of the miser, and the enjoyment of the delightful thing the end of the intemperate man. In the first sense, the ultimate end of man is uncreated, namely God, who alone by his infinite goodness can perfectly satisfy the will of man. In the second sense the ultimate end of man is some created thing existing in him, which is nothing other than the having or enjoyment of the ultimate end.

Aristotle began with the observation that all are agreed that the ultimate point of doing anything at all is happiness. Moreover, there is agreement on the conditions of happiness. It should be self-sufficient, it should be stable and by and large impervious to the slings and arrows of outrageous fortune. Can anything meet these conditions?

The analysis of functions or roles (*ta erga*) provided Aristotle with a way of explaining what we mean when we say of someone or something that they are good. If a thing has a function and performs that function well, it will be called a good thing of that kind. The good butler is one who buttles well, the good punter is one who punts well, the good cook is one who cooks well. It can be said that Aristotle's philosophy reposes on such analyses as that. It makes us feel at ease, we know what's going on. Of course, that's just the way *we* would explain what calling someone a good golfer means, or a good actor, a good speaker, and so on. But Aristotle wants to extend this analysis to man as man.

What can be called the "*qua* locution" picks out a thing under a precise formality. The golfer *qua* golfer putts. The dancer *qua* dancer executes a plié. Fred Astaire *qua* dancer trips the light fantastic and *qua* golfer shoots a bogey on the seventh hole. Does man have a function? Do the golfer, dancer, and tanner have functions but man as such none? Or, do the parts of man, his eye, his leg, his ears, have functions, but the whole man does not? Is there anything that man does *qua* man? If so, he has a function, and if he does it well, he will be accounted a good man.

You can see that this is analogous to Thomas's distinction between human acts and acts of a man. Human acts are true of a man *qua* human. Acts of a man are not true of a man *qua* human, but *qua* animal, vegetable, or mineral. Think of the list of activities ascribed to Socrates in Chapter One. A sign that something is not attributed to a thing *qua* the kind of thing it is will be found in the fact that it is also found in others. Socrates does not see *qua* human being, because things other than men can see. Seeing well leads us to say the eye is good, but not that a man is good *qua* man. We will see later in our discussion of natural law how St. Thomas employs this hierarchy of activities in man when he sketches the human good.

What activity or function is peculiar to man such that he can be said to do it *qua* man? We are not surprised to learn that Aristotle takes rational activity to be man's function. Performing the specifically human function or *ergon* rational activity well makes one a good human person.

The difficulty with this is that rational activity is not a single thing; indeed, it is an analogous term. Because of that, doing it well—*eu* is the adverb that gives rise to the excellence characterizing an activity, its *arete*— is not one thing, and the good for man must accordingly be achieved by a plurality of virtues.

Excellentia autem hominis maxime attenditur secundum beatitudinem, quae est hominis bonum perfectum; et secundum partes eius, idest secundum illa bona quibus aliquid beatitudinis participatur. (IaIIae, q.2, a.2)	Man's excellence is found in happiness which is his perfect good, and in its parts, that is, in those goods whereby he participates in something of beatitude.

Students of Aristotle are divided in seeing man's good in terms of a plurality of activities or in terms of a single activity. Much of what Aristotle says favors the first view, but what he says about contemplation is sometimes taken to mean that this activity is for all practical purposes identical with the human function and that man's ultimate end and happiness can only be found in it. And of course, Aristotle is then charged with elitism.

It is not our present purpose to enter into this question of Aristotelian exegesis. What Thomas took Aristotle to be saying is clear enough. First, he always assumes that Aristotle is talking about what men can attain by their own efforts in this life. Second, on several occasions in the opening five questions of the *Prima secundae,* Thomas observes that Aristotle was aware that in this life only an imperfect happiness can be had. There is nothing which in this life can satisfy the demands of the notion of happiness.

Happiness is an activity, the ultimate perfection of the thing, and in God whose being and activity are one, happiness is identical with the divine essence. Angels are united with God by a single and sempiternal activity.

In hominibus autem, secundum statum praesentis vitae, est ultima perfectio secundum operationem qua homo coniungitur Deo: sed haec operatio nec continua potest esse, et per consequens nec unica est, quia operatio intercisione multiplicatur. Et propter hoc in statu praesentis vitae, perfecta beatitudo ab homine haberi non potest. Unde Philosophus, in I Ethic. (1101a20), ponens beatitudinem	In men however, with respect to the present life, ultimate perfection is found in that operation whereby man is conjoined to God: but this operation cannot be continuous, and thus cannot be unique since it is multiplied because of interruptions. That is why perfect happiness cannot be had in the present. Hence Aristotle in the *Ethics,* putting man's happiness in this life, calls it imperfect, concluding after

hominis in hac vita, dicit eam imper-
fectam, post multa concludens, 'Bea-
tos autem dicimus ut homines.' Sed
promittitur nobis a Deo beatitudo
perfecta, quando erimus 'sicut angeli
in caelo,' sicut dicitur Mt. 22,30.

a lengthy discussion, "happy we say as
men [can be happy]." But a perfect
happiness has been promised us by
God when we will be like "the angels
in heaven" as Matthew says.

This text is found in IaIIae, q.3, a.2, ad 4m. In reply to the fifth objection, he adds that happiness is greater to the degree contemplation is less interrupted, but it is always going to be an imperfect happiness. What man can attain in this life is a "share of happiness: *participatio beatitudinis*."

Et ideo in activa vita, quae circa
multa occupatur, est minus de ratione
beatitudinis quam in vita contempla-
tiva, quae versatur circa unum, idest
circa veritatis contemplationem. (ibid.)

Therefore in the active life which is
busy about many things, there is less
of the notion of happiness than in the
contemplative life which is concerned
with one thing, namely contemplation
of truth.

The picture that emerges is that the various senses of rational activity save or realize in various ways the notion of happiness, but that one of them is pre-eminent, namely, that activity of speculative mind called contemplation. If we could engage in that activity continuously, our happiness would not be imperfect, at least, not as imperfection has thus far been defined. Contemplation is the primary analogate of rational activity; the kinds of rational activity involved in the active life are such only in a secondary sense. In any case, there is an ordered multiplicity of rational activities and, in this life, man's ultimate good and happiness reposes on a plurality of virtues perfecting rational activity in different senses of the phrase.

It can be seen in what sense there is and in what sense there is not a single kind of activity the doing well of which constitutes man's good.

Contemplation and Happiness

The Fathers of the Church reacted differently to pagan philosophy, some seeing it as an error and abomination which had been replaced with revelation, others seeing it as a *praeparatio evangelica* and a cause for marvel at what the mind of man, unaided by revelation, can come to know. The same duality of reaction can be seen in the theologians of the thirteenth century. Thomas, as we have had occasion to mention, was one who found in the pagan philosopher Aristotle a grasp of truths about man, the world, and God that complement and are compatible with the mysteries of the faith. This is no less true in the practical order than in the speculative.

At the outset of his *Metaphysics,* Aristotle presents us with a picture of man's ascent from perception to intellectual knowledge of things perceived which, although first sought with quite practical ends in view, quite soon becomes something desired for its own sake. Aristotle makes the point first with respect to sight. Having opened with the claim that all men by nature desire to know, he goes on to say that a sign of this is the delight we take in seeing even when we have no practical end in view. This adumbration of the theoretical in the realm of perception is developed in the realm of intellectual knowledge as such, where theoretical knowledge is ranked in terms of the objects of its concern. Theoretical knowledge in its most perfect form will bear on eternal things, on divine things, and then it is called wisdom, not in the practical sense of *phronesis,* but in the sense of *sophia.* Wisdom, theology, contemplation ultimately coalesce as the ultimate good at which even the most humble instances of knowing are aimed. By this is meant that any intellectual knowledge shares in and prefigures contemplation which is what alone will fulfill the thirst for knowledge that is definitive of us.

The tenth book of the *Nicomachean Ethics* develops this theme against the background of the manifold components of the "good for man," arguing that the whole practical order is a kind of presupposition to and handmaid of the theoretical, with especial reference to contemplation.

There are standard objections to this made by philosophers as philosophers, that is, without any appeal to revealed truth. The most frequent objection bears on the apparent elitism of the Aristotelian vision of the objectively best life. The contemplation spoken of in the tenth book of the *Nicomachean Ethics* is grounded in the kind of philosophical theology in which metaphysics, and thus philosophy as such, terminates. But metaphysicians on anyone's understanding of the term are rare, and Aristotle has no illusions how difficult it is to engage in metaphysics. This has the unhappy consequence that human happiness can as a matter of principle be achieved only by a small number. But Aristotle asked what is the human good, not what is the good a handful alone can achieve.

This familiar complaint, to which Aristotle could reply, I think, often eclipses the objections Aristotle himself brings against his notion of contemplation as the highest good. The difficulty is not so much that only a few can engage in it as that no one can engage in it except episodically. That which could truly make us happy is an activity that may occupy a portion of a life, but it can never be anyone's exclusive activity. If one is said to lead a contemplative life, this is not because he does nothing but contemplate, but because all his other activities are subordinated to those rare moments when he does contemplate.

We have seen the importance Thomas attaches to Aristotle's teaching that happiness in the full sense of the term cannot be achieved. Since Aristotle wishes to discuss a good achievable by human action in this life, Thomas is quite correct to say that Aristotle does not think perfect happiness is possible in this life. Of course in Aristotle there is no contrast drawn between an imperfect human happiness in this life and a perfect human happiness beyond. Thomas's point is that the highest human activity and its excellent performance will not fulfill the demands of happiness as he has defined it, relying on the common assumptions of men. Indeed, Thomas spells out for us in the *Prima secundae* why speculative science, even metaphysics, cannot be felicific in the desired way.

The object or reality which is the ultimate end is that which best realizes the *ratio boni*. That being which is not merely a good among other good things, but goodness itself, namely God, fulfills the *ratio boni* maximally. Whatever we will we desire under the formality of good. Whenever we will we are implicitly desiring God.

If God is our good and ultimate end, happiness consists in attaining God. One way of attaining him is by way of a scientific grasp of him. That is what the whole of philosophy is ordered to, for Aristotle, insofar as it is precisely a love of wisdom. Wisdom consists preeminently in knowledge of the divine. Philosophy is thus the pursuit of such knowledge of God as we can achieve. But this way of achieving our ultimate end can be productive only of imperfect happiness.

Ad cuius evidentiam considerandum est quod consideratio speculativae scientiae non se extendit ultra virtutem principiorum illius scientiae: quia in principiis scientiae virtualiter tota scientia continetur. Prima autem principia scientiarum speculativarum sunt per sensum accepta, ut patet per Philosophum in principio Metaphys. et in fine Poster. Unde tota consideratio scientiarum speculativarum non potest ultra extendi quam sensibilium cognitio ducere potest. (IaIIae, q.3, a.6)	To see this is so, one need only consider that the speculative sciences cannot range beyond the power of their starting points, because in the principles or starting points of a science the whole science is virtually contained. But the first principles of speculative science are drawn from the senses, as Aristotle makes clear at the outset of the Metaphysics and the end of the Posteriora. Thus the consideration of the speculative sciences taken as a whole cannot go beyond where the knowledge of sensible things can take it.

Thomas often argues that from our knowledge of sensible things we can arrive at knowledge that there are suprasensible substances and by negative contrast with sensible substances mimick the process whereby we move from general to specific knowledge of the essences of sensible substances. But our knowledge of immaterial substances cannot on this basis be quidditative, knowledge of what they are essentially, because sensible objects cannot adequately manifest the essence of immaterial substances.

Unde relinquitur quod ultima hominis beatitudo non possit esse in consideratione speculativarum scientiarum. Sed sicut in formis sensibilibus participatur aliqua similitudo superiorum substantiarum, ita consideratio scientiarum speculativarum est quaedam participatio verae et perfectae beatitudinis. (Ibid.)	Thus it follows that man's ultimate happiness cannot consist in the consideration proper to speculative science. But just as some likeness of higher substances is participated in by sensible forms, so the consideration of the speculative sciences is a kind of participation in true and perfect happiness.

Perfect human happiness can only consist in the perfect attainment of God, not indirectly from the things that are made by way of argument and analogical terms, but in a direct and beatifying vision. Aristotle had pointed out that happiness must be self-sufficient. It cannot therefore consist in a good that does not fully and completely assuage the longing of the human heart.

The following passage summarizes in terms of Aristotelian logic the contrast between imperfect and perfect happiness.

Uniuscuiusque potentiae perfectio attenditur secundum rationem sui obiecti. Obiectum autem intellectus est *quod quid est,* idest essentia rei, ut dicitur in III De anima. Unde intantum procedit perfectio intellectus, inquantum cognoscit essentiam alicuius rei. Si ergo intellectus aliquis cognoscat essentiam alicuius effectus, per quam non possit cognosci essentia causae, ut scilicet sciatur de causa *quid est*; non dicitur intellectus attingere ad causam simpliciter, quamvis per effectum cognoscere possit de causa *an sit.* Et ideo remanet naturaliter homini desiderium, cum cognoscit effectum, et scit eum habere causam, ut etiam sciat de causa *quid est.* Et illud desiderium est admirationis, et causat inquisitionem, ut dicitur in principio Metaphys. Puta si aliquis cognoscens eclipsim solis, considerat quod ex aliqua causa procedit, de qua, quia nescit quid sit, admiratur et admirando inquirit. Nec ista inquisitio quiescit quousque perveniat ad cognoscendum essentiam causae. (IaIIae, q.3, a.8)

The perfection of any power is assessed in terms of the notion of its proper object. But the object of intellect is what a thing is, that is, the essence of the thing, as is said in *On the Soul,* Book 3. Thus intellect is perfect to the degree it knows the essence of the thing. Should then mind know the essence of an effect which cannot enable it to know what the cause is, the intellect would not be said to grasp the cause simply speaking even though it can know of the cause through its effect that it is. Man has a natural desire, when he knows an effect and that it has a cause, to know what the cause is. This desire stems from wonder which triggers inquiry, as is said in the beginning of the *Metaphysics.* For example, if one knowing the solar eclipse considers that it must have a cause and, not knowing what it is, wonders and wondering inquires. Nor will this inquiry come to rest until it achieves knowledge of the essence of the cause.

The Conditions of Happiness

Any thought we might have that the theologian, once having noted what the mere philosopher can say of human happiness, would let it go and concentrate on narrowly theological matters is dispelled by following Thomas's actual procedure in the moral part of the *Summa theologiae*. It seems clear that Thomas does not think that what Aristotle had to say on human happiness and ultimate end has simply been superseded and replaced by revealed truth. Thus he will contrast what we can expect to achieve of happiness in this life with the happiness that awaits us beyond in the beatific vision, nor is the contrast between what pagans can expect in this world and what Christians can. Such a procedure may cause unrest among believers, particularly theologians, when they take it to be an insufficient acknowledgment of the way in which Christian revelation has overturned ordinary human expectations, accounting the wisdom of this world folly and expecting a reciprocal judgment from nonbelievers. It is not a bad idea to have these considerations in mind when we reflect on the contrast Thomas draws between the conditions of imperfect and perfect happiness.

We remember the rejected candidates for the thing that might realize the notion of ultimate end, possible carriers of the formal note: wealth, honor, glory, power, or sense pleasure. These were traditionally rejected by pagan philosophers as well: such things could not be the point of life. The human good and thus human happiness had to attach to that in man which made him better than the beasts, indeed, the epitome of the material world. Obviously, however, things that cannot serve as *the* good may very well be needed for human happiness. Contemplation may be the best use of the highest human faculty but, because it can be engaged in only episodically, cannot be the full story of the moral life.

There are many constituents of the human good, because there are many senses of rational activity. The multiplicity of virtues governing the doing well of rational activity in these various senses is needed if human life is to be integrated. Thomas, who has taken over the Aristotelian analysis and identified it as imperfect happiness, is not of course interested in restricting himself to the good achievable in this life. But his discussion of perfect happiness proceeds by contrasting it with the imperfect kind Aristotle spoke of.

Can human happiness be understood without invoking pleasure? Is not pleasure in fact needed if we are to be called happy in any way that connects with ordinary usage? Consider first this general statement.

Respondeo dicendum quod quadrupliciter aliquid requiritur ad aliud. Uno modo, sicut praeambulum vel praeparatorium ad ipsum: sicut disciplina requiritur ad scientiam. Alio modo, sicut perficiens aliquid: sicut anima requiritur ad vitam corporis. Tertio modo, sicut coadiuvans extrinsecum: sicut amici requiruntur ad aliquid agendum. Quarto modo sicut aliquid concomitans: ut si dicamus quod calor requiritur ad ignem. Et hoc modo delectatio requiritur ad beatitudinem. (IaIIae, q.4, a.1)

Let me say that one thing is needed for another in four ways. First, as antecedent and preparatory to it, as teaching is required for knowledge. Second, as perfecting it, as the body's life needs the soul. Third, as an extrinsic aid, as friends are required to do something. Fourth, as something concomitant, as we say fire requires heat. It is in this last way that pleasure is required for happiness.

Pleasure attaches to an activity and cannot be willed or chosen separately from it. Pleasure in the ordinary use is an accompaniment of sense activity, especially sexual activity. Sense pleasure is a kind of property of eating, drinking, and sexual intercourse. The term is transferred to intellectual activities, the fine arts, and knowledge, which provide a higher and keener pleasure. Contemplation, as the crown of intellectual activity, will afford the highest pleasure. The pleasures of sense will form part of the human good, insofar as sense activities are brought under the sway of reason by the moral virtues.

Which is higher, the vision or the pleasure accompanying it? This is a question Aristotle left unanswered, but for which Thomas provides an answer (IaIIae, q.4, a.2). Calling pleasure the coming to rest of the will and noting that this comes about because of some operation, he argues that we do not will the end of that operation for the pleasure it gives us so much as will it as a good, the pleasure following on that. "Hence it is manifest that the activity in which the will rests is prior to the will's resting in it."

Rectitude of will is required for happiness, both before and during. It is a prior requirement because rectitude of will is precisely the obligatory ordering to the ultimate end, without which the end would not be pursued. Only what is loved is pursued. Right willing is also concomitant with happiness, which consists of the vision of the divine essence. "The will of one seeing the essence of God necessarily loves whatever it loves as ordered to God, just as the will of one not seeing the divine essence necessarily loves whatever it loves under the common notion of the good which he knows" (IaIIae, q.4, a.4). Again, the contrast of perfect and imperfect happiness.

Does human happiness require a body? Insofar as the question bears on imperfect happiness, it seems absurd.

Manifestum est autem quod ad beatitudinem huius vitae, de necessitate requiritur corpus. Est enim beatitudo huius vitae operatio intellectus, vel speculativi vel practici. Operatio autem intellectus in hac vita non potest esse sine phantasmate, quod non est nisi in organo corporeo.... Et sic beatitudo quae in hac vita haberi potest, dependet quodammodo ex corpore. (IaIIae, q.4, a.5)	It is obvious that the body is required for the happiness of this life. For happiness in this life is an operation of intellect, either speculative or practical. But the intellect's activity in this life cannot occur without an image which can only exist in a bodily organ.... That is why the happiness attainable in this life depends in a certain way on the body.

But of course the question is asked because of perfect happiness, something presumably enjoyed now by the souls of departed saints. Thomas rejects the view that the holy souls have to wait until the general resurrection in order to enjoy perfect happiness. He has both authority and reason on his side, he says, citing 2 Corinthians 5:6–8, and pointing out that the vision of the divine essence cannot be grasped from sense images and thus can be enjoyed without the body.

Platonism? How can the happiness of the soul be the happiness of a man, if a man is both body and soul? It cannot be, and that is why, though the beatific vision can indeed be enjoyed by the soul prior to resurrection, because the soul exists not only as a part of a whole but also as that which gives existence to the whole and can itself subsist—that of course is the upshot of the proof for the soul's immortality—the soul's happiness is fulfilled when it rejoins its body. But even then there is a kind of trickle down theory of happiness.

Appetit enim anima sic frui Deo, quod etiam ipsa fruitio derivetur ad corpus per redundantiam, sicut est possible. Et ideo quandiu ipsa fruitur Deo sine corpore, appetitus eius sic quiescit in eo quod habet, quod tamen adhuc ad participationem eius vellet suum corpus pertingere. (IaIIae, q.4, a.5, ad 4m)	The soul desires so to enjoy God that this very enjoyment might also be shared redundantly by the body insofar as this is possible. Therefore so long as it enjoys God without the body, its appetite rests in what it has in such a way that it also wants its body to attain to a share in it.

Does happiness increase when the soul rejoins its body? If the soul desires something it does not yet have, namely that the body share in the happiness it enjoys, it would seem the soul is not perfectly happy. Thomas replies that the will of the soul of the blessed is at rest, because it has what suffices to fulfill it. But he allows that on the side of the soul it does not yet possess God in every way possible for it. "Et ideo, corpore resumpto, beatitudo crescit non intensive, sed extensive: Therefore, having rejoined body, happiness increases not intensively, but extensively" (IaIIae, q.4, a.5, ad 5m).

The perfect disposition of body is required for happiness in this world, both antecedently and concomitantly (IaIIae, q.4, a.6) as are external goods, the latter as instruments and aids of virtuous activity. As for friends, they are required for imperfect happiness as objects of benefaction and as co-operators in both the practical and theoretical order. Friends, the communion of saints, adorn rather than constitute bliss, they being needed for its *bene esse* but not its *esse*.

Attaining Perfect Happiness

Obviously, perfect happiness is not something we can achieve as we can imperfect happiness. Nonetheless, Thomas points out that we are capable of it (*capax perfecti boni*) insofar as we can grasp with mind the universal and perfect good and will it. But the beatific vision exceeds our natural mode of knowing; our experience of sensible things does not suffice for grasping the essence of God. In short, we are capable of it in one sense, but incapable of achieving it. The capability consists, again, in the fact that the will desires its own fulfillment and the exclusion of all evils. But this desire cannot be fulfilled in this life, since there are unavoidable evils such as the darkness of the mind, weakness of will, and bodily ailments.

Think of Camus's Parisian. The description was meant to elicit our sympathy, our judgment that something is wrong here. But if Camus's character is undeniably gloomy, we can tell a similar tale of any human life. One reply to Camus is simply to say: That's the way it is. That's life. The reply is inadequate, however, because Camus has indeed hit upon something. Our lives seem to have built into them a desire that cannot be fulfilled.

Similiter etiam desiderium boni in hac vita satiari non potest. Naturaliter enim homo desiderat permanentiam eius boni quod habet. Bona autem praesentis vitae transitoria sunt: cum et ipsa vita transeat, quam naturaliter desideramus, et eam perpetuo permanere vellemus, quia naturaliter homo refugit mortem. Unde impossibile est quod in hac vita vera beatitudo habeatur. (IaIIae, q.5, a.3)

Similarly the desire for the good cannot be sated in this life. For man naturally wants the good he has to last, but the goods of the present life are transitory, indeed the very life we naturally desire is transitory, yet we would like it to endure forever, because a man naturally shuns death. It is impossible, then, that true happiness be had in this life.

Our reach exceeds our grasp. There lurks in every good enjoyed the realization of its insufficiency. *Post coitum triste,* the pagans said, but the same can be said of the possession of any good.

This intimation of our true good which is implicit in every desire is the link between the natural and supernatural. Religion is derided as pie in the sky, as the promise of some impossible bliss elsewhere, diverting our attention from the things of this world. But the very criticism pays tribute to the natural longing the faith addresses. Pie on earth? Bliss this side of the grave? The utopian alternatives to our true good have the grievous disadvantage that, even if they could be achieved, and no one seriously thinks they can, they would be intrinsically dissatisfying. On the happiest possible outcome, they could provide only imperfect human happiness. One obvious difference between perfect and imperfect happiness is that the former cannot be lost once had, while the latter, alas, can (IaIIae, q.5, a.4). Once again Thomas cites *Nicomachean Ethics* 1101a19 for Aristotle's acknowledgment that the happiness men can achieve in this life falls short of what they themselves mean by true happiness.

Plato, noting that we have ideas that seem to have no instantiation in sensible things, held that we got them from direct contact with the really real. The fact is that the nature of our mind takes us beyond the mode of the things we know. It is not that we were previously acquainted with perfect happiness and see terrestrial possibilities falling short of it. Rather, we notice in the cognitive and appetitive structure of action an orientation to universal truth and universal good. That something answers to these as such is the good news. When we hear it, we realize we have already wanted it and that we have the wherewithal to listen.

Dicendum quod, sicut natura non deficit homini in necessariis, quamvis non dederit sibi arma et tegumenta sicut aliis animalibus, quia dedit ei rationem et manus, quibus possit haec sibi conquirere; ita nec deficit homini in necessariis, quamvis non daret sibi aliquod principium quo posset beatitudinem consequi; hoc enim erat impossibile. Sed dedit ei liberum arbitrium, quo possit converti ad Deum, qui eum faceret beatum. (IaIIae, q.5, a.5, ad 1m)

It should be said that nature did not fail man in necessaries, although she did not give him arms and dress like the other animals, because she gave him reason and the hand whereby he can fashion these for himself; neither does she fail man in things necessary by not giving him a principle whereby he can attain happiness (for that was impossible). But she gave him free will whereby he can turn to God who will make him happy.

Throughout this discussion of ultimate end and happiness, then, we find Thomas acknowledging the truth of Aristotle's account and seeing it in continuity with the beatific vision to which we are called as our ultimate end. The Thomistic and Catholic view is that grace builds on nature and does not destroy it.

Summary

Anything that counts as a human act is undertaken with a view to some end. The end is what is given as answer to the question: What are you doing? Since we intend to do what we do and what we intend is a good, the good for the sake of which the act is performed is an end.

That there is an ultimate end is more difficult to show. It is, however, easy to show how a number of actions cluster, insofar as they are subordinated to some overriding objective: victory in the case of the various activities done by an army, the finished edifice in the case of the many building trades. Is there some activity like that of the general or the master builder that everyone should engage in with respect to his own life, directing various activities to an overriding objective?

Aristotle and Thomas say yes. There is a good with reference to which we appraise eating and drinking as good or bad. This appraisal is not of the biological functions as such, meaning that our digestive system is in good shape. Rather, we mean that eating and drinking now, this much, in these circumstances, are good for me. What criterion is invoked here? My comprehensive or total good.

The first distinction Thomas makes with respect to ultimate end is that between what the phrase means and what is taken to instantiate what the phrase means. On the basis of your laughably limited experience you can yet grasp the meaning of "the most beautiful girl in the world." Then, financed by a philanthropic foundation, armed with your definition concealed in a glass slipper, you go in search of her. Everybody wants "what's good for me" and may be said to choose anything as coming under that conceptual umbrella. This enabled Thomas to make the initially startling claim that everyone is agreed on the ultimate end. He meant that they are agreed that they want what they want and things are wanted as good for the wanter. As to what thing or things will fill that bill, well, here disagreement is rife.

Is the disagreement indicative of irreducibly different tastes, much as you might come back from your search for the most beautiful girl in the world with Fifi LaRue on your arm, while the myopic Bert Parks picks Barbra Streisand? In an excess of romanticism we might even say that every man marries the most beautiful girl in the world. Is it like this when we ask what thing or things really make up what is good for me?

Aristotle, citing rational activity as the human function, dared to say that doing well the activity distinctive of humans will make us good men. But "rational activity" covers an ordered set of activities, and we might say that acting rationally well in all the senses of rational activity is the human good. Aristotle ranks types of rational activity, most notably putting practical reason under theoretical reason. Objectively speaking, contemplation is the highest human activity, because it is the purest kind of rational activity concerned with the most perfect reality, the divine. Theoretical thinking is undertaken with an eye to achieving its own perfection, truth, and this places it above practical thinking, which is aimed at perfecting activities less than reason.

Thomas found Aristotle drawing attention to the imperfect way in which anyone realizes the ideal of happiness. He ranks the contemplator objectively higher than the statesman, but he has no illusions about contemplative activity. Contemplation cannot occupy anyone all the time, it is engaged in episodically, and the contemplative will need the virtues of the activities engaged in when he is not contemplating. Stressing the imperfection of the objectively best instance in Aristotle eases for Thomas, perhaps, the charge of elitism.

There is a perfect happiness, attainable not in this life but the next. God is the highest good, goodness itself, and thus He is what objectively fulfills all our aspirations. But how can we get to Him? Contemplation gets to Him via knowledge of sensible things and thus cannot achieve knowledge of the divine essence. A direct vision of God's essence without any dependence on sense images is perfect happiness. This has been promised us by Christ. The condition is to follow Him. We have the ability, thanks to free will, to respond to this call for conversion.

The discussion of happiness in Questions 2 through 5 of the *Prima secundae* is a choral comparison of imperfect and perfect happiness. The former is not seen as an upstart rival, a product of hubristic and Pelagian pushiness, but as what perfect happiness presupposes and builds upon. Thomas's teaching on the relation of nature and grace is vast and complex. A feature of it that could scarcely be ignored in his treatment of imperfect and perfect happiness is a total lack of negativity in reading Aristotle's effort to answer the question: What does it all mean?

3. The Structure of Human Action

I F WE notice Fifi LaRue fish a Visa card from her purse at the Pan Am counter and ask ourselves what she is doing, we could of course simply say that she is fishing a Visa Card from her purse at the Pan Am counter. We might also say that she is paying for a ticket to Rome or, more vaguely and comprehensively, that Fifi is on her way to Rome.

Now, impulsive though Fifi may be, we would expect that she has given some thought to buying the ticket and to taking the trip before fishing that Visa card from her purse with a flourish that draws admiring stares from several quarters, including of course our own. She did not suddenly spring into existence at the counter, pull out a credit card, and ask for a ticket to Rome. What she is doing implements a notion she has nurtured for some time, however short; it doesn't really matter whether she has been considering the trip for months or minutes. Made weary by the routine of her day, she went shopping, her eye was caught by some fetching travel posters, and she found herself thinking of somewhere altogether elsewhere. Almost anywhere else would do, such was her ennui, but a picture of the Spanish Steps bathed in sunlight, nearly buried in flowers and flower children, arrested her. She sat looking at it, a little smile teasing her sensuous lips. Thoughts of Paris and Madrid fade away. It is Rome she craves. She tells herself she is going and that is that. And so it is that we come upon her at the Pan Am counter in Kennedy airport, fishing a Visa Card from her purse and buying a ticket.

She might have paid cash. She might have written a check. She might have gotten out a Frequent Flyer certificate. In any case, she would be offering something valuable for the ticket, but it is unlikely that we would say that they are different acts. That is, the way she buys the ticket may differ, yet the differences have no moral significance. But is any one of these ways of paying a different act from the act of buying a ticket to Rome? It is true, since there are indeed many ways of paying, that none of them is an essential part of buying a ticket. But they are disjunctively necessary. That is, *some* method of payment must form part of the act of buying the ticket.

She can use the credit card, cash, a check, or a certificate, perhaps a gift certificate, to buy a vial of scent to put behind her pretty ears. That is a different act from buying a ticket to Rome. But any purchase must involve as an element a mode of payment, whether pure or mixed (that is, one might pay part in cash, part by check, etc.).

We can, however, isolate pulling a piece of plastic from her purse from making any purchase at all, and so too with removing bills from her wallet, a certificate from her purse, or writing numbers on a check form. Taken just as such, these might appeal to us as the atoms at which analysis of actions ultimately arrives. And what we would have in mind is that while the act of purchasing may not be separable from some mode of payment, what we are calling modes of payment could well occur without being modes of payment. Fifi's removal of the credit card may be part of a general emptying of her purse in search of her car keys. Or it might form part of any number of intentional acts. Or maybe it is an aborted act. Fifi pulls out her credit card and, as she lays it on the counter, has second thoughts about this impulsive flight to Rome. She hesitates. Whether or not she goes on to buy a ticket, we seem confronted by a distinct human action which, presumably, must be either morally good or bad.

Perhaps, or perhaps we are getting impatient and wonder why we cannot just stick with "going to Rome" as the action Fifi is engaged in, and let it go at that. What is the point of breaking up that fairly simple action into component parts? The cause of our impatience is that there must be a point to making finer grained analyses, and so there must. Otherwise Fifi's taking out her credit card can conceivably be broken up into brain events, the movements of the muscles and bones of her arm, the clutching of the card between thumb and fingers, the drawing of it forth. All these things are going on, all are parts in some sense of what Fifi is doing, but we don't want to hear about them if the question is: What is Fifi doing? The point of that question—Fifi may put it to herself—is to wonder about the morality of the deed.

Something may be either a part of a larger action or an action in its own right. The latter becomes clear when the larger action is interrupted and we are left with just the part which now becomes the only whole we have, the only action performed which can be morally appraised.

Fifi at the counter can be taken to be doing something which includes her wanting to be elsewhere as she glances at travel posters, then concentrating on Rome, determining to go there, deciding to go by plane, picking a day, and going to the counter to buy the ticket. Normally all this will be subsumed into "Fifi is going to Rome." Saying that she is buying her ticket may do service for this larger claim, but were she or someone else to go into all the steps and details that make up that one moral action, we would become restive and wonder why this boring particularity was being visited on us. The only answer can be: *Because sometimes those parts become whole actions subject to moral appraisal on their own.* A single moral act is potentially a plurality of moral acts. Those potential parts become actualized when one arrests oneself, is interrupted, or for some reason does not carry through the original intention. That seems to be the main reason Thomas holds that there is a plurality of will acts.

Constituents of Voluntary Acts

"You Can't Want What You Don't Know." The human act is one that proceeds from deliberate will; it is a knowing wanting. That in us which seeks or desires is specified as this desire or that by its object. I want to go home. I want a girl just like the girl who married dear old dad. Give me land, lots of land, under starry skies above. And so on. For Thomas, as for Aristotle, the nature of a thing is the built-in basis for its activity, because it is an appetite for what is good for the agent whose nature it is. This thought is retained in "Water seeks its own level" and remarks of that kind. The nature of a physical object is the source of appetite and desire, and the more complicated the thing, the more numerous its appetites. (Thus the eventual need to distinguish between nature and appetite, the latter being a faculty or power of the former.)

The transition from nonliving to living things is sometimes described as the transition from the merely natural to the besouled or living. Of course, living things have natures, but "mere nature" is best represented by a thing that has only one drive, is ordered to a single end. Thus Aristotle's elements were determined to move to a given place in the scheme of things. Earth downward, fire upward. This is their nature. By contrast with the inorganic, the simplest living thing has a nature which is the seat of many appetites. Determined activity gives way to spontaneity [*In II de anima*, lect. 7, n. 311–2].

That something should be ordered to a given good or goods is a mark of intelligence. A plan unfolds. It is what we want to know when we study nature. Why does something act as it does? But the knowledge that a plan presupposes need not be had by the things enacting the plan. Animal life is thus a quite new level, where desires are triggered by perception as well as by mere nature. The senses grasp things as pleasing or unpleasing, and the animal seeks or shuns them accordingly. The movement toward what is perceived as good is what Thomas means by sense appetite. Specifically animal desires are consequent on perception, on sense cognition.

These reminders enable us to see what is meant by will. Will is rational appetite, a desire consequent on a knowledge which, unlike perception, surmounts particularity by grasping things *as things of a given kind.* A sense like hearing or sight perceives things only of a given range or kind. Hearing picks up sounds, sight colors. Mind is not restricted to a kind of thing; it can in principle know any and every kind of thing. Its range is not confined to this kind of being, or that, but bears on being as such. That is, it can know anything.

Mind is an appetite for truth; that is its nature. We don't decide to think; we simply are the animal that thinks. Of course we can put our minds to scrambling our minds with drugs, just as we can commit suicide. But each of us is an instance of that very special animal who knows things as the kinds of things they are, can be aware of his awareness of other things, encompasses in his mind the whole universe. Those who seek to depreciate man's uniqueness tell us he is a mere speck in one galaxy among who knows how many galaxies, that even as a species he has been here for a space of time which, cosmically considered, does not even register, and as for individual men, well. . . . But this big put-down self-destructs when we notice that one of those specks is speaking to others and all are assumed to be able to encompass in their grasp the whole cosmos. Some speck. In wiser days that speck was recognized as a microcosm, the whole shebang writ small.

The mind transcends the moment, the particular, and can range over all that is. Will is the appetite that follows on that kind of cognition, on mind. It is the desire consequent on the intellect's universal grasp of what is good. When mind in its practical gear thinks of the good for man, its content specifies the will's desire. You can't want what you don't know.

The human act is a knowing wanting. In reflecting on such situations as those with which we began this chapter, Thomas saw the need to distinguish a number of acts of will, that is, acts of intellectual appetite.

Willing the End

On the assumption that human acts are thus made up of parts that have a moral unity due to the intention that binds them together, Thomas will speak of the constitutive will acts as bearing either on an end or aim, on the one hand, or on the means of achieving that end, on the other.

1. Fifi's eye is caught by travel posters and the thought of taking a vacation interests her.

2. Fifi daydreams over a picture of the Trevi Fountain, a popular ballad echoes in her head. How pleasant it would be. . . .

3. Fifi sees Rome as her destination, as somewhere she means to get to. Fifi intends to go to Rome.

Because Fifi may never go on from [1] to [2] let alone to anything else, Thomas distinguishes this simple stirring of the will by thought and image from other acts of will. She might do [1] and [2] and then shake away the thoughts; [3] will absorb into itself [1] and [2]. If what interests Fifi in the thought of a vacation is moral misbehavior on foreign soil [1] may fortify Fifi in her proclivity to adventure, but she shakes the thought away and does not go on to [2]. If she does go on to take pleasure in the thought of immoral antics in the Azores, she is doing something bad for her character. If she intends to go and fling roses, roses riotously with the throng, her fault is more profound.

I am getting ahead of myself by suggesting these moral appraisals, if only to underscore that, unless there is some such moral payoff on identifying particular acts, we would likely lose interest in distinguishing such possible acts. [1], [2], and [3] exemplify what Thomas calls will (*voluntas*), enjoyment (*frui*), and intention (*intentio*), respectively.

Will is not used here to name the capacity or faculty but rather an activity of that faculty; by will Thomas means a particular want following on an intellectual grasp. Like the will to power. The object of will is the understood good, and acts of will bear on things which are seen as good. These goods are sought as ends, as what finalizes and gives its object to the will act.

Ratio autem boni, quod est obiectum potentiae voluntatis, invenitur non solum in fine, sed etiam in his quae sunt ad finem. Si autem loquamur de voluntate secundum quod nominat proprie actum, sic, proprie loquendo, est finis tantum. Omnis enim actus denominatus a potentia, nominat simplicem actum illius potentiae, sicut *intelligere* nominat simplicem actum intellectus. Simplex autem actus potentiae est in id quod est secundum se obiectum potentiae. Id autem quod est propter se bonum et volitum est finis. Unde voluntas proprie est ipsius finis. (IaIIae, q.8, a.2)

The note of the good, which is the object of the faculty of will, is found not only in the end but also in the things which are for the sake of the end. However, if we speak of 'will' as naming its proper act, then, properly speaking, it is of end alone. For every act bearing the name of its power names that power's simple act, as *understanding* names the simple act of the understanding. The simple act of a power bears on what is as such the object of the power. But it is end which is in itself good and willed. Hence will is properly of end itself.

The reference to *intellectus,* the simple act of intellect which bears on primary intelligibilities, things which are starting points and all but impossible not to know, is a significant analogy, and not only because will is the intellectual appetite. Just as mind first bears on things which are knowable in themselves, directly, immediately (what the tradition in which Thomas moves calls *per se notae*), so the end is first in the order of desirable things: the end is the beginning. Thomas refers to *Nicomachean Ethics* VII, 8 (1151a16), which could be rendered as, "In actions that for the sake of which is the starting point just as axioms are in mathematics." That thought will be echoed when Thomas discusses the natural moral law.

In my end is my beginning, as T. S. Eliot wrote in one of the *Four Quartets*. What is first in thought, what gets us going, is the last thing to be realized.

In executione operis, ea quae sunt ad finem se habet ut media, et finis ut terminus. Unde sicut motus naturalis interdum sistit in medio, et non pertingit ad terminum; ita quandoque operatur aliquis id quod est ad finem, et tamen non consequitur finem. Sed in volendo est e converso: nam voluntas per finem devenit ad volendum ea quae sunt ad finem; sicut et intellectus devenit in conclusiones per principia, quae *media* dicuntur. Unde intellectus aliquando intelligit medium, et ex eo non procedit ad conclusionem. Et similiter voluntas aliquando vult finem, et tamen non procedit ad volendum id quod est ad finem. (IaIIae, q.8, a.3, ad 3m)	In the execution of the deed, the things which relate to the end are means and the end the term. And just as a natural motion sometimes stops midway and does not reach its term, so sometimes a person does what is for the end yet does not achieve the end. In willing, it is the other way round, for will because of the end comes to want what is for the sake of the end, as intellect arrives at conclusions through principles called 'middles.' So the intellect sometimes understands the middle and does not go on from it to the conclusion. Similarly, the will sometimes wills the end, yet does not go on to will what leads to the end.

Here we see the spatial origins in locomotion of the terminology of rational discourse (syllogism) generally and then particularly of practical reasoning. *Medium* or middle, as used of the midpoint of a passage from A to B, is employed in speaking of reasoning as that which links the predicate and subject of the conclusion. The middle term is that of which the predicate is said and which is said of the subject, in the premises, thus providing the conceptual link for the predicate and subject in the conclusion. Those *per se notae* principles alluded to above are immediate in the precise sense of being knowable in themselves (*per se*) without need of a mediating middle term; we see right off the truth of the conjunction of predicate and subject.

Talk of end and means is derived from the same spatial image. The end is the term of the action; what must be done if that term is to be reached are called means, as midpoints that must be passed through in order to arrive at the term or end. This analogy, which helps us understand the terminology, can become an obstacle if we think the means toward an end must be strung out on a chronological line and the end must be some geographic destination. Sometimes that is the case, but not always.

Free Willing

A power or capacity of the soul is, as the name suggests, in potency, potential, not yet actually engaged in the act of which it is the capacity. It is in potency in two ways: to act or not to act; and: to do this as opposed to that. Thomas illustrates this with sight. Sometimes we are not actually seeing, sometimes we are. When we aren't, we can, and when we do, we have actualized the potency, but sometimes we see red, sometimes we see black. Sight needs a cause, first that it should see, and then that it should see this rather than that. That is, it needs a cause of its use or exercise and it needs something to specify or determine its act. It is the will that uses or exercises the other powers, those that come under the dominion of man. If will thus ranges over the other powers as moving or efficient cause, it nonetheless depends upon intellect as its formal cause.

Bonum autem in communi, quod habet rationem finis, est obiectum voluntatis. Et ideo ex hac parte voluntas movet alias potentias animae ad suos	It is the good generally, that has the note of end, which is the object of will. Will therefore moves the other powers of soul to act: for we use the

actus: utimur enim aliis potentiis cum volumus. Nam fines et perfectiones omnium aliarum potentiarum comprehenduntur sub obiecto voluntatis, sicut quaedam particularia bona: semper autem ars vel potentia ad quam pertinet finis universalis, movet ad agendum artem vel potentiam ad quam pertinet finis particularis sub illo universali comprehensus; sicut dux exercitus, qui intendit bonum commune, scilicet ordinem totius exercitus, movet suo imperio aliquem ex tribunis, qui intendit ordinem unius aciei. Sed obiectum movet determinando actum, ad modum principii formalis, a quo in rebus naturalibus actio specificatur, sicut calefactio a calore. Primum autem principium formale est ens et verum universale, quod est obiectum intellectus. Et ideo isto modo motionis intellectus movet voluntatem, sicut praesentans ei obiectum suum. (IaIIae, q.9, a.1)

other powers when we wish. The ends and perfections of all the other powers are included in the object of will as particular goods. The art or power which looks to the universal end always moves to action the art or power which bears on a particular end included under the universal. The general of the army who intends the common good, namely the order of the whole army, by his command moves one of his tribunes who commands one of the platoons. But the object moves by determining the act in the manner of a formal principle, as natural activities are specified: heating by heat. The first formal principle is being and universal truth, the object of intellect. The intellect moves the will in this way, then, presenting to it its object.

Will moves the intellect to perform, but intellect specifies the object of will. The good is the object of appetite or will and thus is the object of intellect not as good, but as true. As the end of intellect, truth is a particular good falling under the general good the will wants, and thus truth is the object of will not as truth but as a good. So too Thomas distinguishes between intellect as a nature and intellect as intellect. As a nature, intellect is determined to the truth, it is an appetite for the truth. Indeed there are some truths it necessarily knows; it cannot fail to know them. As intellect it has a more variable object; it can fall into falsity. It needs to perform lengthy discursive acts to arrive at a given truth. So too will as a nature is ordered and determined to the good as such—determined. Will as will is *ad opposita,* free. The will is not free to want the good; nor is this simply a question of the formal *ratio ultimi finis*. Notice how Thomas articulates the good.

Hoc autem est bonum in communi, in quod voluntas naturaliter tendit, sicut etiam quaelibet potentia in suum obiectum: et etiam ipse finis ultimus, qui hoc modo se habet in appetibilibus, sicut prima principia demonstrationum in intellegibilibus: et universaliter omnia illa quae conveniunt volenti secundum suam naturam. Non enim per voluntatem appetimus solum ea quae pertinent ad potentiam voluntatis; sed etiam ea quae pertinent ad singulas potentias, et ad totum hominem. Unde naturaliter homo vult non solum obiectum voluntatis, sed etiam alia quae conveniunt aliis potentiis: ut cognitionem veri, quae convenit intellectui; et esse et vivere et alia huiusmodi, quae respiciunt consistentiam naturalem; quae omnia comprehenduntur sub obiecto voluntatis, sicut quaedam particularia bona. (IaIIae, q.10, a.1)	This is the common good to which will naturally tends, as any power does to its object, and the ultimate end itself which relates to desirable things as the first principles of demonstration do to intelligibles; and universally whatever befits the willer according to his own nature. For through will we seek not only what pertains to the power of will, but also the things pertaining to each power, and to the whole man. Hence a man naturally wills not only the object of will, but also the others things befitting other powers: like knowledge of the truth, which belongs to intellect; and being and life and other like things which are part of his natural wholeness: all of these are included in the object of will as particular goods.

Among the things the will cannot not will are the objects of the various natural inclinations which enter into man's makeup. This passage is a remarkable foreshadowing of the later treatment of natural law precepts. But what about the freedom of the will? If the will's act is specified by what reason presents to it, what room for maneuver does it have?

There is no doubt that will is not free with respect to goodness itself, to the ultimate end. It is not in our power to will anything other than the good, that is, what is perfective of us. This may seem tautological. I cannot yearn for something other than the point of yearning at all. Whatever particular thing I want will exhibit that note of what-fulfills, what is good.

And as the passage just quoted makes clear, this overall objective can be filled in with the constituents of our overall good. We will not only our good vaguely taken, but also everything we recognize as necessary to our good. Once more, Thomas invokes the running analogy between will and reason—how could he not?—and once more, we have a passage that anticipates IaIIae, q.94, a.2. [It is important that the "Treatise on Law" be seen as a section of the part of the *Summa* in which it is found.]

Finis ultimus ex necessitate movet voluntatem, quia est bonum perfectum. Et similiter illa quae ordinantur ad hunc finem, sine quibus finis haberi non potest, sicut esse et vivere et huiusmodi. Alia vero, sine quibus finis haberi potest, non ex necessitate vult qui vult finem: sicut conclusiones sine quibus principia possunt esse vera, non ex necessitate credit qui credit principia. (IaIIae, q.10, a.2, ad 3m)

The ultimate end necessarily moves the will, because it is the perfect good. Similarly what is so ordered to the end that without it the end cannot be had, like being, life, and the like. Other things, however, without which the end can be attained, are not necessarily wanted by one who wants the end; much as conclusions on whose truth the principles do not depend are not necessarily accepted by one who accepts the principles.

The reason some things do not necessarily move the will is that they are neither the end nor necessary constituents or conditions of the end. Our happiness does not depend on them. The objects of desire that occur to us are all good one way or the other. A bowl of raisin bran looks good, not because of the list of chemicals on the side of the box, but because of remembered pleasant taste. A walk in the rain looks good to Gene Kelly. The Grand Tetons make climbers' feet itch when they think of them. On and on and on. But of just about anything men pursue they can say, "I could live without it." Good as good things are, they are not good through and through. That is, they all have pros and cons. This is the root of our freedom. Our will is not necessarily moved by anything short of goodness itself, and the innumerable carriers of the note of goodness—particular good things—have, as English Benedictines say, their down side. Hence the complexity of the human act. There is no automatic, in the sense of necessary, response to the possible objects of pursuit that come constantly to mind. Fifi at the Pan Am counter is visited by thoughts of what a trip to Rome will do to her bank account, her job, her diet, her morals. Flying, she perceives, is not all ointment.

Freedom is a vast subject. We will not dwell on the discussion, of ancient vintage, as to whether the will can be so buffeted by passion as to lose the name of action. We will not ask whether God necessarily moves the will, save to note that the question must first be distinguished into "moves as efficient cause" and "moves as object or formal cause." As efficient cause, God moves the will He created in a mode appropriate to the will. To see God will be to see the fulfillment of our total being. Preferring anything to God, in vision, is a conceptual impossibility. In this life, alas, even when we know God is goodness itself, because of our deficient way of knowing that, He is a good among many, and other goods are all too often preferred to Him.

Enjoyment and Intention

Years ago there was the joke about the seminarian who confessed that he had read *Commonweal* (nowadays it would be *Crisis*) and was asked by his confessor, "Ah, but did you take pleasure in it?"

The mind inexhaustibly provides to will possible objects of pursuit. To think of anything that can be done or made by us is to think of a good, something that is a possible object of will. Clearly, we screen out the vast majority of these; very few engage the will. Those that do, those whose attractiveness, pull, fittingness, or pleasantness if dwelt on a bit stir up in us a kind of pleasure. It is not that we are committing ourselves to A as opposed to B. We may be stirred by both. Fifi may be half in love with easeful death but also moved by the thought of visiting in Rome the house where Keats died. This enjoyment is of something that promises to fulfill us. It is endlike, and it is pleasant. It holds the promise of putting our desire to rest. As an object before the mind and will, we already in a sense have it and the enjoyment (*fruitio*) is an anticipation of the delight of having it in reality. It is the latter that is enjoyment in the full sense.

We may even go on to intend the end so considered and as considered enjoyed. To intend is to tend toward the thing, to see it as an object of pursuit, as something getting to which may entail doing many as yet unthought of things. (Intention is that which binds together into one moral act a plurality of acts that could occur without reference to one another.)

Et ideo ea quae sunt plura secundum rem, possunt accipi ut unus terminus intentionis, prout sunt unum secundum rationem: vel quia aliqua duo concurrunt ad integrandum aliquid unum, sicut ad sanitatem concurrunt calor et frigus commensurata; vel quia aliqua duo sub uno communi continentur, quod potest esse intentum. Puta acquisitio vini et vestis continetur sub lucro, sicut sub quoddam communi: unde nihil prohibet quin ille qui intendit lucrum, simul haec duo intendit. (IaIIae, q.12, a.3, ad 2m)	Thus it is that many really different things can be the objects of a single intention, insofar as they are made one by reason; either because several things concur to make up another, as proportionate heat and cold enter into health; or because two things are contained under something common that can be intended. Buying some wine and some clothes come under money as under something common, so one whose intention is money is not precluded from intending these two things as well.

The term "intention" may strike us as being linked to thinking rather than willing, and both medieval and modern uses of the term strengthen that. But if we think of "tending toward," its etymology, we will see that the epistemological and logical uses borrow from the sense Thomas has in mind here, not the reverse. Of course, will is intellectual appetite and is dependent on consciousness of an object as a term of pursuit. To intend something is to want something, which will become the reason for wanting other things which are means to it. To tend toward the thing, as a term of a process that may involve as yet unconsidered means, that is intention. Here is Thomas's summary statement of these three will acts bearing on end.

Intentio est actus voluntatis respectu finis. Sed voluntas respicit finem tripliciter. [a] Uno modo, absolute: et sic dicitur *voluntas,* prout absolute volu-	Intention is the act of will bearing on the end. But will looks to the end in three ways. [a] First, absolutely: *will* in this sense occurs when we simply

mus vel sanitatem vel si quid aliud est huiusmodi. [b] Alio modo consideratur finis secundum quod in eo quiescitur: et hoc modo *fruitio* respicit finem. [c] Tertio modo consideratur finis secundum quod est terminus alicuius quod in ipsum ordinatur: et sic *intentio* respicit finem. (IaIIae, q.12, a.1, ad 4m)

want health or any such thing. [b] Second, end is taken as that in which rest can be had, and it is thus that *enjoyment* looks to the end. [c] Third, the end is taken as the term of what is ordered to it, and it is thus that *intention* relates to end.

Means to the End

Having distinguished three acts of will bearing on the end, Thomas turns to the way we will what is for the sake of the intended end. We have already seen that many things and acts can be part of one intention: we intend both the end and that which is for the sake of the end. Thomas distinguishes three acts of will bearing on means: choice, consent, and use. In the course of analyzing these, he will discuss counsel as well, the rational reflection which precedes and guides choice. The rational discourse undertaken at the service of intention and to guide choice is what Aristotle called the practical syllogism.

Syllogism may suggest to us detached and formal reasoning and to that degree the term is unhelpful in this context. If we cannot rid ourselves of the notion that syllogism means only what it means in the *Prior Analytics,* we may speak of the discourse or thinking that is involved before and during action, where action means some activity other than thinking. In any case, we want to make room for the discourse of mind in its practical use.

This is another massively important distinction, that between the theoretical and the practical uses of our mind. These differ because they have different ends in view. In the theoretical use of our mind, we seek the perfection of thinking as such, truth. In the practical use of our mind, we seek beyond truth the perfection of activities other than thinking, activities like choosing, buying and selling, sawing, seeing, see-sawing, etc.

We have seen several passages in which Thomas draws a parallel between mind and will. Just as the mind has starting points in *per se notae* propositions, so the will has its starting point in the ultimate end. Truths other than self-evident ones will claim our assent to the degree that they are linked to the principles. Goods other than the end will move the will necessarily, if they are such that the end cannot be had without them. Not all truths follow necessarily from premises. Not all goods, indeed very few of them, have a necessary relation to the ultimate end.

The principles of practical reason will be judgments which bear on goods. Judgments as to what is good for us, bearing on the end or on things without which the end cannot be had, are principles of practical reason. It is these Thomas will call the precepts of natural law.

The young woman who has the intention of going to Rome has, as we suggested, many possible ways of getting there. Fifi is unlikely to swim, being presently in New York, though if she were in Ostia, she might, like Aeneas, go up the Tiber one way or another. If Fifi in New York consults a travel agent, she will be presented with at least those ways of getting to Rome which promise a percentage to the agent. That there are several indicates that there is no one way of getting to Rome. If there were, Fifi's troubles would be over.

The practical order is a sea of possibilities and contingencies through which we must navigate. There is no single sea lane, just as there is no one port toward which all are sailing. Not that we want to suggest that every practical decision is of the lifeboat variety. That is, twelve people and Tallulah Bankhead have survived the torpedoing of their ship and toss on the frothy waves of the North Atlantic. Food runs out, then water. They look hungrily at one another. Being invited to the captain's table has become fraught with ambiguity. The moral question arises: Who shall become a meal for the others?

Life, thank God, is seldom like that. But pondering what course to take is commonplace. We are prompted to such inquiry, because we intend an end. The will acts bearing on the end presuppose the presentation of the object by mind; the inquiry into ways and means by mind presupposes the intention of the end by will. "Ex hoc quod homo vult finem, movetur ad consiliandum de his quae sunt ad finem: Because he wills the end, a man is moved to take counsel concerning things which are ordered to the end" (IaIIae, q.14, a.1, ad 1m).

Counsel is an inquiry, a questioning. What to do? But in the precise sense: What to do if such-and-such is to be brought about? If such an inquiry arrived at the conclusion that you can't get there from here, that would render the intention of the end idle. *Voluntas* would become *velleitas,* as Thomas says. But that is something that might emerge. If the conditions for getting to Rome cannot be met by me, it is an impossible objective for me, and it doesn't matter that thousands of others go there every day. Only the practically possible can be chosen, and counsel is aimed at choice.

Electio consequitur sententiam vel iudicium, quod est sicut conclusio syllogismi operativi. Unde illud cadit sub electione, quod se habet ut conclusio in syllogismo operabilium. Finis autem in operabilibus se habet ut principium, et non ut conclusio, ut Philosophus dicit in II Physic. Unde finis, inquantum est huiusmodi, non cadit sub electione. (IaIIae, q.13, a.3)

Choice follows on the opinion or judgment that is the conclusion of an operative syllogism. Hence that falls to choice which is like the conclusion in operative syllogisms. The end in doable things functions as a principle, not a conclusion, as Aristotle observes in *Physics,* Book Two. Hence the end as such does not fall to choice.

The intellect's grasp of the end is presupposed by will; so the mind's quest for means of achieving the intended end is presupposed by choice. But Thomas distinguishes another act of will bearing on means that may precede choice, namely, consent. Consent is the directing of the movement of appetite on something within the power of the one doing the directing.

Sed appetitus eorum quae sunt ad finem, praesupponit determinationem consilii. Et ideo applicatio appetitivi motus ad determinationem consilii proprie est consensus. (IaIIae, q.15, a.3)

But the desire of those things which are for the end presupposes counsel's determination. Therefore the directing of the appetitive motion to what counsel has determined is consent properly so called.

Why in the world does Thomas distinguish consent from choice? It turns out that there need be no distinction between them. There is one when counsel turns up a plurality of means, all of them attractive; then of course the choice of one among them is an act of will different from that which finds all the possible means attractive.

Potest enim contingere quod per consilium inveniantur plura ducentia ad finem, quorum dum quodlibet placet, in quodlibet eorum consentitur: sed ex multis quae placent praeaccipimus unum eligendo. Sed si inveniatur unum solum quod placeat, non differunt re consensus et electio, sed ratione tantum: ut consensus dicatur secundum quod placet ad agendum; electio autem, secundum quod praefertur his quae non placent. (IaIIae, q.15, a.3, ad 3m)	It can happen that several means to the end are discovered by counsel, and since each of them pleases, consent is given to each, and from many pleasing alternatives we select one by choosing. But if one alone should be found, there is no real difference between consent and choice, but only in understanding, such that consent might be invoked, insofar as acting is pleasant, and choice, insofar as it is preferred to what does not please.

Thomas speaks of yet another will act bearing on means, one that follows choice, namely use. We use something when we apply it to some operation: *usus rei alicuius importat applicationem rei illius ad aliquam operationem* (IaIIae, q.16, a.1). As following choice, use refers to will's moving the executive powers. So understood, use falls between choice and execution, and the act of will it names would permeate the order of execution when, having sought and found the means to our intended end, we begin to take the necessary steps to attaining it, steps which will involve bodily movements of various kinds and the employment of various things.

Use comes to be employed by the will as moving any other power, and then any cognitive act, whose realization is brought about by will, will be an instance of use. Indeed, the will's causing the activity of any faculty can be called a use of the faculty; in this extended sense, use shows up wherever there is an activity of any faculty that can come under our dominion.

Commanded Acts

The acts of will bearing on end and means are elicited voluntary acts, acts of the will itself; other acts are voluntary insofar as they are commanded by will. They pertain to the will only indirectly, through other powers, powers that the will is said to use. Command (*imperium*) is assigned chiefly to reason by Thomas.

Imperare autem est quidem essentialiter actus rationis: imperans enim ordinat eum cui imperat ad aliquid agendum intimando vel denuntiando; sic autem ordinare per modum cuiusdam intimationis est rationis. Sed ratio potest aliquid intimare vel denuntiare dupliciter. [a] Uno modo, absolute: quae quidem intimatio exprimitur per verbum indicativi modi; sicut si aliquis alicui dicat, "Hoc est tibi faciendum." [b] Aliquando autem ratio intimat aliquid alicui, movendo ipsum ad hoc: et talis intimatio exprimitur per verbum imperativi modi; puta cum alicui dicitur: "Fac hoc." (IaIIae, q.17, a.1)

To command, however, is indeed essentially an act of reason; the one commanding orders the one he commands to do something by way of intimation or declaration; to order in this way, by way of intimation, is an act of reason. Reason can intimate or declare in two ways, [a] first, absolutely. This sort of intimation is expressed by a verb in the indicative mood, as if one were to say to someone, "This ought to be done by you." [b] Sometimes, however, reason intimates something to someone, moving him to it. Such intimation is expressed by a verb in the imperative mood, as for example when to someone is said, "Do this."

Mind or intellect is said to move only insofar as it has received movement from will. "Imperare est actus rationis, praesupposito tamen actu voluntatis: Command is an act of reason which presupposes an act of will" (IaIIae, q.17, a.1). Use follows on command, putting into service whatever is necessary to execute the action.

It may seem that command and the act commanded are simply two different acts; and this will seem even more to be the case when there is an interval between the command and the execution. Nonetheless, they make up a moral whole. "Unde patet quod imperium et actus imperatus sunt unus actus humanus, sicut quoddam totum est unum, sed est secundum partes multa: Whence it is clear that command and the commanded act are one human act, much as a whole is one though it has many parts" (IaIIae, q.17, a.4).

We see in this passage how it is that the many acts Thomas distinguishes here can be parts of what is morally one action. The intention of the end prompts the search for means which lead on to choice, command, and execution. Thomas would then see these parts as embedded in the whole action, potentially many and, at least on occasion, becoming actualized when the action is not taken to term and the only human act to be appraised morally is a truncated one. The analysis of one moral act into a plurality of parts does not suggest then that what we should be inclined to call a single human act has to be recognized as really or actually a plurality of human acts. Rather a single human act contains many parts which are only potentially many; some of them actually come to be separate wholes when something goes wrong.

Command has its natural application to the external acts which execute the choice, but like "use," "command" has other applications as well. An act of will, bearing on means, can be commanded. It makes no sense to speak of commanding the will to seek the good as such. "Primus autem voluntatis actus non est ex rationis ordinatione, sed ex instinctu naturae: The first act of will is not due to the ordering of reason but to the instinct of nature" (IaIIae, q.17, a.5, ad 3m). To command other acts of will presupposes previous will acts which lend their moving power to the command. This is not circular; only the recognition that the moral life is a continuing thing.

Can the act of reason be commanded? This question suggests the way in which the life of the mind, study, research, enter into the moral life.

Sed attendendum est quod actus rationis potest considerari dupliciter. [a] Uno modo, quantum ad exercitium actus. Et sic actus rationis semper imperari potest: sicut cum indicitur alicui quod attendat, et ratione utatur. [b] Alio modo, quantum ad obiectum,

But it should be noticed that the act of reason can be understood in two ways. [a] With respect to the exercise of the act, and thus the act of reason can always be commanded, as when one is told he should listen and use his reason. [b] With respect to its ob-

respectu cuius duo actus rationis attenduntur. (i) Primo quidem ut veritatem circa aliquid apprehendat. Et hoc non est in potestate nostra: hoc enim contingit per virtutem alicuius luminis, vel naturalis vel supernaturalis. Et ideo quantum ad hoc, actus rationis non est in potestate nostra, nec imperari potest. (ii) Alius autem actus rationis est dum his quae apprehendit assentit. Si igitur fuerint talia apprehensa, quibus naturaliter intellectus assentiat, sicut prima principia, assensus talium vel dissensus non est in potestate nostra, sed in ordine naturae: et ideo, proprie loquendo, nec imperio subiacet. Sunt autem quaedam apprehensa quae non adeo convincunt intellectum, quin possit assentire vel dissentire, vel saltem assensum vel dissensum suspendere, propter aliquam causam: et in talibus assensus ipse vel dissensus in potestate nostra est, et sub imperio cadit. (Ia-IIae, q.17, a.6)

ject, and here two acts of reason are found. (i) First, that whereby the truth about something is grasped, and this is not in our power, but comes about in virtue of either a natural or supernatural light. In this respect, then, the act of reason is not in our power and cannot be commanded. (ii) Another act of reason is that whereby we assent to what has been apprehended. Now if the things apprehended are like first principles to which intellect naturally assents, neither assent nor dissent is in our power, but in the order of nature. Therefore, properly speaking, they are not subject to command. Some of the things apprehended do not convince intellect, and assent or dissent are possible, or at least the suspension of assent or dissent for some cause. In things of this kind assent or dissent is in our power and falls under command.

Imagination can be commanded and thus be put to use in a moral act, but what of bodily activities? This question is of keen interest, since we began by distinguishing human acts from acts of a man and said that only human acts are moral and that all moral acts are human acts. This may seem to have as its consequence that the moral life is inside somewhere, a matter of mind and will. But some acts of body can be rational and moral by participation, insofar as they come under command. A sign that digesting and growing escape the range of command and thus the reach of the moral is that we are neither praised nor blamed for digesting well or for growing three inches or losing our hair, and so on, although some doctors may treat indigestion and baldness as moral faults. Thomas entertains an objection that we do indeed praise and blame in this area. After all, are not gluttony and lust morally deficient, bodily acts?

Thomas does not simply set aside digestion and growth taken as such, but rather sees such activities as pertaining obliquely to the moral order, by way of medicine. If something is wrong with our digestion, we can take remedies for it, a couple of Alka Seltzers say, and restore normal functioning. So to use medicine may well be praiseworthy, and not to use it may subject us to blame. The art of medicine and pharmacology aid nature to do its own stuff, so to say. Thus, while it does not make sense to imagine ourselves issuing commands to our digestive tract or telling ourselves to grow a few inches, even these may come under the sway of reason and thus be derivatively morally good or bad. But the objection suggests another tack to Thomas.

Virtus et vitium, laus et vituperium, non debentur ipsis actibus nutritivae vel generativae potentiae, qui sunt digestio et formatio corporis humani; sed actibus sensitivae partis ordinatis ad actus generativae vel nutritivae; puta in concupiscendo delectationem cibi et venereorum, et utendo secundum quod oportet, vel non secundum quod oportet. (IaIIae, q.17, a.8, 3m)	Virtue and vice, praise and blame, do not belong to the acts themselves of the nutritive and generative powers, digestion and the formation of the human body, but to the acts of the sensitive part which are ordered to the acts of the generative or nutritive; for example in desiring the pleasure of food and sex and using them as they should be or as they should not be.

And so Thomas comes to discuss the use of our bodily members, arms, legs, and so forth, in ways which are voluntary and thus moral or immoral. Bodily organs are instruments of the powers of the soul—"organ" means instrument—and the organs come under the sway of reason to the degree that the powers do. When Thomas says that neither the heart nor the reproductive organs are subject to the command of reason, he does not of course mean to suggest that genital activity escapes the range of the moral. What he means is that our heartbeat and certain responses of a sexual kind take place whether we want them to or not. But the desire thereby elicited, itself morally neutral, comes within the range of the moral insofar as it becomes an object of sense or intellectual cognition. Hunger, thirst, and sexual desire are natural. But the desires and pursuits consequent upon them involve awareness and consciousness and thus come into the moral order. It is no fault of Fifi's that after a day or two of not eating she feels hunger, but whether or not she orders a Truckerburger with fries is up to her.

Summary

Thomas is now poised to ask a question of specifically moral moment: in virtue of what are human acts good or bad? To have sailed right into that without these preliminary reflections on human action would have turned up difficulties requiring a backtracking to the analysis of action as such. Questions 7 through 17 of the *Prima secundae* of the *Summa theologiae* provide a good example of the way Thomas blends a variety of traditions into a new whole. We commented on the influence of Aristotle in his discussion of the natural aspects of man's ultimate end or happiness. In the analysis of the various acts of will, those bearing on end, those bearing on means, Thomas casts his net wide for materials from Augustine, John Damascene, Nemesius (or, as he thought, Gregory of Nyssa), and Aristotle. The result is a new whole, a new philosophical whole, by and large, since there is no intrinsic dependence in this analysis of action on revealed truth. When he discusses the way our sexual organs seem to have a life of their own, he attributes this to Original Sin and the removal of the supernatural gift; that is why sexual activities are so difficult to govern. He then turns to Aristotle's *De motu animalium* for an account of this, noting that the heart and the reproductive organs almost act like separate living things within the animal.

Thomas's use of such disparate sources has led some to accuse him of eclecticism, the pasting together of incompatible pieces taken from many places. There is no doubt that, to certain types of scholars, the ability to see unity in diversity is an affront, but Thomas is exhibiting here the same confidence Aristotle had that men speaking of the same issue are likely to say complementary as well as contradictory things and that we should be more alive to the former than to the latter. If one were to point to the baseline of Thomas's discussion, despite its inclusion of things unmentioned by him, it is Aristotle who would be singled out.

Since the basic scheme throughout these questions is the interaction of mind and will, those who deny that Aristotle recognized the will, must be startled by that claim. In Part Two I discuss claims that Aristotle has no concept of the will "as we understand it."

An intellectual grasp of the good in general—implicit in the grasp of anything as good—provides the will with its object, an object it cannot not want. This natural and necessary act of will is called will, and keeping the name of the faculty for the activity is meant to underscore how basic it is. The good that is the object of this basic act of will is the end. The intellectual activity which presides over willing the means to the end is what Thomas refers to as counsel. Counsel is an inquiry, a search for the way to achieve the end, and is itself a complex activity, discursive. When its work is done, the will chooses. The mind's preceptive, commanding act is the prelude to putting to use other powers and our bodily organs to execute the plan arrived at through the process of counsel. What is first in the order of intention is last in the order of execution, and of course vice versa. The end is first present to mind and, having set off the search for ways and means of attaining it, we reach the point where the mental prelude gives way to execution. Counsel arrives at an action that can be done here and now and sets in train a series which eventually will realize the end. The doing or executing of that plan is what we first of all have in mind when we speak of action. That is, what Thomas calls the external or commanded act may seem to be the human or moral act *tout court*. But insofar as it is a human act, it presupposes the internal origins Thomas has been at pains to analyze.

The three major conjunctions of mind and will just mentioned—intellectual grasp of good/will; counsel/choice; command/use—involve the other will acts Thomas discussed, but it is well to keep in mind this basic triad.

Let us end by addressing an uneasiness likely caused by this discussion. Talk of what mind is doing or of what will is doing suggests an inner drama, as if there were rival moral agents within us. But when we say the mind or will does something, we mean of course that a given human being engages in mental activity, a given human being wants something, and so forth. After all, the analysis is aimed at the appraisal of the actions of such agents as Socrates, Abelard, and Cervantes. At the same time, however, we should not allow this uneasiness—it may even become impatience—to lead us to sweep away all talk of different powers and faculties. Rather, we might take the occasion of our unease to reflect on how that talk of distinct powers of the soul came into currency.

Seeing differs from hearing. It is from such indisputable truths that it all begins. I both see and hear, and thus I can be said to have the capacity to see and the capacity to hear. Two capacities? Yes, if the activities are distinct, as they are, the capacities must be. The capacity to hear does not get actualized as seeing. The general rule, then, is that insofar as distinct activities of an agent are recognized, we recognize correspondingly distinct powers or faculties or capacities. This is an inference. The analysis goes on to argue that, because of the distinction of the operations and derivatively the powers, there must be a distinction between them and the soul that is their seat.

It is not our present task to undertake that analysis. But it seems wise at least to refer to it, lest one think Thomas regards all the faculties of the soul, particularly mind and will, as Aristotle did heart and the pudenda, that is, as little animals acting almost autonomously within.

4. Acting Well or Badly

FIFI HAS friends who misbehave and deflect criticism by saying that they are hurting nobody. In steamy novels, soap operas, and Fifi's circle, people who are engaged in extramarital affairs take comfort from the alleged fact that what they are doing harms nobody.

Let us say they are right, since, if they are wrong in this, that is, if they are causing others harm, that would seem to count against what they are doing, morally. To rob a bank in order to frolic on the beach at Runaway Bay would provide grounds for objection. Investors in the bank are likely to balk at unwillingly financing this sordid assignation. But if causing harm to others can provide a negative moral judgment, the fact that what we are doing does not harm others seems an insufficient basis for saying it is morally all right.

Primum non nocere is not only part of the physician's code, it also seems a general rule of justice. Whether the agents may be harming themselves is another matter; indeed, whether such conduct is a matter of indifference to the wider society, however immediately harmless it may seem, is yet another matter. My present point is simply that what might appear to be a basic negative measure of justice does not seem able to function as a broad criterion of morally good action. This recognition may be implicit in the appeal to the no-harm excuse. "I know what I'm doing is wrong, but I'm not hurting anybody." That comes down to saying that what I am doing is wrong, but it could be worse. And we want to know what makes an action wrong and what makes it right.

A positive version of the harm criterion is the benefit criterion. That is, a course of action is commended or defended by pointing to the great benefits that a great number will enjoy as a result. Clearly, many, perhaps most, actions are undertaken in order to bring about some result or other. The various technical, artistic, and athletic activities in which people engage are, as we saw, subject to an internal appraisal of whether or not they meet the requirements of the technology, art, or sport, but they are also subject to a moral appraisal. And the question arises, in what does the moral appraisal consist? Internal judgments of shortstops, watercolorists, and lab technicians, while complex and sometimes difficult, are relatively easier than moral judgments. And one of the great difficulties with moral judgments is knowing what precisely counts pro and con morally. For example, citing the vast benefits to mankind over the foreseeable future is a way of commending a technological breakthrough quite independently of its technical appraisal. Difficulties arise, however, should the project being commended involve killing every tenth person in order to have spare parts for the nine, for example, or should it involve ridding the world of a race judged undesirable from the point of view of certain political goals.

A simpler version of this is Fifi's decision to tell a lie in order to spare, as she thinks, someone else great pain. "Did anyone call while I was out?" Maude Gardner, Fifi's roommate, asks. As it happens, Baxter Hubris called and asked for Maude. "No calls," Fifi lies, just as she had lied to Baxter, when she told him Maude was on an extended trip in the Australian outback and indefinitely incommunicado. Baxter is a brute who in the past has been cruel to Maude; he has a wife and family. He has called with the good news that he has found a job for Maude in his office. Maude has been looking for work for weeks. Fifi, foreseeing a future in which Maude is exploited by Baxter, put through agony, humiliation, and all the rest, lied. Better two small lies than all that, she tells herself.

If Fifi were a philosopher of the professional sort, she might develop a theory according to which failing to pass on the message to Maude does not amount to lying at all. That is, preventing the foreseen bad consequences makes what would otherwise be a lie not a lie. And of course, that is what in its political context would be said as well. If there are huge benefits to society, the act performed to bring them about is in itself morally okay.

On her better days, Fifi might do what she does because God has told her how to act. There are the Ten Commandments, copies of which were sold by furtive men on the edges of the schoolyard when Fifi was a girl. Naughty children bought copies and pinned them to bulletin boards, flouting the Constitution as it was then interpreted. But Fifi learned the Commandments at her mother's knee. Therefore she knows what to say to wicked men who ask her to weekend at Runaway Bay. Violating God's Commandments is wrong, keeping them is right.

These three ways of assigning moral goodness to actions can be called the Contractarian, the Utilitarian, and the Divine Command theories respectively. There is something to be said for each of them, particularly the last, but there are difficulties too. In the case of the Commandments, for example, Fifi is unlikely to think that someone who has not heard of them, someone like the intended product of the public school system, cannot be said to be doing anything wrong if he murders, lies, and steals.

What can Thomas Aquinas tell us about the morality and immorality of actions? What is it that makes an action good or bad?

According to Reason

Ad tertium dicendum quod bonum per rationem repraesentatur voluntati ut obiectum; et inquantum cadit sub ordine rationis, pertinet ad genus moris, et causat bonitatem moralem in actu voluntatis. Ratio enim principium est humanorum et moralium actuum. (IaIIae, q.19, a.1, 3m)

In reply to the third it should be said that the good is presented to the will as an object by reason, and insofar as it falls within the order of reason, it belongs to the moral order and causes moral goodness in the act of will. For reason is the principle of human moral acts.

Moral action occurs when will is guided by reason, and moral action is good when the guiding reason is correct. To know what ought to be done and to will it is what moral goodness amounts to.

We have already seen that the mind's apprehension of the universal good provides an object commensurate with will. The universal good, goodness as such, is something the will necessarily desires. If moral goodness consists in willing what is known to be good, and the first act of will is the desire of goodness as such, moral goodness seems inevitable rather than a task. Indeed, it seems impossible for anyone to be morally bad.

Distinguo, as Thomas might say. While it is true that the will cannot not love goodness as such, the mind and thus will can be mistaken as to what it is in which goodness truly consists. Recall Thomas's distinction between the note of goodness, the *ratio boni,* and the thing or things in which that note is found. I cannot be mistaken about the desirability of goodness nor can I fail to want it, but I can be mistaken about the identity and makeup of true goodness, its carriers, so to speak, and thus desire badly as well.

Reason will be a good guide for will, when it correctly grasps what man's good consists of. Since his good is what fulfills and perfects a rational agent, and rational activity, as we saw, is an analogous phrase, possessed of a variety of ordered meanings, the true account of the human good will comprise many constituents, the particular goods which make up the total good of man. This knowledge will be the starting point of practical reason, reason being practical when it guides will and other faculties. This knowledge will be expressed in precepts or commands which complement on the level of universality the command that precedes use in the concrete and singular voluntary act. The precepts which provide the starting points or principles of practical reason are what Thomas calls natural law. That is the topic of our next chapter.

The end or good being the starting point of moral activity, and the will's love of it following on reason's grasp of it, the continuation is had in the quest for the ways and means of realizing the end, this quest issuing in guides for choice and then commands for the use of the other faculties, the body, arms, and limbs to execute the action judged good. This process issuing in the singular human act, is what Thomas calls the practical syllogism.

When St. Thomas turns to the discussion of moral goodness and badness in the *Prima secundae,* after having analyzed action, he proceeds in three steps, first discussing the goodness and badness of human acts generally (Q. 18), then going on to discuss the goodness and badness of the interior act of will (Q. 19), and finally discussing the goodness and badness of external acts (Q. 20). These are three of the longest questions in the *Summa theologiae.*

The Goodness of Action

Before discussing the goodness of the moral agent as such, Thomas says a few things by way of reminder about the way in which anything that exists can be called good. Insofar as the things of this world come to be as the result of a change, they can be spoken of as the realization of a potency, as the term of a change which is the perfection or fulfillment of the potency. In this sense, each thing is the end or good of a change and is as perfection to some potency. A thing is insofar as a form inheres in matter, and things are ranked insofar as their forms can be ranked. A thing's form is a measure of its existence, limiting existence so to say to this amount or kind. God, by contrast, is the plenitude of being. Evil occurs when a thing does not have something which it ought to have, given its nature. Thus blindness is an evil, the lack of a capacity the thing should have. The goodness and badness of actions is first spoken of in these terms.

Sic igitur dicendum est quod omnis actio, inquantum habet aliquid de esse, intantum habet de bonitate: inquantum vero deficit ei aliquid de plenitudine essendi quae debetur actione humanae, intantum deficit a bonitate, et sic dicitur mala: puta si deficiat ei vel determinata quantitas secundum rationem, vel debitus locus, vel aliquid huiusmodi. (IaIIae, q.18, a.1)

Thus it should be said that any action has goodness to the degree that it has being, and insofar as there is lacking to it anything of the fullness of being that human action ought to have, it is called bad; for example, if it should lack either a determinate amount according to reason, or the right place, or anything like that.

Notice that Thomas is not saying that the human act can be appraised insofar as it is a kind of being first, and then appraised as moral. Rather, moral goodness and badness are being seen on the model of ontological or transcendental goodness, but the special character of the moral is in play: *secundum rationem*. However, when the morally bad action is said not to preclude all goodness, the goodness referred to is not moral goodness.

Actio mala potest habere aliquem effectum per se, secundum id quod habet de bonitate et entitate. Sicut adulterium est causa generationis humanae, inquantum habet commixtionem maris et feminae, non autem inquantum caret ordine rationis. (Ibid., ad 3m)

A bad action can have a *per se* effect insofar as it possesses goodness and being, just as adultery is the cause of new human life insofar as it involves the union of male and female, not insofar as it lacks the order of reason.

A human act is judged good or bad first of all because of its object; what one sets out to do makes the action to be the kind of action it is. It gives it its species or form.

Primum autem quod ad plenitudinem essendi pertinere videtur, est id quod dat rei speciem. Sicut autem res naturalis habet speciem ex sua forma ita actio habet speciem ex obiecto; sicut et motus ex termino. Et ideo sicut prima bonitas rei naturalis attenditur ex sua forma, quae dat speciem ei, ita et prima bonitas actus moralis attenditur ex obiecto convenienti; unde et a quibusdam vocatur bonum ex genere; puta, uti re sua. Et sicut in rebus naturalibus primum malum est, si res generata non consequitur formam specificam, puta si non generetur homo sed aliquis loco hominis; ita primum malum in actionibus morali-

What pertains to the fullness of being seems in the first place to be that which makes the thing to be of a given kind. Just as natural things have species from their form, so action has its species from the object, much as motion has its from the term. Just as the first goodness of the natural thing is read from its form which puts it in a species, so the first goodness of the moral act is read from the appropriate object, which some call goodness in kind, e.g., to use one's own things. And just as the first evil in natural things is failure to achieve specific form, as when something else comes to be instead of a

bus est quod est ex obiecto, sicut acci-
pere aliena. (IaIIae, q.18, a.2)

man, so the first evil in moral actions
is that which is from the object, e.g.,
to take what is another's.

The object of the action is that which the agent sets out to do, to effect.
This is not to say that the goodness or badness of the action is drawn
from its consequences, but it is to say that an action is called good insofar
as it can bring about a good effect. "Et ita ipsa proportio actionis ad effectum, est ratio bonitatis ipsius: It is this proportion of action to effect
that is the reason for its goodness" (IaIIae, q.18, a.2, ad 3m). It is not the
good of the effect that explains the good of the cause, but vice versa.
Actions are good or bad when they are performed; we do not have to wait
for the returns to find out which they are. But the avoidance of conse-
quentialism should not lead us in the direction Kant went. He wanted
the act to be good when performed and tried to find criteria of goodness
that had nothing to do with results. Worrying about results is heteron-
omous, which is German for accidental. As Thomas remarks, when we
act we more often than not act to bring about some effect, but it is the
here and now proportion or relation of the action to the effect that is the
reason for its goodness. This proportion is not dependent on the act's being
successful.

Having stated that the goodness or badness of the act will be read first
of all from its object, what the agent sets out to do, Thomas then asks if
human action is good or bad because of the end. The question suggests
that an action is the kind of moral act it is because of its object, but that
we can set out to do something for the sake of some further end. It has
absolute goodness because of the object, relative goodness because of the
end. Where this is the case, the act has to be appraised both in terms of
its object and in terms of its end. Indeed, Thomas suggests that there is
a fourfold appraisal of action.

Sic igitur in actione humana bonitas
quadruplex considerari potest. Una
quidem secundum genus, prout scilicet est actio: quia quantum habet de

There is then a fourfold goodness of
the human act. One according to its
genus, namely insofar as it is an action because to the degree it has act

actione et entitate, tantum habet de
bonitate. . . . Alia vero secundum specie: quae accipitur secundum obiectum conveniens. Tertia secundum
circumstantias, quasi secundum acci-
dentia quaedam. Quarta autem secundum finem, quasi secundum
habitudinem ad causam bonitatis.
(IaIIae, q.18, a.4)

and being it has goodness. . . . Another according to its species, which is
read from the fitting object. Third
due to circumstances as to certain accidents. Fourth according to the end,
as if according to a relation to the
cause of goodness.

What is this first or generic goodness? Obviously it is not identical with the first goodness drawn from the object of the act. Rather it is this. The act of generation can be successful or good insofar as a child is begun. There is nothing moral in this appraisal; the goodness is ontological, just as the formation of a defective child would be an ontological not a moral evil. The moral appraisal is of sexual intercourse as something one sets out to do as a fitting objective. It will be fitting insofar as it is judged to be so by reason. That judgment will be based on, among other things, whether or not the partners are husband and wife.

To consider the activity of human generation apart from its morality, that is, apart from its being an activity engaged in consciously, *secundum rationem,* is of course an abstraction. It is not as if sometimes human sexual intercourse is a moral, that is, conscious activity, and sometimes not. Rather we recognize that whether it is engaged in morally or immorally sexual intercourse may turn out well or badly when "well" or "badly" refer simply to whether the activity itself achieves its natural term.

The specific moral goodness of the action derives from reason's judgment that doing this now is fitting.

The circumstances can add to the goodness of the action without specifying it as such.

The end is that to which an action already of a given moral kind can be referred.

If I should give alms to the poor in order to be praised, the objectively good act is vitiated by this intention, and the one moral action is bad. An objectively bad action can be ordered to a good end, yet the moral act that binds these two together be bad. In order to be good, simply speaking, the act must be good in kind, done in the appropriate circumstances, and for the sake of a good end. If any of these is defective, the whole act is defective.

The goodness or badness of human acts always involves reason, since to act well is to act according to reason and to act badly is to act against reason. Good and bad are the specific differences of moral actions. The conjugal act and the adulterous act are specifically different from the moral point of view even though they are instances of the same biological action. The adulterous act violates the standards of reason, whereas the conjugal act fulfills them (IaIIae, q.18, a.5, ad 3m).

Interior and Exterior Act

The moral quality of the act has been said to depend on what is done or the object, on the circumstances of time, place, etc., and on the end for the sake of which it is done. Now way back in article 3 of Question 1, Thomas said that the human act is the kind of act it is thanks to its end. But here in Question 18, he has said that the human act is the kind of act it is because of its object, the thing done, not that for the sake of which it is done. Has he changed his mind in the interim? He is certainly aware of the question this raises in our minds, since he formulates it in article 6: Is the act good or bad in kind because of the end?

In actu autem voluntario invenitur duplex actus, scilicet actus interior voluntatis, et actus exterior: et uterque horum actuum habet suum obiectum. Finis autem proprie est obiectum interioris actus voluntarii: id autem circa quod est actus exterior est obiectum eius. Sicut igitur actio exterior accipit speciem ab obiecto circa quod est; ita actus interior voluntatis accipit speciem a fine, sicut a proprio obiecto.

In the voluntary act are found two acts, namely the interior act of the will and the exterior act, and each of these has its own object. The end is properly the object of the interior voluntary act; the object of the exterior act is that on which it bears. Therefore, just as the exterior act is the kind of act it is because of its object, so the interior act of will is specified by the end as by its proper object.

Ita autem quod est ex parte voluntatis, se habet ut formale ad id quod est ex parte exterioris actus: quia voluntas utitur membris ad agendum sicut instrumentis; neque actus exteriores habent rationem moralitatis, nisi inquantum sunt voluntarii. Et ideo actus humani species formaliter consideratur secundum finem, materialiter autem secundum obiectum exterioris actus. (IaIIae, q.18, a.6)

However that which is from will is formal with regard to that which belongs to the exterior act, because the will uses the members as instruments in order to act, and exterior acts only have the note of morality insofar as they are voluntary. So it is that the species of the human act is formally taken from the end and materially from the object of the exterior act.

Why does Thomas begin, in article 2, with the external act, telling us that it is specified by its object, what it brings about, rather than with the internal act, which is specified by the end? If we think of Question 1 of the *Prima secundae,* we could reply that he began by saying the voluntary act is specified by the end. However, I think we can say here that Thomas is beginning with the more obvious. The action as observable performance: using one's own property, taking what belongs to someone else, giving alms, sexual intercourse. These are what they are because of what is done, because of the way the world is made different by them. Because of what they deal with, their "concerning which: *circa quam.*" The external act is the execution, the upshot of the interior acts, and it is as if we think backward from it in order to recognize them. In the order of intention, of the interior act, the end is first and characterizes what the agent is about to do, the kind of act he means to perform. Given that end, a search for the means of realizing it takes place, then choice, command, and, finally, the execution. This article clearly assumes a difference between the end the agent proposes to himself and the means taken to achieve it. So that, in the example Thomas uses, the man sets out to draw approving attention to himself and hits upon alms-giving with appropriate fanfare as the way to do this. Where there is this distinction between end and means, the act bearing on end is formal, that on the means material, because they make up one human or moral action and form/matter are components of substantially one thing (IaIIae, q.18, a.6, ad 2).

There is no essential connection between giving to the poor and vainglory, but the connection is made by the agent, with the result that the two are morally one act. It should not be thought that the external act is without moral character as such and receives it only because it is ordered by reason to the end. The external act—taking another's property, taking another's spouse, helping the poor—is a moral act which is absolutely good or bad. But as a component of a more complex act, other things must be considered before the complex act is called good or bad. The objectively good act may be turned to a bad end. The objectively bad act may be turned to a good end, and then the latter is vitiated. An objectively bad act may be directed to a bad end, and the action is worse because of that. As for the morally indifferent objective act, Thomas will turn to that in a moment.

If the complex act can be specified from the end, as the object of will, and from the object, as what the external act executes, how do these two ways of specifying relate to one another? If Fifi lies to spare Maude grief with Baxter Hubris, is her deed one of deception or of compassion?

How is the external act related to the end willed? Is it essentially connected to it, as a battle is connected with victory, or only accidentally, as taking another's property is to giving to the poor? It is difficult to see how military victory can be achieved without doing battle, whereas Robin Hood's objective can be met in a variety of ways: there is no necessary connection between helping the poor and stealing from the rich. In this second case, where the relation between the external deed and the end it is meant to serve is accidental, that which specifies the external act does not characterize the willing of the end, nor vice versa. "Unde dicimus quod ille qui furatur ut moechetur committit duas malitias in uno actu: thus we say that one who steals in order to philander commits two evils in one act" (IaIIae, q.18, a.7). Where there is a per se connection between the objects of the external and internal acts, the one object characterizes the other. But which characterizes which? Is the rogue Thomas imagines primarily an adulterer or a thief?

Thomas's answer reposes on three assumptions. First, that the difference or characterization of a thing drawn from a more particular form is more specific, as characterizing man from human soul is more specific than characterizing him from things he shares with other animals, with all living things, or with things generally. Second, that the more universal agent is responsible for the more universal characterization. Third, that the more remote the end the more it pertains to the more universal agent, as victory which is the ultimate end of the general is the end he intends, whereas the movement of this company or that is the end intended by officers below him.

Et ex istis sequitur quod differentia specifica quae est ex fine est magis generalis; et differentia quae est ex obiecto per se ad talem finem ordinato, est specifica respectu eius. Voluntas enim, cuius proprium obiectum est finis, est universale motivum respectu omnium potentiarum animae, quarum propria obiecta sunt obiecta particularium actuum. (IaIIae, q.18, a.7)	From these it follows that the specific difference drawn from the end is more general, and the difference drawn from the object essentially ordered to it, is specific in respect to it. For the will, whose proper object is the end, is a universal mover of all the powers of the soul whose proper objects are objects of particular acts.

The activities of the cavalry and of the infantry are both ordered to the ultimate end of victory, but we specify them by their particular objects.

Neutral Acts

It is not unusual to hear it said that the external act has no moral quality, is neither good nor bad in itself, except perhaps in some ontic or ontological sense, but takes on what moral quality it has because of the end intended. If we consider the act of sexual congress just as such, the argument goes, it is good in the way in which natural and nonhuman activities can be said to be good: it functions well, the end is achieved, etc. But this good is compatible with moral badness and moral goodness. Two couples perform the same physical act, and in the one case we speak of married love and in the other of adultery. Clearly, it is concluded, we cannot look to the physical act, to ontic good or evil, to determine the moral character of the human act as such. Isn't this what Thomas himself told us at the very beginning of the *Prima secundae*?

Possibile tamen est quod unus actus secundum speciem naturae, ordinetur ad diversos fines voluntatis: sicut hoc ipsum quod est occidere hominem, quod est idem secundum speciem naturae, potest ordinari sicut in finem ad conservationem iustitiae, et ad satisfaciendum irae. Et ex hoc erunt diversi actus secundum speciem moris: quia uno modo erit actus virtutis, alio modo erit actus vitii. Non enim motus recipit speciem ab eo quod est terminus per accidens, sed solum ab eo quod est terminus per se. Fines autem morales accidunt rei naturali; et e converso ratio naturalis finis accidit morali. (IaIIae, q.1, a.3, ad 3m)

However, it is possible that an act naturally of one kind is ordered to diverse ends of the will, as killing a man, which is one natural kind of act, can be ordered either to the end of the conservation of justice or to the satisfaction of anger. On which basis there are two diverse kinds of moral act, one which is an act of virtue, the other an act of vice. Motion is not specified by its accidental term, but only from that which is its term per se. But moral ends are accidental to the natural thing, and conversely the natural end is accidental to the moral.

If the external act is equivalent to what Thomas here calls "hoc ipsum quod est occidere hominem," a natural event that can be described without assigning guilt and innocence, then it looks as if any moral quality it has derives from the end intended. If this is what Thomas meant to say, it comes down to the assertion that every external act is morally neutral. But he distinguishes morally neutral acts from those which are not. And it is only morally neutral acts which have, when performed, such moral quality as they have solely from the intention with which they are done. It is clearly important, then, to understand what Thomas means by morally neutral deeds.

Actus omnis habet speciem ab obiecto; et actus humanus, qui dicitur moralis, habet speciem ab obiecto relato ad principium actuum humanorum, quod est ratio. Unde si obiectum actus includat aliquid quod conveniat

Every act is specified by its object, and the human act which is called moral takes its species from an object related to the principle of human acts, reason. Hence if the object of the act includes something befitting the order

ordini rationis, erit actus bonus secundum suam speciem, sicut dare eleemosynam indigenti. Si autem includat aliquid quod repugnet ordini rationis, erit malus actus secundum speciem, sicut furari, quod est tollere aliena. Contingit autem quod obiectum actus non includit aliquid pertinens ad ordinem rationis, sicut levare festucam de terra, ire ad campum, et huiusmodi: et tales actus secundum speciem suam sunt indifferentes. (IaIIae, q.18, a.8)

of reason, it will be an act good according to its species, e.g., giving help to the poor. However, should it include something unsuitable to the order of reason, it will be a bad act in its species, e.g., theft, taking another's goods. It can happen however that the object of the act includes nothing pertaining to the order of reason, e.g., picking up a stick, walking in the field, and the like. Such acts are indifferent so far as their species goes.

As a natural occurrence, the action is good or bad in an ontological sense, Thomas notes in response to an objection, these being read without any reference to direction by reason. The event of the stick's being picked up or someone's progress across a field, taken just as such, can be appraised as natural events, but insofar as they contain nothing pertaining to the order of reason, they are morally indifferent—taken in themselves, that is. In its concrete performance, as this person picking up a stick here and now, that person traversing the field now, these acts are not without moral quality. Whence does it come? From the particular circumstances that surround the act, and most notably from the end.

Et oportet quod quilibet individualis actus habeat aliquam circumstantiam per quam trahatur ad bonum vel malum, ad minus ex parte intentionis finis. Cum enim rationis sit ordinare, actus a ratione deliberativa procedens, si non sit ad debitum finem ordinatus, ex hoc ipso repugnat rationi, et habet rationem mali. Si vero ordinetur ad debitum finem, convenit cum ordine rationis: unde habet rationem boni. Necesse est autem quod vel or-

It is necessary that each individual act should have some circumstance by which it becomes good or evil, if only from the intention of the end. Since reason orders, the deliberative act proceeding from reason, if it is not ordered to a fitting end, has the note of evil insofar as it is repugnant to reason. If it is ordered to a fitting end, it agrees with the order of reason and thus has the note of good. It is necessary that it either be ordered

dinetur vel non ordinetur ad debitum finem. Unde necesse est omnem actum hominis a deliberativa ratione procedentem, in individuo consideratum, bonum esse vel malum. (IaIIae, q.18, a.9)

or not be ordered to a fitting end, and thus every act proceeding from man's deliberative reason, taken individually, is either good or bad.

What a person deliberately does, whatever counts as a human act of that person, must be either good or bad as performed, because when it is done, it will be ordered by reason, either right reason or its opposite. An act which as performed is morally indifferent would be an act of man rather than a human act. For example, if I scratch my itching nose. Of course, there are circumstances where such an act could be a signal, a mark of contempt, a bid at an auction, a message in sign language, etc. It is the use to which it is deliberately put that gives it moral quality.

Procreative activities have their character as natural acts, but of course they are never engaged in by humans as merely natural acts; mating by inadvertence, as it were. Consciously to engage in the natural activity is to do so in such a way that the pursuit of its ends is ordered by reason with reference to the good of the agent as a whole, the full implications of the act, etc. The ends of the natural process are subsumed into reason's directing the agent to the good as such; this subsumption is not the denial of the natural end nor its thwarting, of course, but its sublimation into the moral arena of human action.

In any case, there is no support in Thomas for the notion that sexual activity as engaged in by human beings is neither good nor bad and receives its moral quality wholly from elsewhere. Whether procreative acts are engaged in with one's spouse or not are features of the kind of act done; the act is of one moral kind or another depending on such intrinsic features.

Human actions are judged good or bad with reference to their objects, their circumstances, and their ends. All of these must be good in order for the act to be good; if there is failure in any of them, the act itself is bad.

The Interior Act of the Will

After this general discussion of the moral appraisal of human acts, Thomas undertakes separate treatments of the morality of the interior act, of the order of intention, on the one hand, and of the external act, the order of execution, on the other.

With respect to the interior act, the discussion can be reduced to three main headings: (1) The object of willing as source of its moral goodness or badness. (2) Bad conscience. (3) God's will as the measure of the goodness of our willing.

1. The Object of Willing

Good and bad as such pertain to will, just as true and false pertain to mind. Thinking is either true or false, willing is either good or bad. The difference between good and bad willing, moreover, is a specific difference. But acts are specified by their objects. That is why good and bad acts of the will are properly such because of their objects.

The objection arises that the acts of powers other than will are good or bad with reference to the end as well as to the object, so why not will? Thomas replies that "quantum ad actum voluntatis, non differt bonitas quae est ex obiecto, a bonitate quae est ex fine, sicut in actibus aliarum virium: With respect to the act of the will there is no difference between goodness taken from the object and goodness taken from the end, as is the case in the acts of the other powers" (IaIIae, q.19, a.2, ad 1m). What about circumstances? It would seem that when, how, and where the end is willed affects the goodness of the will's act. If so, the goodness of willing cannot be read from the end alone.

Supposito quod voluntas sit boni, nulla circumstantia potest eam facere malam. Quod ergo dicitur quod aliquis vult aliquod bonum quando non debet vel ubi non debet, potest intelligi dupliciter. Uno modo, ita quod ista circumstantia referatur ad voli-	Granted that the will is of the good, no circumstances can make it bad. When it is said that someone wills some good when he ought not or where he ought not, we can understand this in two ways. First, such that these circumstances refer to what

tum. Et sic voluntas non est boni: quia velle facere aliquid quando non debet fieri, non est velle bonum. Alio modo, ita quod referatur ad actum volendi. Et sic impossibile est quod aliquis velit bonum quando non debet, quia semper homo debet velle bonum: nisi forte per accidens, inquantum aliquis, volendo hoc bonum, impeditur ne tunc velit aliquod bonum debitum. Et tunc non incidit malum ex eo quod aliquis vult illud bonum; sed ex eo quod non vult aliud bonum. Et similiter dicendum est de aliis circumstantiis. (IaIIae, q.19, a.2, 2m)

is willed. And then the will is not of the good, because to want to do something when it ought not be done is not to will the good. Second, such that it refers to the act of willing. And then it is impossible that someone should will the good when he should not, because a man ought always will the good; unless perhaps it should happen that someone, in willing this good, is thereby prevented from willing an obligatory good. But then evil does not arise from the fact that one wills the one good, but because he does not will the other good. Other circumstances can be handled in much the same way.

Wouldn't it be better to say that the goodness of the will's act depends on reason and not on its object? The fact is that to say the one is to say the other, and for this reason. If the goodness of will properly depends on its object, that object is proposed to it by reason. For the good as understood is the object of the will proportioned to it. Sensible or imagined good is not proportioned to will but to sense appetite. The will is the appetite that can tend to the good as such, the universal good, and that is what reason apprehends. "Et ideo bonitas voluntatis dependet a ratione eo modo quo dependet ab obiecto: Therefore the goodness of will depends on reason in the same way that it depends on its object" (IaIIae, q.19, a.3).

Reason grasps the good under the aspect of truth: such-and-such is perfective of me. The will bears on the good as good, that is, as desirable. But the second presupposes the first.

Dicendum quod bonum sub ratione boni, idest appetibilis, per prius pertinet ad voluntatem quam ad rationem. Sed tamen per prius pertinet ad rationem sub ratione veri, quam ad voluntatem.

It should be said that the good under the aspect of goodness, that is, as desirable, pertains to will first, not reason. Nonetheless, it first pertains to reason under the note of truth, before

untatem sub ratione appetibilis: quia appetitus voluntatis non potest esse de bono, nisi prius a ratione apprehenda- tur. (IaIIae, q.19, a.3, 1m)	it pertains to will under the note of the desirable, because the will's appe- tite can be of the good only insofar as it is first grasped by reason.

True judgments about the good are the condition of a good will. This priority of reason is built into the concept of voluntary activity which is deliberate willing, an appetite consequent upon the grasp of the good. Willing the end or good triggers off other acts of thought and desire, as we saw, but at the outset it is the mind's grasp of goodness as such, a grasp implicit in the grasp of anything as good, *sub ratione boni,* that presents to will its commensurate object. What the will seeks is goodness as such and particular things insofar as they share in some way in goodness.

2. Bad Conscience

We have seen that in order to count as an instance of human action a deed must be knowingly done. In order for it to be a good act, it must proceed from a judgment of what is the good thing to do. Various puzzles can be generated from this, among them the following. If a person's judgment of what is the good thing to do is as a matter of fact false, would he not act well if he acted contrary to that judgment? The bringing to bear of knowledge on an action is the work of conscience, is in fact a dictate of reason, so the puzzle can be restated thus: Is one who acts contrary to bad conscience acting well? Or: Does a bad conscience bind? It may seem odd to say that we are held to follow a bad conscience, that is, obliged to do what we judge is right even when we are wrong, but that is what Thomas holds.

He develops his own view against the background of another. Some, having pointed out that there are three kinds of act, some which are good in kind, others bad in kind, and others indifferent, say that if conscience judges that one should do a specifically good act, there is no error. So too when it tells us not to do a specifically bad act. The errant conscience tells us to do what is specifically bad or not to do what is specifically good.

Similarly conscience errs when it tells us some indifferent act, like stepping on a crack in the sidewalk, is wrong. The people Thomas has in mind say that when conscience commands or prohibits an indifferent act, it obliges, and the will which departs from the judgment is bad. In the other instances of errant conscience—commanding what is evil, prohibiting what is good—we are not obliged to follow, and the will which does not is not bad.

Thomas calls this irrational. The object of will is proposed to it by reason, and insofar as reason judges something to be bad, willing it is bad. Thomas does not see that the distinction of acts into indifferent and into those good or bad in kind is relevant. How reason judges determines the moral quality of will as in accord or discord with that judgment.

Puta, abstinere a fornicatione bonum quoddam est: tamen in hoc bonum non fertur voluntas, nisi secundum quod a ratione proponitur. Si ergo proponatur ut malum a ratione errante, feretur in hoc sub ratione mali. Unde voluntas erit mala, quia vult malum: non quidem id quod est malum per se, sed id quod est malum per accidens, propter apprehensionem rationis. (IaIIae, q.19, a.5)	To abstain from fornication, for example, is a kind of good, yet the will does not bear on this good save as proposed to it by reason. If therefore it should be proposed as evil by a mistaken reason, it would bear on it under the note of evil. So the will will be bad because it wills the bad, not indeed what is bad in itself, but that which is bad per accidens, because of reason's understanding.

Note how Thomas retains the notion of what is good or bad in itself. Without that point of reference, there would be no way to speak of the conscience as erroneous, of course. But the one with the erroneous conscience is unaware of the discrepancy between what he thinks good or bad and what is good or bad, so he is unaware that his conscience is erroneous. But what if his reason should tell him to do something against divine law? If he himself is aware of this conflict, then his conscience is not completely erroneous, and he is obliged to follow divine law, not his own defective judgment. The same would be true of a Catholic who thinks he ought to do something he knows is contrary to Church teaching. To be aware of the discrepancy is to know that he ought to follow Church teaching. Here an erroneous conscience would be one that mistakenly judges it to be God's will or Church teaching that he do what God or the Church forbids (IaIIae, q.19, a.5, 2m).

This raises another question. If an erroneous conscience always binds, does it excuse the bad action one performs in following conscience? In order to deal with this question, Thomas remarks, we must recall what was said earlier of ignorance. Sometimes ignorance makes what would have been a voluntary act involuntary, but not always. When the act is rendered involuntary by ignorance, it is no longer to be appraised as a human act and is neither morally good nor morally bad. When ignorance itself is willed, whether directly or indirectly, that is, by choice or by neglect, there is moral fault.

Si igitur ratio vel conscientia erret errore voluntario, vel directe, vel propter negligentiam, quia est error circa id quod quis scire tenetur; tunc talis error rationis vel conscientiae non excusat quin voluntas concordans rationi vel conscientiae sic erranti, sit mala. (IaIIae, q.19, a.6)	If then reason or conscience should err by a voluntary error, whether directly or because of negligence, being an error about something one is held to know, then such an error of reason or conscience does not excuse or make the will agreeing with reason or conscience so erring other than bad.

One who has an erroneous conscience thus seems obliged to do an objectively bad act, but he is not excused for doing it. Not to follow his conscience would be bad; to follow it is bad. It seems that he is damned if he does, and damned if he doesn't. But it doesn't seem right that a person sins no matter what he does. If there is no chance of doing well, he may seem to be deprived of the status of moral agent. He seems *perplexus*: condemned to do evil.

Nec tamen est perplexus: quia potest intentionem malam dimittere. Et similiter, supposito errore rationis vel conscientiae qui procedit ex ignorantia non excusante, necesse est quod sequatur malum in voluntate. Nec tamen est homo perplexus: quia potest	He is not however perplexed, because he can set aside his evil intention. Similarly, supposing an error of reason or conscience which does not arise from excusable ignorance, it is necessary that evil should follow in the will. Yet the man is not perplexed,

ab errore recedere, cum ignorantia sit vincibilis et voluntaria. (IaIIae, q.19, a.6, 3m)	because he can recede from his error, since his ignorance is vincible and voluntary.

If one through no fault of his own found himself in a situation where no matter what he did or did not do he did wrong, then he would be *perplexus* in Thomas's sense. But he does not think anyone is in or could be in such a spot. If one through his own fault gets into such a spot, that is another thing entirely.

3. God and Goodness

After Thomas shows that reason is the measure of the goodness of will because it presents to the will its object, he asks if the goodness of will depends upon eternal law. This is a first adumbration of matters that will be discussed formally in the Treatise on Law, which begins at Question 90. Reason is the measure of will, insofar as reason is measured by eternal law.

Quod autem ratio humana sit regula voluntatis humanae, ex qua eius bonitas mensuretur, habet ex lege aeterna, quae est ratio divina.... Unde manifestum est quod multo magis dependet bonitas voluntatis humanae a lege aeterna quam a ratione humana: et ubi deficit humana ratio, oportet ad rationem aeternam recurrere. (IaIIae, q.19, a.4)	That human reason should be the rule of human will according to which its goodness is measured derives from eternal law which is divine reason.... Hence it is manifest that the goodness of will is much more dependent on eternal law than on human reason; and where human reason is defective, it should have recourse to eternal reason.

That the goodness of the human will depends on conformity with divine will is proved in this way. The goodness of will depends on intending the end, and the ultimate end of the human will is the highest good, that is, God. "Requiritur ergo ad bonitatem humanae voluntatis, quod ordinetur ad summum bonum quod est Deus: the goodness of the human will requires that it be ordered to the highest good who is God" (IaIIae, q.19, a.9). But the object of the divine will is God Himself. Thus, in willing the highest good, the human will is measured by the divine will.

The general point being made, Thomas addresses the problems which arise from making the goodness of our will depend upon conformity with the divine will. Does this conformity extend to the particular objects willed? Thomas's discussion of this gathers together much of what he has already said and casts new light upon it.

The will bears on its object as this is presented to it by reason. But reason can consider an object in diverse ways, seeing it as good under one aspect and as not good under another. That is why, with respect to the same thing, one person's will is good because it wills it to be insofar as it is good, and another's will is good because it wills it not to be insofar as it is not good. He exemplifies this with a memorable case. The judge has a good will insofar as he wills the death of the criminal, because this is just; the man's relatives, who do not want him killed because of the evil of death, also have good wills. If opposed acts of will can both be good, it is unclear what bite there is to saying our wills are good when they conform to the divine will. If they do this insofar as they choose good or avoid evil, and if opposite acts involving the same object are both good, the measure seems unhelpful.

A further point. Since will follows on reason's grasp, the will will bear on a more common good insofar as mind grasps something under a more common aspect of goodness. Take the example of the condemned man again. The judge's concern is the common good, which is justice, and in the light of that wills the death of the criminal, the death being good in relation to the common condition. The man's wife considers the more limited good of the family, and in the light of that she does not want her guilty spouse to be killed. It is the good of the entire universe that is grasped by God, He being its maker and governor; what He wills, He wills in the light of the common good, namely His goodness, which is the good of the whole universe. The creature's knowledge is naturally of a particular good proportioned to its nature. It can happen that something is good from a narrower perspective that is not good in the wider one, and vice versa.

Et ideo contingit quod aliqua voluntas est bona volens aliquid secundum rationem particularem consideratum, quod tamen Deus non vult secundum rationem universalem, et e converso. Et inde est etiam quod possunt diversae voluntates diversorum hominum circa opposita esse bonae, prout sub diversis rationibus particularibus volunt hoc esse vel non esse. Non est autem recta voluntas alicuius hominis volentis aliquod bonum particulare, nisi referat illud in bonum commune sicut in finem: cum etiam naturalis appetitus cuiuslibet partis ordinetur in bonum commune totius. Ex fine autem sumitur quasi formalis ratio volendi illud quod ad finem ordinatur. Unde ad hoc quod aliquis recta voluntate velit aliquod particulare bonum, oportet quod illud particulare bonum sit volitum materialiter, bonum autem commune divinum sit volitum formaliter. Voluntas igitur humana tenetur conformari divinae voluntati in volito formaliter, tenetur enim velle bonum divinum et commune, sed non materialiter ratione iam dicta. (IaIIae, q.19, a.10)

It can happen that a certain will is good in willing something considered in a particular aspect, which God, regarding in the light of the universal, does not will, and conversely. That is why different men can will opposites, and their wills yet be good insofar as they will this to be or not to be under different particular aspects. But the will of a man willing some particular good is not rectified unless it refers it to the common good as to the end, just as the natural appetite of any part is ordered to the common good of the whole. It is from the end that the formal reason for willing that which is for the sake of the end is taken. So in order that one will with a rectified will a particular good, it is necessary that the particular good be willed materially and the divine common good be willed formally. The human will is held to conform itself to the divine will with respect to the thing willed taken formally, but not materially, for reasons already given.

If, when a particular good is willed with reference to the common good as end, it is the common good that is formally willed, then the created will, willing any particular good under the aspect of the common good, is formally conformed with the divine will. In passing, Thomas notes that the good that is the object of a particular appetite must be referred to the good of the whole, if the agent is to act well.

Thomas adds that the human will can be conformed to the divine will

as efficient cause, because no matter what it wills, its activity presupposes
divine causality, and one can thus be said to will what God wants him
to will.

External Action

The external, commanded act of will can be good because of the kind
of act it is, something determined by its object, e.g., giving alms to the
poor. But it can also be ordered to a further end, as in the example of the
one who gives alms out of motives of vainglory. But the further end may
itself be good, say, the peace and order of the community which are threat-
ened by the desperate poor. The goodness of the will in intending the end
then spills over to the external act, just as its badness, as in the case of the
vainglorious almsgiver, vitiates the external act.

Bonitas autem vel malitia quam habet
actus exterior secundum se, propter
debitam materiam et debitas circumstantias, non derivatur a voluntate,
sed magis a ratione. Unde si consideretur bonitas exterioris actus secundum
quod est in ordinatione et apprehensione rationis, prior est quam bonitas
actus voluntatis: sed si consideretur
secundum quod est in executione operis, sequitur bonitatem voluntatis,
quae est principium eius. (IaIIae,
q.20, a.1)

The goodness or badness the external
act has in itself because of its fitting
matter and circumstances does not
derive from will but rather from reason. Hence if the goodness of the external act is considered as it is in the
ordering and grasp of reason, it is
prior to the goodness of the act of
will; but if we consider it as it is in
the execution of the deed, it follows
the goodness of will, which is its
principle.

Insofar as the mind proposes to will the external act as something good,
the will is good as desiring what reason has so judged; in this way, in the
order of intention, it is the good of the external act which is prior to the
good will. In the order of execution, the external act is an effect of will
and follows on and is affected by its moral goodness or badness (ibid., ad
1m). Thus, there is a twofold goodness of the external act, that which
derives from its object and circumstances and that which derives from the

end to which it is ordered. The second kind of goodness depends upon the goodness of will.

| Illa autem quae est ex debita materia vel circumstantiis, dependet ex ratione: et ex hac dependet bonitas voluntatis, secundum quod in ipsam fertur. (IaIIae, q.20, a.2) | That however which stems from fitting matter and circumstances depends on reason, and the goodness of the will depends on this insofar as it bears on it. |

If the will is good because of its proper object and of its end, the external act will be good. But the goodness of the external act cannot depend on being ordered to a further good end alone. If what is done is not judged by reason to be a good act, it cannot be made good by being ordered to a good end. And a good kind of act is vitiated, if it is ordered to a bad end. Thomas likes to remind us that one defect makes an act bad, but in order for it to be good, it must be good in terms of object, circumstances, and end.

Is it one and the same goodness whereby the internal and external acts are good, or are these several instances of goodness? The interior act of will and the external act constitute morally one act, and the question finally is about that moral act. Is it good or bad? When the external act has no moral quality of its own, when it is morally neutral, then the goodness of the one moral act is read from the end intended. But the external act can be of a kind which of itself has moral quality, and then its goodness does not derive from the end.

| Sic ergo dicendum quod quando actus exterior est bonus vel malus solum ex ordine ad finem, tunc est omnino eadem bonitas vel malitia actus voluntatis, qui per se respicit finem, et actus exterioris, qui respicit finem mediante actu voluntatis. Quando autem actus exterior habet bonitatem vel malitiam secundum se, scilicet secundum materiam vel circumstantias, tunc bonitas exterioris actus est una | So it should be said that when the external act is good or bad only from being ordered to the end, then the goodness or badness of will, which as such looks to the end, is wholly the same as that of the external act, which looks to the end via the act of the will. But when the external act has goodness or badness of itself, i.e. because of its matter and circumstances, then the goodness of the ex- |

et bonitas voluntatis quae est ex fine, est alia: ita tamen quod et bonitas finis ex voluntate redundat in actum exteriorem, et bonitas materiae et circumstantiarum redundat in actum voluntatis. (IaIIae, q.20, a.3)

ternal act is one, and the goodness of the will drawn from the end another, but such that the goodness of the end redounds from the will to the external act, and the goodness of matter and circumstances redound to the act of will.

What, if anything, does the external act add to the goodness or badness of the interior act? The interior is not only concerned with end, but also with the act that is the means of bringing it about. The external act derives its goodness from reason and will, not vice versa. Thus it can seem that the actual execution of the external act does not add to the goodness or badness of what is being morally done. This is a conundrum advanced by Abelard in his *Scito Teipsum*.

In reply, Thomas says that if we are asking about the goodness the external act derives from the willing of the end, it could be said that the external act adds nothing to its goodness, unless the will itself could be said to be better or worse. That, he suggests, might come about in three ways.

Fifi, about to give some money to a beggar, is jostled by passersby and fails to get the dollar into the outstretched hand. She is swept on down the street, where another extended hand provides an opportunity, and she presses the money into it. The duplication of acts of the will amounts to an increase of goodness.

Or, Fifi might have given up on that first try whereas Maude persisted, fended off the onward flow of pedestrians, and gave the beggar money. Maude's will to give alms is greater, because it lasts longer.

And the intensity with which one wills the end would seem to make the will better or worse.

But what about the moral quality that the external act has from its object and circumstances? Abelard contended that actually building houses for the poor added nothing to the goodness of the intention to do so.

Si autem loquamur de bonitate actus exterioris quam habet secundum materiam et debitas circumstantias, sic comparatur ad voluntatem ut terminus et finis. Et hoc modo addit ad bonitatem vel malitiam voluntatis: quia omnis inclinatio vel motus perficitur in hoc quod consequitur finem, vel attingit terminum. Unde non est perfecta voluntas, nisi sit talis quae, opportunitate data, operetur. Si vero possibilitas desit, voluntate existente perfecta, ut operaretur si posset; defectus perfectionis quae est ex actu exteriori, est simpliciter involuntarium. (IaIIae, q.20, a.4)

If we are speaking of the goodness the external act has from its matter and circumstances, then it is compared to will as term and end. And in this way it adds to the goodness or badness of will, because every inclination or motion is perfected when it reaches its end or attains its term. Hence there is no perfected will unless, given the opportunity, it acts. If the possibility be lacking, the perfected will remaining but unable to act, then the defect of perfection with respect to the external act is simply involuntary.

It was Abelard's contention that the external act was neither good nor bad in kind, but owed its goodness or badness solely to intention. Because intention alone is good, the actual execution of the intention neither added to nor detracted from its moral quality. This requires, of course, that every external act is morally neutral and becomes good because it is done with a good intention, that is, for the sake of a good end, and becomes bad for the opposite reason. Difficulties arise when we ask for the criteria of a good intention. Unless it is the intention to bring about some good, whether means or end, there seems to be no way of speaking of good intention. But then there must be states of affairs and kinds of action which are good quite independently of my intending them.

Summary

The human voluntary act will be good, insofar as will is measured by reason. The act of willing in the first instance bears on the end or good which has been first grasped by reason. The good is that which is desirable as perfective of the one desiring it. Only when mind judges that something is good does the will, the intellectual appetite, have something to want.

Anything that the mind judges to be good, sees as good, is thereby brought under the common formality of goodness. That common formality cannot not be desired. In seeing things as good, the mind is implicitly grasping that in virtue of which good things are good. This is the *ratio boni*. No particular good commands the will's desire, since in some aspects it will not be desirable or good.

Mind's grasp of the good is the measure of the will's goodness. When the will desires the end or good presented by reason and prompts the search for means of attaining it, the thing judged to be a means will share in the goodness of the will desiring the end. Sometimes the act that serves as a means has no moral quality of its own and is good or bad solely with reference to the end. Some possible ways of attaining the end have their own moral quality, because of their object and circumstances. That they have moral quality is a judgment of reason different from the judgment that they are ordered to the end.

Reason is not an arbitrary measure of the will. The assumption is that true judgments as to the human good provide guidance to the will. These true judgments as to what is to be done are a measured measure, and their ultimate measure is the divine will or eternal law. We turn now to the principles that guide reason in its quest for true knowledge of the good, since everything that has been said about the goodness of voluntary action is, as we have seen, dependent on that.

5. Natural Law

T HE AIM or end of action is what is first in the order of intention but
last in the order of execution. Goodness as such, goodness in all its
amplitude, is the object of the faculty of will. Since it is the very nature
of will to be ordered to the good, the will necessarily wills the end of
goodness as such, goodness in all its amplitude, when this is presented to
it by the mind.

But, we may say, it is not goodness as such but this or that good thing
we think of, and desire may or may not follow on such thoughts. Whoever
thought of goodness as such? Everyone, the answer is, though only implicitly, insofar as any of those particular things are seen as good. What
does it mean to say that something is grasped as good except that it is
seen to be the carrier of this formality: "that which is fulfilling or perfective
of me"? The judgment that "X is good," however, is never equivalent to
"X is goodness." If it were, then we would necessarily want not only the
aspect under which the mind grasps the thing, but the thing itself. We
could not not love it. As we have seen, for Thomas, since God is goodness,
He is an object we will be unable not to love, when we see Him. But in
this life, the love of God can compete with the pursuit of pleasure, wealth,
fame, or diversion. In this life, any possible object of will, of love, has pros
and cons, and the will is thus free in its regard. In order for an X that is
good to engage us, those moves that Thomas calls enjoyment (*fruitio*) and
intention must take place.

But is it the case, perhaps, that the things the mind grasps as good are
all equal, because none of them is identical with goodness? The aspect
under which something is thought when it is judged to be good is, again,

goodness, the *ratio boni*, the ultimate end, happiness. For our present purposes, let these be equivalent. The point just made can be made in terms of ultimate end, by saying that while all men necessarily desire the ultimate end that is happiness, they are far from agreement on what constitutes happiness. Does this mean that just any judgment as to what constitutes happiness or the ultimate end is as good as any other? Surely not. Thomas was at some pains to show that certain things—wealth, pleasure, power—cannot effectively play the role of ultimate end of the human agent. He is not denying that some, perhaps many of us, make such things our ultimate end. There are those, St. Paul said, *cuius deus venter est*: whose god is their belly. Let us have before us again a passage we considered on an earlier occasion.

Hoc autem est bonum in communi, in quod voluntas naturaliter tendit, sicut etiam quaelibet potentia in suum obiectum: et etiam ipse finis ultimus, qui hoc modo se habet in appetibilibus, sicut prima principia demonstrationum in intelligibilibus: et universaliter omnia illa quae conveniunt volenti secundum suam naturam. Non enim per voluntatem appetimus solum ea quae pertinent ad potentiam voluntatis; sed etiam ea quae pertinent ad singulas potentias, et ad totum hominem. Unde naturaliter homo vult non solum obiectum voluntatis, sed etiam alia quae conveniunt aliis potentiis: ut cognitionem veri, quae convenit intellectui; et esse et vivere et alia huiusmodi, quae respiciunt consistentiam naturalem; quae omnia comprehenduntur sub obiecto voluntatis, sicut quaedam particularia bona. (IaIIae, q.10, a.1)

That then is the good as such, to which the will naturally tends as any power tends to its object; it is also the ultimate end, which plays the same role in desirables that the first principles of demonstration do in intelligibles; and generally whatever befits the nature of the one willing. For we do not desire with our wills only what pertains to the power of will, but also what pertains to each power and to the whole man. Hence universally a man wills not only the object of will, but also all those things appropriate to the other powers: such as knowledge of truth which is appropriate to intellect, and to exist and live and the like, which are required for the integrity of his nature. All these come under the object of will as certain particular goods.

It is Thomas's view then that we necessarily desire not only the ultimate end, but also whatever is necessary for it, e.g., existence, life, etc. "And similarly whatever is ordered to this end, such that without them the end could not be had, like to exist and to live and the like: et similiter illa quae ordinantur ad hunc finem, sine quibus finis haberi non potest, sicut esse et vivere et huiusmodi" (IaIIae, q.10, a.2, 3m).

Things that cannot serve as the ultimate end may nonetheless be such that without them the ultimate end cannot be attained. As such they enter into the account of the good for man, although not of course on an equal footing. If those who make a god of their belly culpably attempt to make the slaking of hunger and thirst the point of life, it is nonetheless obvious that food and drink are necessary for human existence and thus things without which the good more proportionate to our nature as rational cannot be had. In short, there is a hierarchy among the goods constitutive of the good of man. Remember Thomas's discussion of whether a bodily good could be our ultimate end.

. . . dato quod finis rationis et voluntatis humanae esset conservatio humani esse, non tamen posset dici quod finis hominis esset aliquod corporis bonum. Esse enim hominis consistit in anima et corpore: et quamvis esse corporis dependeat ab anima, esse tamen humanae animae non dependet a corpore, ut supra ostensum est; ipsumque corpus est propter animam, sicut materia propter formam, et instrumenta propter motorem, ut per ea suas actiones exerceat. Unde omnia bona corporis ordinantur ad bona animae, sicut ad finem. (IaIIae, q.2, a.5)

. . . even granted that the end of reason and will were the conservation of human existence, it could not be said that the end of man is a bodily good. To be a man involves soul and body, and although the existence of body depends on soul, the existence of the human soul does not depend on body, as was shown earlier; the body is for the sake of the soul, as matter is for the sake of form, and instruments for the sake of the agent in order that he may act through them. Hence all goods of the body are ordered to goods of the soul as to their end.

The discussion of ultimate end and happiness, like the discussions of voluntary action and the various will acts that make up voluntary action, puts the emphasis on will, since the good is the object of will. Nonetheless, as we are reminded throughout, the good must first be grasped as a truth, *ut verum,* before it can be desired as good, *ut bonum.* That is, cognitive activity is a continuing complement of willing, intending, choosing, using the body, etc. Let us turn now to a formal consideration of the knowledge that guides the will.

Reason and Will

We can begin by recalling more of the hints about practical reason that have been dropped by Thomas, when his discussion focused on will acts.

That the thought bearing on action is practical is obvious enough. So too it is obvious that the good achievable by action is what is meant by the human end or good. Does this mean that man's ultimate end consists in some operation of practical reason? Thomas says no. The activity in which the ultimate end is achieved, contemplation, is a theoretical use of the mind, and its object is not an operable object, but God. The activity of practical intellect is thus ordered to, subservient to, the activity of theoretical intellect. Practical intellect is clearly in play in what Thomas calls the contemplative life, but as a means to the end of theoretical reason.

Many exhibit impatience or incredulity when confronted with Aristotle's insistence that contemplation is the most perfect act of the defining faculty of man and thus is that in which his good, happiness, or perfection primarily consists; and the object of contemplation is the divine. Mortimer Adler dismisses this as a mistake, wanting ethics and politics to bear on the virtues of the practical life. It is of course true that the ends of moral virtues are just that, ends, endlike, not mere means. But they are ends which can be ordered to a further end, and should be, if the human good in the highest sense is to be had.

Intellectus practicus ordinatur ad bonum quod est extra ipsum: sed intellectus speculativus habet bonum in seipso, scilicet contemplationem veritatis. Et si illud bonum sit perfectum, ex eo totus homo perficitur et fit bo-

The practical intellect is ordered to a good outside itself, but speculative intellect has its good in itself, namely, contemplation of truth. And if that good is perfect, the whole man is perfected by it and made good, some-

nus: quod quidem intellectus practicus non habet, sed ad illud ordinat.
(IaIIae, q3, a.5, 2m)

thing practical intellect does not have,
but it is ordered to it.

This is not to say that the ultimate end is within us, as if contemplation bore on itself. God is of course distinct from our intellect, and He is our ultimate end, but we attain Him through the activity of speculative mind, namely, contemplation (ibid., 3m). Practical intellect is ordered to the directing and perfecting of activities other than its own activity.

Let us recall Thomas's discussion of whether the goodness of an act depends on its being in conformity with the divine will. Insofar as the will bears on the ultimate end, goodness as such, the formality under which it desires anything, the will is conformed to the divine will. The reason is that goodness as such is the object of the divine will. Furthermore, insofar as the will loves according to the natural inclination God gave it, it acts in conformity with the divine will (IaIIae, q.19, a.10). Moreover, if the will is good insofar as it follows the correct guidance of reason, reason is a measured measure, and what it is measured by is eternal law. "Quod autem ratio humana sit regula voluntatis humanae, ex qua eius bonitas mensuretur, habet ex lege aeterna, quae est ratio divina: that human reason is the rule of human will by which its goodness is measured derives from the eternal law, which is the divine reason" (IaIIae, q.19, a.4).

There is a recurrent analogy in the questions of the *Prima secundae* that we have been considering, an analogy Thomas takes from the *Nicomachean Ethics*: the first principle or starting-point in matters of conduct is the end proposed, which corresponds to principles in the disciplines (1151a16). In fact, *voluntas,* the primary natural act of will which is determined to its object, goodness, corresponds to *intellectus,* the primary mental grasp. Indeed, what mind naturally grasps as the human good, the will naturally loves and desires.

The notion of "means" is derived from locomotion and applied to both mind and appetite. Just as there are midpoints through which the moved passes in order to reach its term, so those things which are for the sake of the end are called *media* or means (IaIIae, q.8, a.2. sed contra). Because we desire the end, we come to desire the things which are for the sake of the end, just as intellect arrives at conclusions from principles which are called means (IaIIae, q.9, a.3, 3m). This connects with the structure of counsel or deliberation, which depicted the inquiry of practical reason as moving syllogistically from principles to a conclusion which guides choice.

This suggests that practical reason is in possession of first principles and that its inquiry moves in the direction of judgments more and more proportionate to the singular acts it would guide. The principles of practical reason are what Thomas calls the precepts of natural law. After looking at what he has to say on this score, we will move on in the next chapter to discuss the process or discourse that characterizes practical reason.

Principles of Practical Reason

Since reason regulates, guides, rules the will, it is not surprising that the principles whereby this regulating is achieved receive the name law. Thomas notes that the etymology of law suggests binding and obliging. Will is the starting point of action, but it receives its starting point from reason. The starting points or principles that reason grasps and will is guided by are accordingly referred to as laws. The term law, Thomas will show, is an analogous one. That is, it has an ordered plurality of meanings, and if we should ask which of those meanings is regulative of the others, the answer would be that which refers to the sort of things legislatures come up with. That is, the controlling meaning of "law" is human positive law, which unproblematically exemplifies the definition of law as "quaedam rationis ordinatio ad bonum commune, ab eo qui curam communitatis habet, promulgata: a promulgated rational ordering to the common good on the part of one with authority in the community" (IaIIae, q.90, a.4).

Et quia ratio etiam practica utitur quodam syllogismo in operabilibus, ut supra habitum est, secundum quod Philosophus docet in VII Ethic.; ideo est invenire aliquid in ratione practica quod ita se habeat ad operationes, sicut se habet propositio in ratione spe-	Because practical reason too uses a kind of syllogism about things to be done, as was said earlier according to Aristotle's teaching in the *Ethics,* we should look in practical reason for something that relates to actions, as in speculative reason the proposition re-

culativa ad conclusiones. Et huiusmodi propositiones universales rationis practicae ordinatae ad actiones,
habent rationem legis. Quae quidem
propositiones aliquando actualiter
considerantur, aliquando vero habitu-
aliter a ratione tenentur. (IaIIae, q.90,
a.1, 2m)

lates to conclusions. This kind of universal proposition in practical reason
ordered to action has the note of law.
Such propositions are sometimes actually thought about, sometimes are
held by reason as by a habit.

The earlier analogy between will and intellect gives rise to this further analogy between practical and speculative intellect. Just as there are start-ing points of reasoning generally, so too there are starting points of the practical reasoning that guides choice and action. "Primum autem prin-cipium in operativis, quorum est ratio practica, est finis ultimus: the start-ing point in things to be done, with which practical reason is concerned, is the ultimate end" (IaIIae, q.90, a.2). It is well to notice such connecting links between the discussion in the so-called "Treatise on Law," which begins with Question 90, and what has gone before it in this part of the *Summa theologiae*. The "Treatise on Law" is often read as if it were an autonomous and self-sufficient discussion of law in all its senses. Consid-ered in abstraction from its literary setting, the discussion of law may be read in such a way that its dependence on what has gone before is over-looked or misunderstood. Seeing it in conjunction with the preceding, one is struck by the backward references, the link-ups, the continuity of the discussion with its prologue.

By calling the first principles of practical reason a law, more precisely, natural law, Thomas links it to human positive law as well as to a number of other senses of the term, namely, eternal law, already mentioned, and divine law in the sense of revealed law, both old and new. Comparison with these other senses of the term, all of which, insofar as they are called law, are parasitic on human positive law, sharpens our understanding of what is meant by natural law.

We have already seen that by natural law Thomas means the principles in practical reason that function in a way analogous to principles in spec-ulative reason. Another characterization of natural law follows on his discussion of eternal law. God's providence can be considered on an analogy with human positive law, as God's rational direction of the cosmos He has created. The whole of creation is governed by divine reason, which can thus be thought of as the *law* of creation. Now if God is the law of creation, creatures can be said to participate in that law, insofar as they are governed by it. It is because the rational creature man is governed by eternal law in a peculiar way, not simply as directed by it, but as capable of formulating in his own mind what, given eternal law, ought to govern his acts, that another kind of law is spoken of. Law is something of reason. All creatures as governed by God can be said to manifest the divine reason, and this is true of man as well. But man has his own reason, whereby he can judge what is good or bad, and this is what is called natural law.

"Multi dicunt: quis ostendit nobis bona?" cui quaestioni respondens, dicit: "Signatum est super nos lumen vultus tui, Domine," quasi lumen rationis naturalis, quo discernimus quid sit bonum et malum, quod pertinet ad naturalem legem, nihil aliud sit quam impressio divini luminis in nobis. Unde patet quod lex naturalis nihil aliud est quam participatio legis aeternae in rationali creatura. (IaIIae, q.91, a.2)

"Many ask, who will show us what is good?" replying to which he says, "The light of your countenance is sealed upon us, Lord," as if the light of natural reason whereby we discern what is good and evil, which pertains to natural law, is nothing other than the impress of the divine light on us. Thus it is clear that natural law is precisely the participation in eternal law by the rational creature.

Natural law is reason's natural grasp of certain common principles which should direct our acts. Just as speculative intellect moves from common and certain truths toward ever more particular truths about the things that are, so practical reason moves off from basic, common, and certain directives toward ever more particular guides for choice and action. The starting points of speculative reason are indemonstrable; so are those of practical reason. Furthermore, the particular directives give rise to another kind of law. "Et istae particulares dispositiones adinventae secundum rationem humanam, dicuntur leges humanae, servatis aliis conditionibus quae pertinent ad rationem legis: these particular dispositions discovered by human reason are called human law—if the other components of the definition of law are present" (IaIIae, q.91, a.3).

The meaning of that final phrase is this. Not every discovery of a more particular guide for action is called a law, but only those that direct public actions to the common good and emanate from public authority and are promulgated. As opposed to what? To moral philosophy, understood as the quest for more informative though still general guidelines; also, the guidelines that emerge from anyone's experience, and which he may or may not voice. Not every less common directive for action has the force of law.

Thomas's procedure here may seem circular. In Question 90, he proceeds on the assumption that if we know any kind of law it will be human positive law, and his definition pretty obviously applies to it. Now he seems to be arriving at the notion of positive law from that of natural law. And in the previous article, he described natural law as a special participation in eternal law. If the various kinds of law form an ordered set, how do we determine what is first and what secondary in the set? Human positive law seems sometimes to be first, and sometimes to be secondary.

In things named analogically, it is sometimes the case that what first saves the account of the term is also prior in being or reality. But sometimes what is first named is ontologically least. Whenever a term is shared by God and creature, the creature will save the meaning of the term first and most obviously, but God, who is named secondarily, is prior in existence. So in the case before us, although eternal law can be understood as law only by thinking of human positive law, what we refer to as eternal law is really first and, when we know this, we can see the other sorts of law as dependent on it. Man's capacity to discern what is good or evil is received from God the Creator. Insofar as God's ordering of His creation is called a law, this rational sharing in ordering and guiding is called natural law. Insofar as natural law consists of indemonstrable and very common principles, human law can then be seen as determining and applying these to particular situations. Thus, that which primarily saves the meaning of "law" is seen to derive from what only secondarily and derivatively is called law.

Divine positive law is needed, insofar as man is called to an end surpassing his nature.

Dicendum quod per naturalem legem participatur lex aeterna secundum proportionem capacitatis humanae naturae. Sed oportet ut altiori modo dirigatur homo in ultimum finem supernaturalem. Et ideo superadditur lex divinitus data, per quam lex aeterna participatur altiori modo. (Ia-IIae, q.91, a.4, 1m)	It must be said that in natural law the eternal law is participated in a way proportionate to the capacity of human nature. But man must be directed in a higher way to the supernatural, ultimate end. Therefore a law divinely given was added through which eternal law is participated in a higher way.

It is also the case that, insofar as natural law is explicitly formulated in Revelation, our natural capacities are reinforced and shored up in the face of the debility of human reason and the corrosive effect of bad habits. The Magisterium's reinforcement of natural law is one of the strongest examples of the divine mercy, in a time when even the most elementary truths about human behavior are obnubilated by widespread decadence.

When it is pointed out that man shares in eternal law in a peculiar way, because of his reason, it should not be thought that he does not also share in eternal law in the way other creatures do.

Sed quia rationalis natura, cum eo quod est commune omnibus creaturis, habet aliquid sibi proprium inquantum est rationalis, ideo secundum utrumque modum legi aeternae subditur: quia et notionem legis aeternae aliquo modo habet, ut supra dictum est; et iterum unicuique rationali creaturae inest naturalis inclinatio ad id quod est consonum legi aeternae; "sumus" enim "innati ad habendum virtutes," ut dicitur in II Ethic. (Ia-IIae, q.93, a.6)	Since rational nature, along with what is common to all creatures, has something proper to itself as rational, it is in both ways subject to eternal law. First it has in a certain way knowledge of eternal law, as was said above, and also there is a natural inclination in every rational creature to that which is consonant with eternal law: "We are so made as to have virtue," as Aristotle said in the *Ethics* (1103a25).

Question 94

The treatment of law that begins with Question 90 of the *Prima se-cundae* is all but unique in the writings of Thomas. Not only is there no parallel to the treatise itself, many of the individual articles making up the various questions of the treatise have no parallel elsewhere in the writings of St. Thomas. This deprives us of further light, however oblique, on some of the central points in the treatise. All the more reason, then, to see the treatise as emerging out of the discussions that have preceded it in the work where it is found.

Is natural law a habit of intellect in the way that science is? This is the first question Thomas poses in Question 94, which is devoted specifically to natural law. What is the sense of the question? We have seen that Thomas often compares *intellectus* as the first act of mind with *voluntas* as the first act of will, each bearing necessarily and unerringly on its object. By means of the first act of intellect we grasp indemonstrable truths. Does *intellectus* refer to the grasp or to the truths? The faith sometimes means those truths which are grasped by the supernatural virtue of faith. Thomas takes natural law to refer to the first principles of practical reason, not to practical reason's grasp of those principles. As it happens, there is a traditional term for the intellect's grasp or ability to grasp those principles: *synderesis*. The following analogy is suggested:

intellectus	*synderesis*
first principles	natural law

"Synderesis dicitur lex intellectus nostri, inquantum est habitus continens praecepta legis naturalis, quae sunt prima principia operum humanorum: synderesis is called the law of our intellect insofar as it is the habit containing the precepts of natural law, which are the first principles of human acts" (IaIIae, q.94, a.1, 2m). It is just this parallel between the speculative and practical uses of our minds that provides the structure for the famous article 2 of Question 94.

The principles that underwrite both theoretical and practical thinking are *per se nota,* indemonstrable, self-evident. A principle is known through itself, as opposed to being demonstrated from others, if its predicate enters into the understanding of its subject. This is the first mode of perseity Aristotle speaks of in the *Posterior Analytics* and elsewhere. Such propositions are called immediate because no middle term is required to connect predicate and subject. Here is an example: "Man is rational." Why so? Because, Thomas says, "Qui dicit hominem, dicit rationale: who says man, says rational." That does not seem to be true. If I say man, I say man, not rational, and vice versa. The terms are not synonyms. Let's try again. "That which is indicated by 'man' is indicated by 'rational'?" Not much help there. On that basis, "Socrates is bald" or "Man is on the moon" would be *per se notae*. "Rational is a constituent of the nature signified by 'man.'" Rational is part of man's meaning. What does man mean? Rational animal. In the sentence above, rational is predicated *per se* of man, meaning it is affirmed of the nature as such, it names the nature from a constituent of the nature. Only when we know what "man" means do we see that "man is rational" is *per se nota*.

From Boethius, Thomas makes the distinction between propositions which are *per se notae* in themselves but not to us. Only those which are the former can be the latter, the added ingredient being that we know what the terms mean. There are some *per se notae* propositions which are such that no one can fail to know the meanings of their terms and thus fail to see that they are so. Other self-evident propositions involve terms whose meanings depend on special experience or learning, and these are *per se notae* only to the relevantly wise.

These distinctions are not idle. In both the speculative and practical orders there are *per se notae* propositions whose terms are commonly known. Grasp of their truth accordingly is not confined to the sophisticated; indeed, it is these truths which form the great common bond among men of varying degrees of talent.

In his autem quae in apprehensione omnium cadunt, quidam ordo invenitur. Nam illud quod primo cadit in apprehensione, est ens, cuius intellec-	There is a certain order among the things that everyone grasps, for what is first apprehended is being, the understanding of which is included in

tus includitur in omnibus quae-
cumque quis apprehendit. Et ideo
primum principium indemonstrabile
est quod "non est simul affirmare et
negare," quod fundatur supra rationem entis et non entis: et super hoc
principio omnia alia fundantur, ut
dicitur in IV Metaphys. Sicut autem
ens est primum quod cadit in apprehensione simpliciter, ita bonum est
primum quod cadit in apprehensione
practicae rationis, quae ordinatur ad
opus: omne enim agens agit propter
finem, qui habet rationem boni. Et
ideo primum principium in ratione
practica est quod fundatur supra rationem boni, quae est, "Bonum est
quod omnia appetunt." Hoc est ergo
primum praeceptum legis, quod
bonum est faciendum et prosequen-
dum, et malum vitandum. Et super
hoc fundantur omnia alia praecepta
legis naturae: ut scilicet omnia illa
facienda vel vitanda pertineant
ad praecepta legis naturae, quae
ratio practica naturaliter apprehendit
esse bona humana. (IaIIae,
q.94, a.2)

whatever else anyone grasps. Therefore the first indemonstrable principle
is that one cannot simultaneously affirm and deny, which is based on the
notion of being and nonbeing. On
this principle all others are based, as
is said in *Metaphysics* IV. Just as being
is what is first grasped absolutely
speaking, so the good is the first
thing grasped by practical reason
which is ordered to a work: for every
agent acts for the sake of an end
which has the note of the good.
Therefore the first principle of practical reason is based on the notion of
the good, which is, "The good is that
which all things seek." This then is
the first precept of the law: Good is
to be done and pursued, and evil is to
be avoided. On this are based all the
other precepts of the law of nature;
such that all things to be done or
avoided pertain to precepts of natural
law that practical reason naturally
grasps as human goods.

Is Thomas suggesting, when he says that the first thing our mind grasps
is being, that in our baby book under the heading "First Word Spoken"
we should find the entry "being?" Since it is doubtful that we will, we
may think that Thomas has been carried away in the course of doing
philosophy and theology and has forgotten what it is like with most of
us—even while he purports to be speaking of what is commonly known
by men.

Notice what Thomas says about the understanding of being as included in whatever else is understood. What he is saying is quite compatible with the common experience of mankind that children first say words like "Mama," "hot," "car," "baby," and so on. Our experience is of particular beings, and our ideas and words refer either to instances or kinds of being. But this means that in knowing X, we implicitly know X as a being. That this is indeed latent in our ability to speak and get around in the world becomes clear when, mistaken that X is this or that, we say, "Well, in any case, it's something." It is. It is a being. We don't come to learn that things are beings after we have known and talked about them. If anything, we come to see that all along we have known them as kinds of being and thus that all of them are values of the variable in "X is being."

Of course there is nothing special in the vocable "being." It is a voiced sound like others. You might name your cat Being. Roadside monsters are announced from miles away on billboards simply as The Thing. And as Aristotle pointed out, children tend to call all women "mother" and all men "father." Words whose meanings may be clarified and their range restricted begin with a generic serviceability. What "being" means lurks in every meaning and can for particular purposes be made explicit.

This is also true of the first principle of reasoning as such, the so-called principle of contradiction. "She's married," you say, dashing my hopes, and I protest, "But you said she wasn't married." In quite ordinary conversations we hear, "Which is it? Make up your mind. Will you donate your body to science or not?" And little kids, when they argue, sometimes end in a choral exchange: "It is." "It isn't." "It is." "It isn't." These being elided as faces empurple and breath grows short to: 'tis and 'snot. It is in such homely ways that knowledge of the rock bottom first principle is revealed.

The reference to *Metaphysics IV* is important, since you will wonder why Thomas expressed the first principle of all reason in terms of affirmation and denial. Why didn't he say that the first principle is: A thing cannot be and not be at the same time and respect? That predicates cannot be affirmed and denied simultaneously of the same subject and that propositions cannot be simultaneously true and false follow on the ontological truth. Aristotle in the text and Thomas in his commentary take up these matters. They are important. Presumably the first principle of all reasoning is not the only self-evident principle. But all other self-evident principles will presuppose and thus depend on it. And there may be dependencies among the later self-evident principles. There is a kind of discourse here, as there is in the order of definition, but it is not the discourse of demonstration. We must not think that first principles in the plural simply zap the mind one at a time and in total independence of one another.

No more should we imagine that the practical use of our mind is wholly divorced from its speculative use. It is sometimes said that if there are self-evident principles of the practical order, then they must stand on their own without any relation of dependence on theoretical truths and perhaps quite independently of one another. This seems a view quite alien to that of Thomas.

Respondeo dicendum quod intellectus practicus et speculativus non sunt diversae potentiae. Cuius ratio est quia, ut supra dictum est, id quod accidentaliter se habet ad obiecti rationem quam respicit aliqua potentia, non diversificat potentiam: accidit enim colorato quod sit homo, aut magnum aut parvum; unde omnia huiusmodi eadem visiva potentia apprehenduntur. Accidit autem alicui apprehenso per intellectum, quod ordinetur ad opus, vel non ordinetur. Secundum hoc autem differunt intellectus speculativus et practicus. Nam intellectus speculativus est, qui quod apprehendit, non ordinat ad opus, sed ad solam veritatis considerationem: practicus vero intellectus dicitur, qui hoc quod apprehendit, ordinat ad opus. (Ia, q.79, a.11)

I reply that it should be said that the practical and speculative intellects are not diverse powers. The reason, as was shown above, is that what relates accidentally to the notion of the object of a potency does not diversify the potency. It is accidental to the colored object that it be a man or large or small which is why all such things are apprehended by the same power of sight. It is accidental to what intellect grasps that it be ordered or not be ordered to a work. Yet this is how speculative and practical intellect differ. For the speculative intellect is that which does not order to some work what it understands, but only to the consideration of its truth; the practical intellect is that which orders what it understands to a work.

In the *sed contra est* of that same article, Thomas quotes as the motto of the discussion Aristotle's remark in the *De anima*: "intellectus speculativus per extensionem fit practicus: the speculative intellect becomes practical by extension." But one faculty does not become another. Therefore they are not two faculties.

We live in a time when, under a persistent Kantian influence, practical reason is accorded an autonomy quite alien to the classical understanding of it that Thomas adopts. Moreover, nonsense such as the "naturalistic fallacy" clouds minds, and it is thought that Thomas must be so interpreted as to be saying that the truths of the practical order are utterly independent of the way the world is, independent of nature and facts, of descriptive truths. Dichotomies between fact and value do not provide us with innocent alternative ways of expressing what Thomas teaches. There is a whole sad history behind such matters, one that increasingly is being recognized as bankrupt. It is grievously wrong to imagine that Thomism must be corrected from such quarters. Therapy must go in the opposite direction. In any case, we shall want to read Thomas straight.

So read, we will notice that the principle of contradiction is sometimes called the first principle of the speculative use of our mind, sometimes the first principle of thinking as such. Needless to say, it is a principle which reigns over the practical as well as the speculative order. Indeed, sometimes Thomas takes *intellectus* to be the habit of both speculative and practical first principles (IaIIae, q.58, a.4). But let us return to the text of Question 94, article 2.

Quia vero bonum habet rationem finis, malum autem rationem contrarii, inde est quod omnia illa ad quae homo habet naturalem inclinationem ratio naturaliter apprehendit, ut bona, et per consequens ut opere prosequenda, et contraria eorum ut mala et vitanda. Secundum igitur ordinem inclinationum naturalium est ordo praeceptorum legis naturae. Inest	Because good has the note of end, and evil the contrary note, reason naturally grasps all those things to which man has a natural inclination as goods and consequently as what should be pursued in deed, and their contraries as evils to be avoided. There is then an order of the precepts of the law of nature which follows the order of natural inclinations. For

enim primo inclinatio homini ad bonum secundum naturam in qua communicat cum omnibus substantiis: prout scilicet quaelibet substantia appetit conservationem sui esse secundum suam naturam. Et secundum hanc inclinationem pertinent ad legem naturalem ea per quae vita hominis conservatur, et contrarium impeditur. —Secundo inest homini inclinatio ad aliqua magis specialia, secundum naturam in qua communicat cum ceteris animalibus. Et secundum hoc dicuntur ea esse de lege naturali "quae natura omnia animalia docuit," ut est coniunctio maris et feminae, et educatio liberorum et similia. —Tertio modo inest homini inclinatio ad bonum secundum naturam rationis, quae est sibi propria: sicut homo habet naturalem inclinationem ad hoc quod veritatem cognoscat de Deo et ad hoc quod in societate vivat. Et secundum hoc ad legem naturalem pertinent ea quae ad huiusmodi inclinationem spectant: utpote quod homo ignorantiam vitet, quod alios non offendat cum quibus debet conversari, et cetera huiusmodi quae ad hoc spectant.

there is first in man an inclination to what is good, according to the nature he shares with all substances, insofar namely as any substance seeks to preserve its existence according to its proper nature. On the basis of this inclination those things whereby man's life is preserved and the contrary impeded pertain to natural law. Secondly man has an inclination to more special things according to the nature he shares with other animals. On this basis those things are said to be of natural law "which nature teaches all animals," like the union of male and female and the education of offspring and the like. Third, man has an inclination to the good according to reason, which is proper to him: thus man has a natural inclination to know the truth about God and to live in society. According to this, those things which look to this inclination pertain to natural law; e.g. that a man should avoid ignorance and not offend the others with whom he must live, and other such things.

Practical reason is concerned with perfecting activities other than its own reasoning, and the theater of its directing and guiding activity contains the other inclinations which enter into the human makeup, some of them unlike reason in that we share them with other beings. The most widely shared inclinations are the most basic, the most natural. The natural drive to preserve itself in being is taken by Thomas to be true of anything. As present in us, it comes down chiefly to pursuing food and drink and avoiding harm. These are not inclinations we decide to have. The human task is to guide such inclinations so that they achieve their end or good in a way compatible with and even enhancing the good of the whole man. Eating and drinking make for a healthy continuation in existence, and health is a good of the whole man and dispositive to his seeking goods higher than health.

In much the same way, like other animals we do not decide to be attracted to the opposite sex or feel an impulse to mate; nor is continuing concern for offspring simply the result of a decision. If the first inclination is ordered to the preservation of the individual, this second level of inclination is ordered to the preservation of the species. Sexual activity and the raising of children must be rationally guided in such a way that they achieve their natural ends and contribute to the good of the agent as a whole. The ends of these inclinations, like the ends of the first, are particular goods, which must find their setting within the comprehensive good stated in the most basic precept of all.

Thirdly, there are inclinations peculiar to man as a rational animal. The desire to know is not something we decide to have; it is there as we are. So too is living with others. Thought experiments of the kind indulged in by John Rawls in *A Theory of Justice,* in which individuals imagine a society they will contract to enter, can have the unfortunate consequence of blurring the overwhelmingly obvious fact that no individual human is born or survives independently of others, nor can he reach fulfillment worthy of the name save in the company of his fellow men. Being social is not a choice; it is a fact of our nature. The moral dimension bears on how men direct their actions with an eye to the common good, since we can live well or badly in society. Likewise, the desire for knowledge has to be directed.

What this text gives us are the areas where natural law precepts will show up, the activities they will seek to regulate, and the overall good, which is the measure of these particular goods.

What strikes us immediately is the hierarchical nature of the account. The levels of inclination in man are attributed to natures, not because man is a bundle of substances, but because there are creatures which exhibit only the first level of inclination, others which exhibit the first and second, but only man subsumes these under a rational nature. Man is, in short, a microcosm and, like the macrocosm, an order.

We also discern the hierarchy involved in comparing goods which are proper to individuals with those which are goods of individuals, insofar as they are members of families and of the wider society. The good we have in common with others is more perfect than our merely private good, and this provides a measure of action.

What we do not find is any list of first principles of the practical order, any list of precepts of natural law. Indeed, the only things that look like precepts are found at the end and might be formulated: One ought to avoid ignorance; one ought not cause harm to his fellows. And of course we are struck by the fact that they are stated negatively.

About the paucity, not to say almost total absence, of formulation of any precepts of natural law after the very first one, we could say that the same dearth obtains in the discussion of speculative principles. We do have "Every whole is greater than its part," and "Two things equal to a third are equal to one another," and that makes three in all. But we can say we have three on the practical side as well.

We can, however, discern the shape of the precepts that would be formulated with regard to the first and second levels of inclination. "The pleasures of food and drink should contribute to the good of man as a whole." "Sexual congress should further the good of procreation in a way contributing to the whole good of man." The activities consequent upon these inclinations must be guided by reason, in order that the agent reach fulfillment as an individual, as a member of a family and a city, and as one whose highest perfection consists in knowledge of God Who is the common good of the universe.

Nonetheless, just as an exhaustive list of self-evident truths of a theoretical kind does not exist, so there is no exhaustive listing of precepts of natural law. The decalogue contains some of the more important, and here again most of them are stated negatively. Why is that?

Lex suis praeceptis habet communem instructionem. Ea vero quae agenda sunt in periculis non possunt ad aliquid commune reduci, sicut ea quae sunt vitanda. Et ideo praecepta fortitudinis magis dantur negative quam affirmative. (IIaIIae, q.140, a.1, 2m)

Law's precepts provide a common instruction, and the things that ought to be done when imperiled cannot be reduced to something common as the things to be avoided can. That is why the precepts of fortitude are given negatively rather than affirmatively.

The general moral task is to act well with respect to the goods that are the ends of inclinations that enter into our makeup, that is, to insure that the pursuit of particular goods does not jeopardize the good of the whole man, something that happens when the pursuit of the ends of lesser inclinations impedes the pursuit of the ends of higher inclinations. The tempering of the lower appetites and making them amenable to rational guidance is what is meant by moral virtue. One who reads Question 94, article 2 against the background of the *Prima secundae* will think of the cardinal virtues, as he reads Thomas on the levels of inclination and the precepts called for by each. And in the next article, he makes it clear that it is virtuous activity that natural law precepts command.

Temperantia est circa concupiscentias naturales cibi et potus et venereorum, quae quidem ordinantur ad bonum commune naturae, sicut et alia legalia ordinantur ad bonum commune morale. (IaIIae, q.94, a.3, 1m)

Temperance is concerned with the natural desires for food and drink and sex which indeed are ordered to the common good of nature, just as the other legal matters are ordered to the common moral good.

Knowing Natural Law

Before saying more about specific natural law precepts, let us consider an evident difficulty. The preceding few pages may strike even the well disposed as obscure. It is easy to have the sense, in reflecting on the texts before us, that we are dealing here with very *recherché* and sophisticated matters indeed. We cannot imagine Uncle Earl following the discussion at all, whatever difficulties we ourselves might be having. And that is a problem.

Natural law is made up of the very first directive judgments that we make. These are not achievements so much as starting points, and if the theory of natural law means anything, it means that everyone already has, in a significant sense of "has," these precepts in his standard repertoire. No one can fail to know them. That is the claim. Natural law is not a theory we are asked to accept on the basis of things we already accept. This theory maintains that you are already holding it. And isn't that preposterous?

Natural law, Thomas said, is the peculiarly rational participation in eternal law. Who would want to volunteer to go down to McDonald's and ask everyone who holds that to raise his hand? We have also been told that natural law precepts are to the practical order what self-evident principles are to the theoretical order. It is equally unlikely that this would claim the allegiance of each and every customer. Was Thomas hanging out with a pretty extraordinary bunch of Dominicans, whose elevated conversation misled him about what everybody knows?

Consider the parallel. "In the theoretical order, there are first principles which are immediately known because their predicate is included in the definition of their subject." This claim isn't going to bring down the house at McDonald's either. So it looks as if Thomas and his mentor Aristotle have attributed to the many what some of the learned may know.

Distinguo. We must not identify the *account* of first principles with the first principles themselves. Thomas is not suggesting that Aristotle's and Boethius's discussion of first principles would be readily intelligible to anyone; no more is Question 94 op-ed material. Nonetheless, if at McDonald's the clerk says there is pickle on your burger and you say there isn't, you and he and everyone else know that one of you is wrong. Either there is or there is not pickle on your burger. So too when he admits his mistake, however mystified he may be that one has been made, and says, "I gotta do the right thing. Have a pickle," you will nod, everyone will nod, no one will think he has said anything controversial. Doing the right thing, doing the good thing, avoiding the opposite—of course.

This distinction enables us to state the claim clearly: Everyone can be presumed already to know the first principles of practical reason but not any theory about them, nor even the description of them as "first principles of practical reason." What anyone can be presumed to know is that he ought to act in a way that furthers the good, ought not drink himself blotto, seduce young maids, prevent his kids from learning, and so on.

But this clarification does not deal with another problem. It would not take a trip of Captain Cook extent to find someone who had never stated in his native tongue the equivalent of: Good is to be done, and evil avoided. Or even that he should eat to live not live to eat. If language can be taken to express what one knows, and one has never expressed such judgments, on what basis can we claim that he knows them?

The parallel in the theoretical order is again indispensable. You and I have relatives who have never uttered in English or otherwise the sentence: "It is impossible for a thing to be and not to be in the same respect." It is not inconceivable that there are human beings who have never uttered, "Either it is or it isn't." What then can it mean to claim that they know things they have never said?

As we suggested earlier in discussing the first part of article 2, the claim that everyone knows the first principle of reasoning does not depend on their having formulated it in its abstract form. It suffices that it is known as embedded in particular judgments, such as that about the pickle on the burger. The disputants there need not express their agreement by intoning, "It is impossible for a thing to be and not to be at the same time and in the same respect." Nonetheless, that principle is known to them already as their agreement attests. Furthermore, the fact that we say "of course" to the abstract formulation—once its tongue-twisting syntax is mastered—indicates recognition, not learning. In a significant sense, this is something we have already known.

A sign that a proposition is *per se nota* in this sense is that it cannot be coherently denied. The defense of first principles takes the indirect form of showing that their contradictories are incoherent. In short, the tack taken is a *reductio ad absurdum*. The upshot is to show that, while someone might think or say the opposite of a first principle, he cannot mean it, because what he says is meaningless. Aristotle's defense of the first principle of reasoning proceeds in just this way, as a perusal of Book IV of the *Metaphysics* will show. Aristotle imagines someone voicing the opposite of the first principle. "It is possible," this imagined Athenian says, "for a thing to be and not to be at the same time and in the same respect." And of course a form of this would be that it is possible for a proposition and its contradictory to be simultaneously true, since they would be expressing the possibility the dissenter asserts. Now the fast form of the refutation would simply apply this admission to the denial and say that one who says the contradictory of a proposition can be true when that proposition is true, and who maintains that it is true that the contradictory of the principle of contradiction is true, is thereby committed to the truth of the principle of contradiction. Thus, far from denying it, he is asserting it in a somewhat Pickwickian way.

Aristotle chooses a far simpler route. The dissenter speaks. Either the words he uses mean some things and not others, or they do not. If a word means both a and ~a, this will affect the sentence in which it figures, which will then mean p and ~p. Thus, in order successfully to deny the principle of contradiction, one must invoke and honor it. Therefore the denial is frivolous.

The reason such efforts annoy is that they seem to be a form of verbal prestidigitation. Nonetheless, sometimes they are necessary and, more importantly, the claim that there are indemonstrable, nongainsayable principles, commits one to such a defense. But if there are such principles in the practical order, their denial must leave the dissenter in the soup. This is a corollary of the claim that everyone already in some sense holds the precepts of natural law. I mention this, because I do not think it is sufficiently taken into account in discussions of natural law. Later, I will give some indication as to how such *reductiones ad absurdum* in the practical order look.

Levels of Natural Law

"Do and pursue the good and avoid evil" is the first and most common precept of natural law. Every other precept will be based upon it, presuppose it, be less common than it. Precepts that guide action with respect to the first level of inclination will be more restricted in range, which is what is meant by less common or general. Still, these precepts will be of breathtaking generality, something that can be seen when the Golden Rule is said to be a precept of natural law.

Dicendum quod verbum illud non est sic intelligendum quasi omnia quae in Lege et in Evangelio continentur, sint de lege naturae, cum multa tradantur ibi supra naturam: sed quia ea quae sunt de lege naturae plenarie ibi traduntur. Unde cum dixisset Gratianus quod "ius naturale est quod in Lege et in Evangelio continetur," statim, exemplificando, subiunxit, "quo quisque iubetur alii facere quod sibi vult fieri." (IaIIae, q.94, a.4, 1m)

That remark should not be taken to mean that everything contained in the Law and Gospels belongs to natural law, since many things handed down there are above nature, but that what is of natural law is treated there in a full way. Thus when Gratian says that "natural law is what is contained in the Law and Gospel," he immediately adds by way of example "where one is told to do unto others as he would have done to himself."

So too, once the inclinations and their ends are known, a common precept covering them all can be recognized. "Unde hoc est apud omnes communiter rectum, ut secundum rationem dirigantur omnes hominum inclinationes: hence it is universally right for everyone that all our inclinations should be directed by reason" (IaIIae, q.94, a.4, 3m).

When precepts become less general and more informative, they lose in universal applicability and admit of exceptions. That the property of others ought to be returned is taken by Thomas as something that follows from the general precept that we should act according to reason's dictate. (We will discuss later what he means by such derivations.) But the precept about returning what is borrowed admits of exceptions. If someone asks for his weapon in order that he might subvert the country we would reasonably demur.

Such "proper conclusions" from more common precepts are of natural law only in the sense that they are derived from it. That is, insofar as natural law precepts are said not to admit of exceptions, these less general precepts must be distinguished from them. St. Thomas calls such "proper conclusions" secondary precepts of natural law on occasion, and when he does, he will explain the immutability of natural law precepts in two ways. With regard to the first precepts, there are no exceptions to their applicability. With respect to secondary precepts (*praecepta secunda*), he will say they are changeless only in this sense that it will always be the case that by and large one ought to return borrowed items.

Since nature sometimes inclines in a quite definite way but sometimes does not, he makes another distinction in how things pertain to natural law.

Aliquid dicitur esse de iure naturali dupliciter. Uno modo, quia ad hoc natura inclinat; sicut non esse iniuriam alteri faciendam. Alio modo, quia natura non induxit contrarium: sicut possemus dicere quod hominem esse nudum est de iure naturali, quia natura non dedit ei vestitum, sed ars adinvenit. Et hoc modo "communis omnium possessio et omnium una libertas," dicitur esse de iure naturali: quia scilicet distinctio possessionum et servitus non sunt inductae a natura, sed per hominum rationem, ad utilitatem humanae vitae. Et sic in hoc lex naturae non est mutata nisi per additionem. (IaIIae, q.94, a.5, 3m)

Something can be said to belong to natural law in two ways. First, because nature inclines to it, like: no injury should be done another. Second, because nature does not indicate the contrary, as we might call it natural law that man is nude, because nature did not clothe him, but rather art. In this way "the common ownership of all and one freedom for all" is said to be of natural law, namely because the distinction of possessions and servitude are not brought about by nature but by the minds of men as useful for human life. In this then the law of nature is changed only in being added to.

Presumably this distinction is one between more and less basic precepts. In any case, Thomas distinguishes in Question 94 between levels of precept: the first and most common, common precepts, and proper conclusions.

More and more particular judgments as to what is to be done are found in two principal places, in the civil law and in such less authoritative places as ethics books. The law is concerned with overt behavior in a society and regulates it with respect to the common good. Law and justice, unsurprisingly, complement one another. There is no reason for the moralist to confine his advice as to what we should do to overt behavior. His advice will carry weight, not because he has authority over us and can apply punitive sanctions if we fail to perform, but because of the force of his arguments. In the next chapter, I will argue that moral philosophy can be thought of as a kind of dry run at the discourse which is embedded in particular actions. The moralist anticipates actions, formulates in advance rules of behavior which enunciate how the good can be achieved in circumstances of a given kind. In short, he does in a formal way what anyone informally does when he considers what he should do in a future situation, whether impending or not.

One of the most succinct statements about the levels of moral precept occurs when Thomas is discussing the decalogue. Morality, he reminds us, consists of the rational direction of action, and the judgment of practical reason proceeds from naturally known principles.

Ex quibus diversimode procedit potest ad iudicandum de diversis. Quaedam enim sunt in humanis actibus adeo explicita quod statim, cum modica consideratione, possunt approbari vel reprobari per illa communia et prima principia. Quaedam vero sunt ad quorum iudicium requiritur multa consideratio diversarum circumstantiarum, quas considerare diligenter non est cuiuslibet, sed sapientum, sicut considerare particulares conclusiones scientiarum non pertinet ad omnes, sed ad solos philosophos. Quaedam vero sunt ad quae diudicanda indiget homo adiuvari per instructionem divinam: sicut est circa credenda. (IaIIae, q.100, a.1)

From which it proceeds diversely to judge of diverse things. For some things about human acts are so explicit that right away, with minimum consideration, they can be approved or disapproved by appeal to those common and first principles. Some, however, are such that judging them requires long consideration of diverse circumstances, a task that does not fall to all; no more is the consideration of particular conclusions of the sciences the task of all, but only of philosophers. Some things indeed are such that, in order to judge them, man needs to be helped by divine instruction, as in what is to be believed.

Thomas goes on to say that, insofar as all moral judgments derive from those first principles, they can all be said to belong to natural law, but of course in different ways. First, those which are derived right off with little need to ponder. Examples? "Honor your father and mother." "Do not kill." "Do not steal." "Et huiusmodi sunt absolute de lege naturae: Without any qualification these belong to natural law" (IaIIae, q.100, a.1).

Examples of the second kind of derivations, those which emerge from the more subtle consideration of the wise, are: "Rise in the presence of the aged, and honor a person of old age." "Et ista sic sunt de lege naturae, ut tamen indigeant disciplina, qua minores a sapientioribus instruantur: and these belong to natural law, but in such a way that they require learning whereby the many are instructed by the wise" (ibid.).

Third are precepts which need divine instruction. For example: "Do not make graven images," and "Do not take the name of the Lord in vain" (IaIIae, q.100, a.1).

This discussion and its sequel make clear that such precepts as "Do not kill" are not among the first principles of natural law. This is not to say simply that they are less common than "Do good and avoid evil." Precepts less common than the very first one come *before* the moral precepts of the decalogue, which are of the first kind mentioned above.

Illa ergo praecepta ad decalogum pertinent, quorum notitiam homo habet per seipsum a Deo. Huiusmodi vero sunt illa quae statim ex principiis communibus primis cognosci possunt modica consideratione; et iterum illa quae statim ex fide divinitus infusa innotescunt. Inter praecepta ergo decalogi non computantur duo genera praeceptorum: illa scilicet quae sunt prima et communia, quorum non oportet aliam editionem esse nisi quod sunt scripta in ratione naturali quasi per se nota, sicut quod nulli debet homo malefacere, et alia huiusmodi; et iterum illa quae per diligentem inquisitionem sapientum inveniuntur rationi convenire, haec enim preveniunt a Deo ad populum

Those precepts pertain to the decalogue that God enables man to know by himself. Of this kind are those which immediately after slight consideration can be seen to follow from first common principles, as well as those known straightaway by the infusion of divine faith. Two kinds of precept are not included in the decalogue, those which are first and common, no other statement of which is needed than their inscription in natural reason as self-evident, such as that a man ought not do evil to anyone, and the like; and those which by diligent inquiry are found to be reasonable, for these come from God to His

mediante disciplina sapientum. (Ia-   people via the learning of the
IIae, q.100, a.3)   wise.

These two kinds of precept pertain to the decalogue only in the sense
that the first are presupposed by the Commandments and are contained
in them as principles are included in proximate conclusions; the second
in the way in which conclusions are contained in the principles from which
they are derived. This makes clear that the precepts of the decalogue
occupy a logical space midway between such precepts as "Harm no one"
and "In defending yourself use only so much force as is necessary." The
precepts presupposed by the decalogue are characterized as *per se nota,*
those of the decalogue as *conclusiones proximae.* The further precepts would
seem to include not only those of legislators but also the advice of the wise
moralist.

When it is thus seen that such fundamental proscriptions as those
against murder and theft are, as it were, conclusions from such more
common precepts as "Harm no one," and when we notice that it is those
more common precepts which are said to be *per se nota,* the question must
arise as to the status of "Do not lie" and "Do not murder." Is it the case
that they are not *per se nota* precepts? Or is the phrase *"quasi conclusiones"*
meant to suggest a discursive derivation less than argument and demonstration? And, however that is decided, are the moral precepts of the
decalogue absolute in the sense of exceptionless and indispensable?

We will turn to these questions in the next chapter, and look at Thomas's discussions of bigamy and divorce that found their way into the
Supplementum of the *Summa theologiae,* Questions 65–67. But there is still
one more matter to be taken up now.

Nongainsayability

The parallel between first principles in the speculative and practical
orders suggested this question to us earlier. If the first principle of all
reasoning cannot coherently be denied, can the same be expected of the
first principles of practical reason? The answer is clearly yes. First principles are starting points, they are what everything else in a given order

presupposes, and they are not put forward as hypotheticals but as propositions whose truth can establish that of others derived from them. By calling the first principles of practical reason *per se nota,* Thomas is promising just this. The promise is easily kept with respect to the most common principle of all, the principle of contradiction. A similar *reductio* is available for the most common principle of practical reason: Good ought to be done and pursued, and evil avoided.

Anyone who says that evil ought to be done is saying in effect that it should be pursued; but the definition of good is "that which all things seek." Thus, like Milton's Satan, the dissenter is saying, "Evil be thou my good," and this is not a dispute about whether or not good should be sought and evil avoided, but presumably one about what counts as good.

Not much, but something. Can we go on to show that certain prohibited modes of conduct are similarly incoherent? I think such *reductiones* are possible in the case of suicide, and of drunkenness, of wholesale slaughter, and the like. If this is true, then the *quasi conclusiones* are themselves *per se notae,* and we have in the practical order a situation similar to that in the speculative order, where there are many *propositiones per se notae,* which are hierarchically ordered and all of which come under the very first. Think of the axioms in plane geometry.

It may well be asked whether precepts can be regarded as *per se* in any of the modes of perseity Thomas took over from Aristotle. In speaking of the first principles of the speculative order, it is only the first mode of perseity that is invoked, namely, that which obtains when what the predicate term signifies enters into the account or definition of the subject term. But how precisely does that apply to "It is impossible to affirm and deny the same proposition"? What *is* the subject of that proposition? We have to rephrase it to make clear what the subject is.

A proposition cannot be simultaneously affirmed and denied. Presumably a proposition is that which is either true or false and what is being said here is that any attempt to affirm and deny the same proposition is a denial of what a proposition is. Affirmation and denial are linked to truth, which in turn is linked to being. The reason a proposition cannot be both affirmed and denied *simul,* nor be simultaneously true or false is that a thing cannot at the same time be and not be. What is a being? Something that is. But something that is cannot at the same time be something that is not.

The first mode of perseity thus seems to apply to the first principle of reasoning. Does it apply as well to the first principle of practical reason? The *ratio boni* offered in the context of this discussion is that *quod omnia appetunt.* The further assumption is that, whatever is desired is desired as perfective of the desirer. This is as true of the apparent good as of the real good, so that from the point of view of the *ratio boni,* there is no need to distinguish between what is desired and what ought to be desired, between the desired and the desirable. This being the case, that the good ought to be pursued, follows from the meaning of "good."

Thus, Thomas must be taken to speak quite formally, when he says of the first principles of speculative and of the first principles of practical reason that they are *per se notae* in the sense that their predicates enter into the account of their subjects.

6. Carrying On

REASON is the mark of the moral, the agent consciously directing himself to goods and ends. This is what is meant by human action, as opposed to other activities and operations of ours which do not follow on deliberate will. Cognitive and appetitive elements multiply as we move away from the great overriding objective of our doings—that we be happy, perfected, or fulfilled—toward the quite particular thing a deed is.

Our will is fulfilled by the good, but who will show us what is good? *Quis ostendit nobis bona?* Thomas loves to quote this verse of Psalm 4, because its continuation is taken by him to be a statement of what must measure our acts if they are to be morally good. "Signatum est super nos lumen vultus tui, domine: the light of thy countenance is impressed upon us, O Lord."[1] Our mind is so made as to have the capacity to formulate the guidelines and precepts which direct our acts to the desired end and forbid paths that lead to darkness. This is the peculiarly human participation in eternal law, effecting another, natural law written in our minds in the sense that it is made up of the precepts men naturally formulate as they pursue happiness.

There are certain truths about the world that no one can fail to know. That a claim either is or is not true, that one either is or is not saying something, that a thing either is or is not such-and-such, are truths which underwrite our thought and language, because thought and language re-

---

1. In the new Vatican edition of the Vulgate, Psalm 4, 6–7 is given thus: "Multi dicunt: Quis ostendit nobis bona? Leva in signum super nos lumen vultus tui, Domine." The Jerusalem Bible gives this: "'Who will gives us sight of happiness?' many say. Show us the light of your face, turned toward us."

flect the way the world is. These truths are known at least implicitly by every normal human being of sufficient age. "Implicitly" here is the acknowledgment that almost no one has expressed them abstractly; rather, they are embedded in our daily doings and can be made explicit. When they are, there is instant acquiescence, perhaps a little embarrassment too that things so obvious should need to be said; acquiescence here is the sign that everyone already knows them. It is not a matter of learning. (One can of course learn the trappings of the theories which discuss them—immediate propositions, *per se notae*, first principles, nongainsayability, etc.)

Such truths provide the boundaries of discourse, because they express the way it is with the world. It is seldom that such principles require saying in their abstract form. Regional versions suffice. "Are you in or out? Ante up." "Is you is or is you ain't my baby?" "Instant replay will establish whether or not he caught the ball with both feet in bounds." (In obscure cases, "judgment calls" permit the game to continue, rules requiring either/or, not both/and, applications.) When they are abstractly stated, they make explicit that the truth holds for anything that is. This is of course to know the least, not the most, that can be said of anything. Information decreases as generality increases. To know of something only that it exists is but one step beyond knowing nothing about it at all. Quite a step, of course, and one that will wake our wonder. Why, it has been asked with awe, is there anything at all rather than nothing? The minimal statement about things—that they either are or are not—expresses what is most marvelous about them all.

Natural law is the claim that there are common, general guidelines for action, easily formulated by practical reason, with universal application. Thomas refreshes us on first principles of reasoning generally, because they provide a helpful analogy to grasping the nature of common precepts. Like first principles of thinking as such, the first principles of practical reasoning are implicitly known by everybody. The analogy suggests that when they are explicitly formulated, assent is given as to the already known, not to the newly learned; it also suggests that efforts to hold the opposite of these precepts lead the dissenter into incoherence, not to an alternative. Furthermore, the fact that there is a very first principle of all reasoning suggests an order with at least two levels among *per se nota* principles. But there are more than two levels of self-evident proposition, even when the terms involved are those whose meaning is known to every-one. Discourse and argument are anticipated even more closely in the case of self-evident truths containing terms whose meanings are known only to the expert. So too it is in the practical order.

The principles of practical reasoning are called precepts, because they do not state the way things are so much as, given the way things are, the way they ought to be. "Intellectus speculativus per extensionem fit prac-ticus: speculative mind becomes practical by extension."

Praeceptum legis, cum sit obligato-rium, est de aliquo quod fieri debet. Quod autem aliquid debeat fieri, hoc provenit ex necessitate alicuius finis. Unde manifestum est quod de ratione praecepti est quod importet ordinem ad finem, inquantum scilicet illud praecipitur quod est necessarium vel expediens ad finem. (IaIIae, q.99, a.1)	A precept of law, since it is obliga-tory, concerns what ought to be done. That something ought to be done stems from the necessity of some end. Thus it is clear that the meaning of precept suggests an order to the end, insofar, that is, as what is prescribed is necessary or expedient to the end.

A modern reader might ask at this point if all precepts are hypothetical imperatives, meaning: is the action prescribed or proscribed obligatory only given the end, such that, if we take away the end, obligation ceases? The question comes down to one that will have occurred to you. Is it only means that are obligatory? Are we not obliged to seek the end itself?

Praeceptum importat rationem debiti. Intantum ergo aliquid cadit sub prae-cepto inquantum habet rationem de-biti. Est autem aliquid debitum dupliciter: uno modo, per se; alio modo, propter aliud. Per se quidem debitum est in unoquoque negotio id quod est finis, quia habet rationem per se boni; propter aliud autem est	A precept suggests the note of obliga-tion. Something falls under a precept then to the degree that it is obliga-tory. But something is obligatory in two ways: first, in itself; second, on account of another. In any enterprise, what is obligatory as such is the end which has the note of good in itself; that which is ordered to the end is

debitum id quod ordinantur ad fi-   obligatory on account of it.
nem. (IIaIIae, q.44, a.1)

The first precept of all is that which expresses with sweeping generality the end of human acts. In acting, we must seek and do the good and avoid its opposite. That this should have the air of a platitude is not a mark against it; it *is* a platitude, a truism. And it is true. We must, in acting, seek that which is truly fulfilling and perfective of us, our good, and avoid what thwarts and stunts the flourishing of our nature. The level of platitude is surpassed, when we distinguish between what may appear to be and what truly is fulfilling of us. While men cannot meaningfully deny that it is the good they should do, they disagree, sometimes dramatically, as to what constitutes that good. What is the field over which further precepts will range?

Omnes inclinationes quarumcumque   All the inclinations of whatever part
partium humanae naturae, puta con-   of human nature, for example, the
cupiscibilis et irascibilis, secundum concupiscible and irascible, pertain to
quod regulantur ratione, pertinent ad natural law insofar as they are regu-
legem naturalem, et reducuntur ad   lated by reason, and they are reduced
unum primum praeceptum. (IaIIae,   to one first precept.
q.94, a.2, ad 2m)

Precepts telling us how to act and how not to act will bear on the ends of these inclinations. Obviously, since the inclinations are natural, that is, given, it is not our choice whether to have them or for them to have the objects they do. What does fall to us is to regulate the pursuit of these goods, and precepts do this by ordering these goods to the good of the whole man, to the common good. This is what is meant by "*regulantur ratione*: regulated by reason."

There are three levels of inclination—those we share with everything, those we share with other animals, and those peculiar to us as men—and there are also levels of precept among and within these three orders. The first and most common in the three orders would be, respectively, that our pursuit of food and drink should be regulated by reason, that our sexual lives should come under the governance of reason, and that we should not harm our fellows or wallow in ignorance. Such precepts are so obvious that they require no stating. That is why Thomas says they are presupposed by the precepts of the decalogue, the latter being quasi conclusions from them and, in their turn, principles of more particular precepts derivable from them (IaIIae, q.100, a.3).

That there is a hierarchy of precepts of natural law in terms of greater and lesser universality is clearly Thomas's teaching. But he also held that there is an order among precepts, which follows on the order of natural inclinations. Which inclinations are more human, more natural to us as human? The very question can seem idle, given the description of the inclinations. Some are said to be peculiar to us—to live in society, to seek knowledge—and are clearly more human. Are they more natural?

Any precept is an ordinance of practical reason and by that very fact is expressive of what is peculiar to man. However, when we consider the matter of the precepts, the orders of inclination, that order which is most natural is what we share with all things. The principle of inclination is called a nature, and these natures are parts of human nature (IaIIae, q.94, a.2, 2m). Nature is a principle of motion and rest, of operation, and in the most basic sense is determined to one end: *determinatur ad unum*. Not every nature making up our nature is equally determined to one. On that basis, there is a hierarchy among inclinations insofar as they are natures.

The view of the cosmos that Thomas holds calls the first and most basic level of reality nature and sees everything else as moving out from it. Thus, when he contrasts the living and the nonliving natural thing, Thomas will contrast nature and soul. Both are principles of operation, but "nature" is reserved for operations determined to one end. The life-world is such that even the most primitive form of life exhibits variety and diversity of operation. Thomas contrasts the element whose natural movement is in one direction with the plant, which pushes its root downward, its stem upward, and its leaves to the various points of the compass. Variety and spontaneity thus become marks of perfection. In that sense, the less natural a thing, the more perfect it is, the higher in the cosmic hierarchy.

We saw how Thomas spoke of reason as a nature and then as reason, and the same with will. "Prius salvatur in posterioribus: the most fundamental is mimicked in the derived." Even the highest powers, at the outset, exhibit the mode of nature, that is, determination to one. This is the sense of the adverb *naturaliter* that Thomas uses to characterize the mind's sure grasp of the ends of the inclinations as goods. This means immediately. The mode of reason as such is inquiry, the sifting of possibilities, the amassing of support for this as opposed to that—reason as reason is discursive. But discursive reason presupposes certain things as naturally, that is, nondiscursively, known. These are the first principles, whether of the speculative or practical order.

So too the will, as nature, is determined to the good; it is the desire of the good. But as will, it must be determined to this good or that by reason.

First principles and the precepts of natural law thus exhibit reason's act insofar as reason is a nature. But, insofar as some truths are more basic than others and grasped first, Thomas speaks of a modicum of consideration as entering into the grasp of principles on the next level. On the side of knowledge, then, some principles are more naturally known than others. As mind carries on, moving away from the principles, the characteristic activity of reason, discourse, begins, and what Thomas calls "proper conclusions" (as opposed to quasi conclusions) are arrived at.

From the point of view of the matter or object of the precepts, there is a similar gradation. It is noteworthy—to some, notorious—that Thomas takes from Ulpian the definition of natural right (*ius naturale*) which occurs in the text of Question 94, article 2: "quae natura omnia animalia docuit: what nature taught all animals." Natural right is opposed to *ius gentium,* which might be rendered "the law of nations." Is this a distinction between natural and positive law? No. *Ius gentium* is the level of natural law peculiar to men, whereas the *ius naturale* is common to men and animals. That is, the distinction is between the second and third levels of natural inclinations.

Notice that it is *ius*—right—rather than *lex*—law—that is at issue here. The object of justice is *ius,* the just, the objective right it is the law's purpose to serve.

The right or the just implies equality, hitting the right measure. We justify margins on the page, we adjust the weight in a boat. Natural right, or the naturally just, is exemplified by giving an amount equal to what one gets. A just price represents proportional equality. Positive right or the positively just is that which is established by agreement, whether between individuals or communities (IIaIIae, q.57, a.2). The distinction between *ius naturale* and *ius gentium* is a subdivision of the naturally just.

Ius sive iustum naturale est quod ex sui natura est adaequatum vel commensuratum alteri. Hoc autem potest contingere dupliciter. Uno modo, secundum absolutam sui considerationem: sicut masculus ex sui ratione habet commensurationem ad feminam ut ex ea generet, et parens ad filium ut eum nutriet. Alio modo aliquid est naturaliter alteri commensuratum non secundum absolutam sui rationem, sed secundum aliquid quod ex ipso consequitur: puta proprietas possessionum. Si enim consideretur iste ager absolute, non habet unde magis sit huius quam illius: sed si consideretur quantum ad opportunitatem colendi et pacificum usum agri, secundum hoc habet quandam commensurationem ad hoc quod sit unius et non alterius, ut patet per Philosophum in II Politic (1263a21).

Absolute autem apprehendere aliquid non solum convenit homini, sed etiam aliis animalibus. Et ideo ius quod dicitur naturale secundum primum modum, commune est nobis et aliis animalibus.... Considerare autem aliquid comparando ad id quod ex ipso sequitur, est proprium rationis. Et ideo hoc quidem est natu-

The naturally just or right is that which of its nature is adequate or commensurate to another. This can come about in two ways. First, by an absolute consideration, as male by definition has a commensuration to the female that he might beget with her; and parent to child that she might nourish him. Second, something is naturally commensurate to another, not of its nature considered absolutely, but because of something consequent upon it, e.g., private property. For if this field is considered as such, there is no reason why it should belong to you or to me, but if it be considered in terms of the opportunity of cultivating it and its peaceful use, it can have a commensuration to you rather than me, as Aristotle makes clear in *Politics*, II.

To grasp something absolutely belongs to the other animals as well as man. So what is called natural right in the first sense is common to us and other animals.... But to consider something in terms of that which follows on it is proper to reason. Therefore this is naturally right for man because of natural reason which dictates it.

rale homini secundum rationem naturalem quae hoc dictat. (IIaIIae,
q.57, a.3)

This is not a distinction between inclination and the rational direction
of it, nor is it the distinction between natural and unnatural inclinations.
The second distinction is between what befits nature, like food, drink,
and the like, and the delightful which follows on knowledge, "sicut cum
aliquis apprehendit aliquid ut bonum et conveniens, et per consequens
delectatur in ipso: as when one apprehends something as good and befitting and consequently takes pleasure in it" (IaIIae, q.30, a.3). The first
kind of desire is common to men and animals, whereas the second is
proper to man whose reason introduces wants and pleasures beyond what
nature requires: "praeter id quod natura requirit." Precepts bear on the
first kind of inclinations and express rational direction of their pursuit.
The distinction, then, is not between inclination and knowledge, but
rather between levels of precept.

Dicendum quod ius gentium est quidem aliquo modo naturale homini,
secundum quod est rationalis, inquantum derivatur a lege naturali per
modum conclusionis quae non est
multum remota a principiis. Unde de
facili in huiusmodi homines consense-
runt. Distinguitur tamen a lege naturali, maxime ab eo quod est
omnibus animalibus commune. (Ia-
IIae, q.95, a.4, ad 1m)

It should be noted that the law of nations is in a way natural to man, according as he is rational, insofar as it
is derived from natural law in the
mode of a conclusion not much dis-
tant from the principles. That is why
men easily concur on these. It is distinguished from natural law, however,
especially from that which is common
to all animals.

It seems clear that Thomas regards the precepts bearing on the first
and second orders of natural inclinations to be natural law in a stronger
sense than those which bear on what is peculiar to man. Precepts having
to do with preservation in existence, first of the individual, then of the
species, are as principles from which as quasi conclusions the precepts
associated with the *ius gentium* follow.

Marriage and Natural Law

That the goods to which we are naturally inclined are not all of a piece, equal, but hierarchically ordered, and that the precepts directive of them reflect this, comes to the fore especially in Thomas's discussion of marriage. As we know, Thomas did not complete the *Summa theologiae*. The Third Part ends with Question 90 and the discussion of the sacrament of penance. Thomas had also discussed baptism, confirmation, and the Eucharist. The Supplement completes the discussion of the sacraments and ends with a treatment of the Last Things. These discussions in the Supplement are cannibalized from Thomas's commentary on the *Sentences* of Peter Lombard. The discussion of marriage is a long one, running from Question 41 through Question 68. Thomas is chiefly concerned with the sacrament of matrimony, but of course he subsumes into it marriage as the natural conjunction of man and woman for purposes of procreation and mutual help in the raising of their offspring.

But is marriage natural? Thomas can think of a number of reasons why one might say no. First, if *ius naturale* is what nature teaches all animals, and if sexual intercourse in animals takes place without anything like marriage, it seems we cannot say marriage is natural. Furthermore, if it were natural, it would always have obtained, but Cicero speaks of a wild early condition of mankind when adults did not know which children were theirs. Again, the natural would seem to be the same everywhere, but men notoriously differ in marriage customs. Finally, if the ends of nature can be served without marriage, and they can, marriage is not natural. Nature intends the survival of the species, and this can take place outside marriage, as by fornication (Supl. q.41, a.1).

On behalf of an affirmative answer to the question, Thomas cites Gratian and Aristotle, who said that man is by nature a political animal, but he is even more naturally a marrying animal (*Ethics* VIII, 1162a17). Typically, St. Thomas begins his discussion with a distinction. Something can be called natural in several ways; first, as necessarily caused by the principles of the nature, in the way that stones fall naturally. Marriage is not natural in this sense, however much we may truly be said to fall in love.

Alio modo dicitur naturale ad quod natura inclinat, sed mediante libero arbitrio completur: sicut actus virtutum dicuntur naturales. Et hoc modo matrimonium est naturale: quia ratio naturalis ad ipsum inclinat dupliciter. Primum, quantum ad principalem eius finem, qui est bonum prolis. Non enim intendit natura solum generationem prolis, sed traductionem et promotionem usque ad perfectum statum hominis inquantum homo est, qui est status virtutis. Unde, secundum Philosophum, tria a parentibus habemus, scilicet "esse, nutrimentum et disciplinam." Filius autem a parente educari et instrui non posset nisi certos parentes haberet. Quod non esset nisi esse aliqua obligatio viri ad mulierem determinatam, quae matrimonium facit.

Secundo, quantum ad secundarium finem matrimonii, qui est mutuum obsequium sibi a coniugibus in rebus domesticis impensum. Sicut enima naturalis ratio dictat ut homines simul cohabitent, quia unus non sufficit sibi in omnibus quae ad vitam pertinent, ratione cuius dicitur homo naturaliter politicus; ita etiam eorum quibus indigetur ad humanam vitam, quaedam opera sunt competentia viris, quaedam mulieris. Unde natura monet ut sit quaedam associatio viri ad mulierem, in qua est matrimonium. (Supl. 41.1)

Something is called natural in another way if nature inclines to it, but free will is needed to bring it off, as the acts of virtue are called natural. Matrimony is natural in this sense, because natural reason inclines to it in two ways. First, with respect to its principal end which is the good of the child. Nature intends not only the generation of the child, but also its rearing and training to the perfect state of man as man, which is the state of virtue. Hence, according to Aristotle, we get three things from parents, existence, nutrition, discipline. But a child cannot be educated and instructed by his parents unless he has certain parents. And this happens only if a man is bound to a definite woman, and that's matrimony.

Second, with respect to the secondary end of matrimony, which is the mutual help of the spouses in the domestic tasks they have. For just as natural reason dictates that men should live together, since the individual cannot suffice to himself for everything needed for life, thanks to which man is said to be naturally political, so too in the necessities of life, some tasks are men's work, others women's. So nature instructs that there should be an association of man with woman, and that is matrimony.

We should not imagine that the primary and secondary ends of marriage are identical with the procreative and unitive meanings of the con-jugal act that Pope Paul VI mentioned in *Humanae Vitae* and which have become such a prominent part of Pope John Paul II's teaching. Those two meanings inhere in the act whereby man and wife freely help nature achieve her primary end. The secondary end of marriage here has to do with the continuing union of the couple for the good of the child, under-stood not merely as coming into existence but being raised to the full status of a human person.

In discussing the first objection to calling matrimony natural, Thomas observes that nature inclines different species differently, since the young of some animals are self-sufficent at birth or shortly afterward. Since hu-man babies are born helpless and require years of care and nurture, nature inclines the male to stay with his mate in order that the primary end of matrimony might be achieved. As for Cicero's primitive men, Thomas is dubious, not least because of the Bible's account of the first couple. Diverse marriage customs? Of course. The nature that inclines is variable, and its inclination is variously expressed. Several times Thomas remarks that "na-tura humana mutabilis est: human nature is mutable," and there have not been lacking those who see this as undercutting the stability required by his doctrine of natural law. Not at all. Matrimony is not natural in the sense of necessarily caused by nature. Rather, reflection on nature brings the swift realization that the conjunction of male and female cannot be a random and fleeting thing if the fruit of the union is to become a perfect member of the species. It is not simply that sexual union produces off-spring; men recognize this and direct themselves in the light of it. Vari-ations in the manner of this direction, from time to time and people to people, far from being an argument against matrimony's being natural, draw attention to the way it is natural. The final objection works only if one thinks that the production of the child suffices. Since the child will survive only if cared for and will become human only if disciplined and instructed in virtue, the objection that fruitful fornication fulfills the end of nature fails.

Needless to say, when Thomas goes on to speak of matrimony as a sacrament, the discussion becomes richer. That discussion begins with

Question 42. Since I am a mere philosopher, it would not be appropriate for me to discuss that. Rather, I want to pick out from Thomas's discussion of bigamy points helpful for understanding the ranking of natural law precepts that we have been discussing.

Why Not Many Wives?

There are Henny Youngman style answers to the question we need not dwell upon. "Take my wife. Please. I have more." In the Old Testament, God permitted polygamy because of the hardness of hearts.

Is it against natural law to have several wives at the same time? What authorities suggest that bigamy is against natural law? In Question 65, article 1, Thomas cites the "two in one flesh" of Genesis, the physical impossibility of the male's simultaneous availability to several wives, and then this argument: "Don't do to others what you would not have them do to you." "No man would want his wife to have another lover. Ergo, etc." Finally, striking a romantic vein, Thomas mentions the jealousy lovers have of one another, and how wary they are of rivals. Three's a crowd.

In developing his own thoughts on the subject, Thomas speaks of what is natural to the agent because of his genus, and what is natural to him because of his specific difference. Things natural to him in the first sense make up *ius naturale*. Things natural to him in the second sense make up *ius gentium*. Both of these pertain to natural law, but the first is more basic and fundamental than the second. The distinction between generic and specific properties is not of course confined to humans. The lodestone, as a stone, falls like other stones, but as lodestone it attracts iron.

Given that distinction, Thomas introduces another.

Omnibus rebus insunt quaedam principia quibus non solum operationes proprias efficere possunt, sed quibus etiam eas convenientes fini suo reddunt, sive sint actiones quae consequantur ex natura sui generis, sive consequantur ex natura specie. (Supl. 65. 1)

There are in each thing principles thanks to which it not only effects its proper activities, but which also render it conformed to its end, whether these be actions following on the nature of its genus or the nature of its species.

The principles in the agent who has cognition are the cognitive power and the appetite consequent upon it. "Unde oportet quod in vi cognitiva sit naturalis conceptio, et in vi appetitiva naturalis inclinatio, quibus operatio conveniens generi sive speciei reddatur competens fini: Hence in the cognitive power there must be a natural conception, and in the appetitive a natural inclination, by which an operation befitting its genus or species renders it conformed to the end." What is peculiar to man is that he grasps the notion of end—he knows things qua good, qua end—and he knows the relation or proportion of actions to that end, what will bring it off. Animal cognition guiding action is called the estimative power by Aristotle and must be distinguished from that which directs man in his proper operation. The latter is called *ius naturale* or *lex naturalis*.

Lex ergo naturalis nihil aliud est quam conceptio homini naturaliter indita qua dirigitur ad convenienter agendum in actionibus propriis: sive competant ei ex natura generis, ut generare, comedere, et huiusmodi, sive ex natura speciei, ut ratiocinari et huiusmodi. Omne autem illud quod actionem inconvenientem reddit fini quem natura ex opere aliquo intendit, contra legem naturae esse dicitur. (Supl. 65. 1)	Therefore natural law is precisely the conception naturally given man whereby he is directed in performing his proper activities in a fitting manner, whether these pertain to him from the nature of his genus, i.e., procreation, eating, and the like, or from the nature of his species, reasoning and the like. Whatever renders an action unconformed to the end nature intends by a given activity is said to be contrary to natural law.

St. Thomas here conflates the first two orders of inclination of IaIIae, q.94, a.2. The reason is that both are ordered to continuation in existence, the first of the individual, the second of the species.

An action that is not conformed with, is inharmonious with, thwarts, the end intended by nature will be contrary to natural law. But an action can be so appraised either with respect to the principal or to the secondary end of the activity, and in either case can be said to be thwarting of it in several ways.

Uno modo, ex aliquod quo omnino impedit finem: ut nimia superfluitas	In one way, when something completely impedes the end, as too much

aut defectus comestionis impedit salutem corporis, quasi principalem finem comestionis; et bonam habitudinem in negotiis exercendis, qui est finis secundarius. Alio modo, ex aliquo quod facit difficilem aut minus decentem perventionem ad finem principalem vel secundarium: sicut inordinata comestionis quantum ad tempus indebitum. Si ergo actio sit inconveniens fini quasi omnino prohibens finem principalem, directe per legem naturae prohibetur primis praeceptis legis naturae, quae sunt in operabilibus sicut sunt communes conceptiones in speculativis. Si autem sit incompetens fini secundario quocumque modo, aut etiam principali ut faciens difficilem vel minus congruam perventionem ad ipsum, prohibetur non quidem primis praeceptis legis naturae, sed secundis, quae ex primis derivantur, sicut conclusiones in speculativis ex principiis per se notis fidem habent. Et sic dicta actio contra legem naturae esse dicitur. (Supl. 65. 1)

or too little food impedes the body's health, which is the principal end of eating, and a good disposition to carry on one's work, which is the secondary end. In another way, by something which makes the achieving of either the principal or secondary end difficult or less fitting, such as inordinate eating at the wrong time. If then an action is unconformed to the end as wholly thwarting the principal end, it is directly prohibited by natural law's first precepts, which are the analogue in action of the common conceptions of the speculative order. If however it is unbefitting the secondary end in some way, or even the principal end, by making its attainment difficult or less decent, it is forbidden, not indeed by the first precepts of natural law, but by the second, which are derived from the first as in speculative matters conclusions from self-evident principles have a claim on our assent. And in this sense the action can be said to be against natural law.

Applying this to matrimony, Thomas identifies its principal end as the begetting and raising of children, and this is an end humans share with the other animals. The chief good of marriage is thus the child. In men there is a further, secondary end, which is sharing in the activities aimed at the necessities of life. Mutual fidelity is a good of marriage from both points of view. For believers, matrimony has a further end insofar as it signifies Christ's love of His Church. "Unde primus finis respondet matrimonio hominis inquantum est animal; secundus inquantum est homo; tertius inquantum est fidelis: Thus the first end of matrimony is sought by man insofar as he is animal, the second insofar as he is human, the third insofar as he is a believer."

Thomas is now in a position to address the question before him: Is it contrary to natural law to have several wives at once? It is not contrary to natural law in the sense that it thwarts or even makes difficult the principal end of marriage. A man can father families with several wives at once, and he can raise and educate them as well. But the secondary end of matrimony, though it is not completely thwarted, is made difficult, since such a household will be one where peace is impeded by the fact that the man's affections are not simultaneously available to all his wives, jealousies will arise, trouble threaten. The third, sacramental end, is completely destroyed by such an arrangement. So, in a way, a plurality of wives is against natural law, and in a way it is not.

Such a conclusion makes no sense if we have a univocal, flatland view of natural law precepts, as all simply self-evident and on the same basis, so that ranking and any more or less are ruled out. It should by now be crystal clear that such an approach has little in common with that of St. Thomas.

If the discussion of the way polygamy is said to be contrary to natural law—only in an attenuated sense—reveals a different valence and degree of natural law precept, this is equally true in the discussion of polyandry. Polyandry is contrary to natural law with respect to its primary precepts and principal end. Why? The father cannot fulfill his obligation toward his children, if it cannot be determined whether or not they are his or belong to one of the other men in his wife's life. But the rearing as well as the begetting of children is the principal end of marriage. This being wholly impeded by polyandry, polyandry is against natural law.

But what of the invocation of the Golden Rule to rule out both polygamy and polyandry? If a man wouldn't want his wife to have another man, he shouldn't have another wife. That sounds like the principle of fairness and impartiality. Indeed, universalizability has been advanced in recent years as the very mark of moral reasoning. If I want to exempt myself from the demands of a principle, I must be ready to exempt all others who are relevantly the same as myself. Not to do so is said to be the abandonment of the moral point of view, not a version of it. In the case in point, Thomas confronts an argument that may seem to display an attitude in advance of its time, the repudiation of a double standard for men and women. But if we turn with a keen anachronistic interest to his discussion of the argument, we will be disappointed.

Dicendum quod illud praeceptum legis naturae, "Quod tibi non vis fieri, alteri non feceris," debet intelligi, "eadem proportione servata": non enim, si praelatus non vult sibi resisti a subdito, ipse subdito resistere non debet. Et ideo non oportet quod, ex vi illius praecepti, quod si vir non vult quod uxor sua habeat alium virum, quod ipse non habeat aliam uxorem: quia unam uxorem habere plures viros est contra prima praecepta legis naturae, eo quod per hoc quantum ad aliquid totaliter tollitur, et quantum ad aliquid impeditur bonum prolis, quod est principalis matrimonii finis. In bono enim prolis intelligitur non solum procreatio, sed etiam educatio. Ipsa enim procreatio prolis, etsi non totaliter tollatur, quia continget post impraegnationem primam iterum mulierem impraegnari, ut dicitur in IX De animal., tamen multum impeditur, quia vix potest accidere quin corruptio accidat quantum ad utrumque fetum vel quantum ad alterum. Sed educatio totaliter tollitur, quia ex hoc quod una mulier plures maritos haberet, sequeretur incertitudo prolis respectu patris, cuius cura necessaria est in educando. Et ideo

It should be said that this principle of Natural Law, "Do to others what you would have them do to you," has to be understood as "guarding the same proportion." A bishop may not want a priest to disobey him, but that does not require him to obey the priest. Thus it does not follow, on the strength of this precept, that if a man doesn't want his wife to have another man he should not take another wife, because for one wife to have several husbands is contrary to the first precepts of natural law, since in some respects completely and in others partially it impedes the good of the child, which is the principal end of matrimony. By the good of the child is meant not only procreation but education. The begetting of the child, though it is not wholly impeded, since Aristotle tells us that a pregnant woman can become doubly pregnant, nonetheless is greatly jeopardized, because it can happen that one or both fetuses die. Education is completely impeded, because the children of the wife with many husbands will be of uncertain paternity, and the father's care is necessary in educating the child. That is why no law nor custom

nulla lege vel consuetudo est permis-
sum unam mulierem habere plures
viros, sicut e converso. (Supl. 65. 1,
7m)

permits a woman to have many husbands, though the reverse happens.

Apart from that novel theory of twins, St. Thomas is saying that there is something in the nature of things that the mind recognizes as ruling out a given course of action. It is interesting to see the Golden Rule called a precept of natural law. Doubtless it is one of those presupposed by the precepts of the decalogue; perhaps an alternative expression of "Do harm to no one." The *ius* on which justice bears and thus the law is an objective measure, in the nature of things. The proportion between man and woman on the matter of the primary end of marriage is such that the way things are absolutely rules out polyandry and more or less rules out polygamy.

Pondering these things, you will of course be thinking of a science fiction epic you mean to write. The bombs have fallen, but, by a nuclear fluke which will remain unexplained for thousands of years, the earth has been returned to a Garden of Eden status. In the Garden State and nowhere else, human life has survived the Mad exchange. There is a statuesque woman, one Cha Cha LaStrada, whose mien brings to mind Leda, the White Goddess, the earth mother, and also three men, Larry, Curly, and Moe. Your story opens at twilight, birdsong and the rosy light of the setting sun have rendered the garden a veritable bower. Moe has unearthed a six pack of Coors, Larry a deeply frozen quart of Chocolate Revel ice cream, Curly brings flowers. Your plot will show how, having the future of the race firmly in mind, these four make marital arrangements which only weeks before would have shaken New Jersey to its foundations. Unnatural? We live in changing times, as Eve said to Adam on the way out of the garden. Desperate remedies are called for. You cannot resist the following scene: Cha Cha, reading the *Supplementum* to the *Summa theologiae* to her many children, smiles a Giocanda smile.

How would Thomas discuss such a situation? The passages we have quoted at perhaps unpardonable length make one thing very clear. Natural law is not something Thomas appeals to as to a set of intuitions one either has or does not. Even the Golden Rule involves surprises. Natural law is the rational direction of action, the formulation of precepts stating how the good is to be achieved, how evil avoided. Even within the realm of natural law proper, there are levels, such that reason as reason comes more and more to the fore. A modicum of consideration delivers up the implications of the very first principles, but to carry on from there requires a good deal of thinking, and the precepts derived, while they can still be called of natural law in the sense that they are derived from it, no longer have the characteristic of universality. Only by and large will they guide us to the good.

Practical Reasoning

Important as natural law is, since it gives us our bearings in the moral order and lays out the great guidelines that cannot be gainsaid, it is far from being proportioned to the particular acts we must do. This is not of course to say that because it is general it is applicable only to generalities. Genera are predicated of individuals and tell us of what kind the individuals are. If contraception thwarts the principal end of matrimony, it is always and everywhere wrong, not just in general, but in every instance of it. It is well to state even something as obvious as this, since it is sometimes suggested that natural law is acceptable on the level of generality, but it must give way in the realm of singular action to other factors. Either those factors can be stated and discussed, or they cannot. If they are ineffable, this is likely because there is nothing to be said for them. The principle that evil may not be done in order that good might result is not a bargaining chip when one acts. It governs each and every action.

Practical reason has as its aim the directing of activities other than reason, ordering them all to the common good. The movement in the practical order exemplifies the general movement of the human mind, from confusion to clarity, from the common to the specific, from the general to the particular. The great difference is that the actions mind must direct are singular. The ultimate desideratum in the practical order is not to come up with precepts of however low a level of generality, but to apply them to singular circumstances.

One way of continuing the discussion just engaged in would be to look at what Thomas has to say of the derivation of nonabsolute or *ut in pluribus* precepts from natural law precepts. There are many suggestive passages in his treatment of human positive law, so going on to that discussion in the "Treatise on Law" is tempting, but not in the circumstances. I would like to end by drawing attention to the main lines of Thomas's teaching on the reasoning process of the practically wise person, the prudent person.

Synderesis is the name given to the mind's quasi-habitual knowledge of the first precepts of natural law. Prudence is the name given to the virtue of practical intellect which directs our choices.

A virtue is that which makes someone good by rendering his activity good. The recurrence of "good" in this Aristotelian account, which Thomas took over, prepares us for the fact that virtues in the strict sense will be habits of appetite, since good is the object of appetite. Appetite's first natural operation may be determined to one, but after that there is indeterminacy, and a habit is necessary to introduce a second nature, thanks to which one regularly and with pleasure seeks the good. The second nature or habit which determines an otherwise indeterminate appetite to the true good is what is meant by virtue.

Mind too is determined to one in its first, natural moves, but after that requires habits which will insure that it regularly and with ease finds the truth. Thus it is that the second natures or habits of mind are called virtues, but they are virtues only in an extended sense of the term.

In a word, "virtue" is an analogous term for St. Thomas. Habits which inhabit appetite are virtues in the full sense of the term. Thanks to them, we have not only a capacity to perform in a certain way, but an inclination to use that capacity. Intellectual virtues, by contrast, give the capacity, but not the inclination to use it.

Cum igitur habitus intellectuales speculativi non perficiant partem appetitivam, nec aliquo modo ipsam respiciant, sed solam intellectivam;

Since therefore the habits of speculative intellect do not perfect the appetitive part, but only the intellective, they can indeed be called virtues in-

possunt quidem dici virtutes inquantum faciunt facultatem bonae operationis, quae est consideratio veri (hoc enim est bonum opus intellectus): non tamen dicuntur virtutes secundo modo, quasi facientes bene uti potentia seu habitu. Ex hoc enim quod aliquis habet habitum scientiae speculativae, non inclinatur ad utendum, sed fit potens speculari verum in his quorum habet scientiam; sed quod utatur scientia habita, hoc est movente voluntate. Et ideo virtus quae perficit voluntatem, ut caritas vel iustitia, facit etiam bene uti huiusmodi speculativis habitibus. (IaIIae, q.57, a.1)

sofar as they cause the capacity of good operation, which is the consideration of truth (for this is the good work of intellect); but they cannot be called virtues in the second sense, as if they caused the good use of the power or habit. One's having the habit of a speculative science does not incline him to use it, but he becomes capable of thinking truly concerning the objects of his science. But that he should use the science possessed is due to the movement of will. Therefore a virtue which perfects will, like charity or justice, causes the good use of speculative habits of this kind.

Virtues of speculative intellect are virtues in a lesser sense than the virtues of appetite. But what of art and prudence, the virtues of practical intellect? Art is reason directing the making of things, prudence is reason directing doing or behaving. Both are thus ordered to something beyond the perfection of cognition as such; truth is sought in order to be put to work, applied to an opus. Nonetheless, Thomas says that art is like the virtues of speculative intellect in this, that it gives the capacity to work well, but not the inclination to use that capacity well. Like the virtues of speculative intellect, art is more concerned with its object than with how the human will relates to the object. Whether the geometer is happy or sad is irrelevant to his doing geometry, and the same can be said of the artist. Art and science depend on moral virtues for their good use (IaIIae, q.57, a.3).

If art has affinity with the virtues of speculative intellect, prudence is closer to the moral virtues, the habits of appetite. One who has the virtue of prudence has both the capacity and the disposition to use that capacity, much as with the moral virtues. The starting point of the practical order is the end.

Et ideo ad prudentiam, quae est recta ratio agibilium, requiritur quod homo sit bene dispositus circa fines: quod quidem est per appetitum rectum. Et ideo ad prudentiam requiritur moralis virtus, per quam fit appetitus rectus. (IaIIae, q.57, a.4)

Thus in order to have prudence, which is right reason in things to be done, a man must be well disposed regarding ends, which is brought about by rectified appetite. Therefore prudence requires moral virtue through which appetite is rectified.

The practically wise man is one who acts wisely. That is, his deeds are guided by the judgment he makes as to the appropriate way to act here and now. In order for this to go off smoothly, his appetites must be ordered to the true good. Appetite resists this direction and may either throw off the process of reasoning before mind issues a command as to what is to be done here and now, or it follows reason only with pain and resistance. The good man has achieved wholeness and integrity of person such that his lower appetites are responsive to the guidance of reason, which appraises what is to be done with an eye "to the things which pertain to man's whole life and to the ultimate end of human life: de his quae pertinent ad totam vitam hominis, et ad ultimum finem vitae humanae" (IaIIae, q.57, a.4, 3m).

St. Thomas's first discussion of prudence occurs in the IaIIae, Question 57, between his discussion of the various acts of will that are elements of the complete human act and his discussion of natural law. He returns to prudence in the IIaIIae (qq. 47–56), where he discusses the cardinal virtues (temperance, fortitude, prudence, and justice). Thanks to prudence, practical reason issues the command on which use follows. It may be well to schematize the interplay of mind and appetite in the analysis of the complete human action.

Synderesis (natural law)	Will's natural desire of end
Counsel	Choice
Command	Use

There is no mention of prudence in the treatment of counsel or deliberation in Question 14 of the *Prima secundae*. The reason for this may be that taking counsel is only a part of what prudence does. We are talking here, not simply of the thinking that precedes action, but of the thinking that is embedded in the singular act, animating it and giving it direction.

Circa agibilia autem humana tres actus rationis inveniuntur: quorum primus est consiliari, secundus iudicare, tertius est praecipere. Primi autem duo respondent actibus intellectus speculativi, qui sunt inquirere et iudicare: nam consilium inquisitio quaedam est. Sed tertius actus proprius est practici intellectus, inquantum est operativus: non enim ratio habet praecipere ea quae per hominem fieri non possunt. (IaIIae, q.57, a.6)

With respect to human doings three acts of reason are found, the first of which is taking counsel, the second judging, the third commanding. The first two answer to the speculative intellect's acts of inquiry and judgment: for counsel is a kind of inquiry. But the third is the act proper to practical intellect insofar as it is operative: for reason only commands those things which can be done by man.

Practical reasoning includes moments when we are looking for possible means to an end and judging that one is best. Thomas likens these to activities of the speculative intellect, and indeed the truth of such judgments, such as it is, is speculative truth. The mind is concerned with contingent particulars, and there is little of fixed truth there. "Cognitio autem veritatis in talibus non habet aliquid magnum, ut per se sit appetibilis, sicut cognitio universalium et necessariorum: sed appetitur secundum quod est utilis ad operationem, quia actiones sunt circa contingentia singularia: knowledge of the truth about such things is no big deal, nor is it desirable for itself, as knowledge of universal and necessary truths is, but it is sought as useful to action, since actions are concerned with contingent singulars" (IaIIae, q.14, a.3).

We have seen that Thomas speaks of the discourse of practical reason on the model of the syllogism. Since the end is the principle in practical matters, the premiss from which the practical syllogism takes off is a general precept as to what is to be sought, expressive of the end. Whether this is a precept of natural law, affirmative or negative, or a precept of a lesser order, one of positive law or of moral philosophy, expressing in general terms how the end can be achieved, the task is to see how it is to be obeyed in the circumstances in which one finds oneself. What functions as the next premiss of the practical syllogism is a judgment about those singular circumstances. This judgment may be the result of a previous inquiry or deliberation; it specifies choice and, thanks to the habitual orientation to the end involved in the precept, has efficacy as well. Practical reason's command or precept is the culminating act of prudence and, as Thomas suggests, alone of the components of prudence is peculiar to practical intellect.

Once more we can see the unwisdom of trying to separate as well as distinguish the theoretical and practical uses of the mind. The practical syllogism incorporates speculative truths. But what marks off the practical most decisively from the theoretical is the sense truth has as applied to the characteristic act of practical reason.

Verum intellectus practici aliter accipitur quam verum intellectus speculativi, ut dicitur in VI Ethic. (1139a26). Nam verum intellectus speculativi accipitur per conformitatem intellectus ad rem. Et quia intellectus non potest infallibiliter conformari rebus in contingentibus, sed solum in necessariis; ideo nullus habitus speculativus contingentium est intellectualis virtus, sed solum est circa necessaria. Verum autem intellectus practici accipitur per conformitatem ad appetitum rectum. Quae quidem conformitas in necessariis locum non habet, quae voluntate humana non fiunt: sed solum in contingentibus quae possunt a nobis fieri, sive sint agibilia interiora, sive factibilia exteriora. Et ideo circa sola contingentia ponitur virtus intellectus practici: circa factibilia quidem, ars; circa agibilia vero prudentia. (IaIIae, q.57, a.5, 3m)

Truth in practical intellect is not the same as truth in speculative intellect, as is said in *Ethics* VI. For the true in speculative intellect arises from the conformity of the intellect with the thing. And because the intellect cannot infallibly conform itself to contingent, but only to necessary, things, there is no speculative habit of contingent things which is an intellectual virtue, but only of necessary things. The true in practical intellect arises from conformity with rectified appetite, a conformity which has no place in necessary things which do not come about because of the human will, but only in contingent things which can come to be because of us, whether they are interior actions or exterior makings. Therefore only a virtue of practical intellect is concerned with contingents, art with makeables, prudence with do-ables.

Prudence is not a calculative skill that can function independently of the appetitive disposition of the agent. It is true that on the level of generality even the libertine is able to discuss the demands of chastity, perhaps impress us with his ability to imagine a regimen conducive to the good of bringing one's sexual appetites under the sure guidance of reason. Meanwhile, he stalks the world like a raging lion, seeking maidens to devour.

Similar objections are regularly raised to the Aristotelian tenet that the good ruler must be a good man. Aurele Kolnai once lectured at length on Rasputin as a counterexample of this.

Thomas's point is untouched by such examples. Discussions are general, actions are singular and concrete. When we act, we are not drawing a conclusion; we are choosing, doing, being. The contrast is that Kierkegaard drew between thought and existence. To bring off a singular action in the light of a principle, when our appetite has been schooled to pursue the opposite, is all but impossible. If done at all, the deed will be painful. Don Giovanni decides to practice custody of the eyes, but, given his sordid history, the temptation to peek through his fingers at concupiscible passersby will overwhelm him.

The wise man is able with ease and pleasure to act in accord with his principles, because his heart is in the right place, his appetites have been schooled by moral virtues to desire the true good.

Envoi

It will not seem odd to us that the whole enterprise of moral philosophy and theology comes down to influencing singular acts, fleeting deeds that come and go. Moral theory is not sought for its own sake. It offers little for the mind in terms of satisfying knowledge. The whole point of it is to anticipate and guide action so that our end may be achieved.

But out of these singular acts our character is formed, and we are either good or bad. Character is more permanent than the deeds that form it or, once formed, emanate from it. However endlike the life of moral virtue, it cannot be for us the ultimate end. Moral character disposes for the pursuit of knowledge of the things of this world in their noncontingent characters and ultimately to knowledge of the divine. The desire to know truth as such, God, is implicit in any inquiry, any quest of truth. St. Augustine had a predilection for Truth as the name of God. Hence his description of heaven: *gaudium de veritate*: delight in the truth.

The purpose of these six chapters of Part One has been to give an overview of St. Thomas's moral philosophy and to place his doctrine on natural law within the whole. The advantage of this is that what otherwise might be obscure remarks in the "Treatise on Law" are seen to be echoes of themes struck from the very outset. In all but confining ourselves to the *Summa theologiae,* we sought to give the precise expression of the wider whole of which the discussion of natural law forms a part. There is no developed parallel to the treatment of natural law we find in the *Prima secundae,* just as there is no true parallel to Thomas's discussion of the elements of the complete human act in that same part of the *Summa theologiae.* Thus, there is really no alternative to relying on the *Summa,* if one seeks to give an overview of Thomas's moral thought, which, while fundamentally Aristotelian, voraciously incorporates elements from the whole tradition in which Thomas as a theologian stands.

It is not only the world that does not end with a bang. In a series of micro-essays, which form Part Two, matters that could not be incorporated into these chapters will be found. Part One remains at most a sketch, but one that can be filled in by going again and again to St. Thomas Aquinas.

PART TWO

7. Aristotle and Thomas: Père Gauthier

A LTHOUGH it is no easy thing to attempt a brief statement of the moral
doctrine of St. Thomas Aquinas, I have been guilty of several such
efforts in the past, each time—I say this in extenuation—at the invitation
of someone. Once the impossibility of the exercise is accepted, there is a
certain exhilaration to be had from plunging forward nonetheless. To do
the thing at all, it is necessary to select an angle of approach with the hope
that the very selective and partial account based on it is nonetheless faithful
to all the unmentioned features of the doctrine.

For purposes of this summary, and of course with an eye to the wider
purpose, I will say some things about the way in which Thomas incorporated Aristotle into his moral theology. You recognize at once that this
is far from being noncontroversial. No less a scholar than René Antoine
Gauthier, editor and translator (with Jean Yves Jolif) of the L'Ethique à
Nicomaque[1] and editor of the critical Leonine edition of St. Thomas's
Sententiae super libros Ethicorum[2] insists that St. Thomas must be put in
the forefront of those who did violence to Aristotle's thought by forcing
it into the Procrustean bed of Christian theology.[3]

1. Aristote, L'Ethique à Nicomaque, Introduction, Traduction et Commentaire, par
René Antoine Gauthier et Jean Yves Jolif, deuxième edition avec une introduction
nouvelle. 3 vols. Tome I, Introduction par René Antoine Gauthier (Louvain, Paris,
1970).

2. St. Thomas Aquinas, Sententiae Libri Ethicorum, vol. 47 of Opera Omnia Sancti
Thomae de Aquino (Rome, 1969).

3. Vol. 1, Introduction, pp. 274–75: "Les responsables en sont les théologiens, no-
tamment un Thomas d'Aquin, précisément parce que, théologiens, ils ont dû faire

If Gauthier is right, then the Aristotelianism found in Thomas can be of interest only to theologians. Aristotelians, and indeed historians of philosophy, would have to recognize it as an abuse of Aristotle for purposes unshared by the Stagirite.

To this it could be replied that Thomas wrote a commentary on the *Nicomachean Ethics* and that we can look there rather than in the moral parts of the *Summa theologiae* and other theological writings for a purer Thomistic Aristotle. Alas, Gauthier stands athwart this path as well. Thomas's fellow Dominican and editor is one of the most caustic critics of the commentary, warning that it is nothing like a modern one.[4] There are those who might detect oblique praise of Thomas here, but that is not Gauthier's intention. Gauthier's animadversions on the quality of Thomas's writing must be unique among critical editors. So extreme a criticism seems unlikely to be true; if it were, the tack I am taking in this book would be worse than misguided. What I want to suggest is that those who do not share Thomas's religious beliefs, those for whom moral theology holds no charm, can nonetheless read with philosophical profit both the commentary on Aristotle's *Ethics* and the moral part of the *Summa theologiae*.

This claim could perhaps be made without differing from Gauthier. That is, one might agree that Thomas radically distorts Aristotle for theological purposes, but that, nevertheless, there is an extractable philosophical doctrine contained in the moral theology which, when extracted, could be described both as non-Aristotelian and as moral philosophy. This, it might be said, is the moral philosophy of St. Thomas Aquinas.

---

violence à la sagesse grecque pour la faire tenir dans le lit de Procruste de leur système."

4. Ibid., p. 275: "Saint Thomas n'a donc écrit ni une philosophie morale, ni une interprétation d'Aristote pour Aristote; mais il n'en a que davantage marqué l'exégèse aristotélicienne, car, pour pouvoir utiliser la philosophie morale d'Aristote dans une théologie animée par un esprit étranger à l'esprit d'Aristote et construite selon des exigences étrangères aux exigences de la philosophie, il lui a fallu en bouleverser le sens et l'équilibre." In short, Thomas's moral thought is "la négation de l'enseignement exprès de l'Aristote historique."

Some, hearing this, will be reminded of disputes between Etienne Gilson and Fernand Van Steenberghen.[5] Gilson came to insist more and more on the fact that Thomas was chiefly a theologian, and this led him to maintain that the only order of doctrine in Thomas is that displayed by the *Summa theologiae.* James Collins's demur[6] did not prove to be a rallying point for a rival school, and it can be said that, by and large, students of St. Thomas came to see more opposition between Thomas and Aristotle than anything else—the "real" Aristotle, that is. The Aristotle who figures in the work of Thomas under the honorific *Philosophus* is something of an imaginary character whose speeches, taken out of literary context, mean things in Thomas they could not have meant for Aristotle.

This is not an esoteric point of disagreement. The relation between Thomas and Aristotle is one of the most pressing topics before Thomistic scholars, at least in my opinion. The apparently innocuous cliché that Thomas baptized Aristotle has taken on a meaning, as with Gauthier, which—let us be frank—calls into question either the honesty or intelligence of St. Thomas. Knowingly to distort a text is a serious matter, and it will not do to say this was the literary custom of the time, surely a question-begging explanation.[7] The truth seems rather to be that Thomas meant to say what Aristotle meant when he attributes a position to Aristotle. If he is systematically wrong about this, there is a word to describe such a deficiency.

My own view is that which we find expressed if not embraced by Pico della Mirandola: *sine Thoma Aristoteles mutus esset.* I hold that Thomas's commentaries on Aristotle are precious aids for understanding the text of Aristotle. I think it is nonsense to state universally that these commentaries do not achieve what they clearly set out to achieve, but that somehow this does not matter. Chenu's view is incredible to anyone who has spent years

5. See Etienne Gilson, *History of Christian Philosophy in the Middle Ages* (New York, 1955), and Fernand Van Steenberghen, *La philosophie au XIIIe siècle* (Louvain, 1966).

6. James Collins, "Towards a Philosophically Ordered Thomism," *New Scholasticism* 32 (1958), pp. 301–26.

7. M. D. Chenu, *Introduction à l'étude de Saint Thomas d'Aquin* (Montreal, Paris, 1950), pp. 173–98.

with those commentaries. I am happy to say that my position is not a completely isolated one at the present time. Giovanni Reale's magnificent study of Aristotle's *Metaphysics* goes a long way toward validating the approach to the text taken by Thomas in his commentary on that most difficult work.[8] If *that* commentary can be defended, the task of defending the others is much easier.

Difficulties of another sort await me on this side, of course. If it be granted that Thomas set out to understand and explain the text of Aristotle as such, he could still have been *honestly* mistaken in his views. No doubt. But this possibility is one amenable to the usual kind of philosophical and textual discussion—just the sort of thing I take Thomas to be engaged in. I need not maintain that Thomas's interpretations are noncontroversial in order to deny that he proceeded in the way suggested by Gauthier and others.

To put an end to these introductory matters, let me say that if I did not take the position I do, if I agreed with Gauthier, I would exclude Thomas from the ranks of moral philosophers. Not that I want to suggest that Père Gauthier is the village idiot, of course, though his caustic style is contagious. (His comments on books listed in his bibliography surely mark a low point in contemporary scholarship.) I propose to take one of his remarks and examine it closely with a view to showing (a) something of Thomas's understanding of Aristotle, (b) the way Aristotle is subsumed into moral theology, and (c) how this is not without interest to philosophers.

Gauthier asserts that there is a profound, crucial, and unbridgeable difference between Aristotle and St. Thomas because of their views on ultimate end, a difference which can go unnoticed because of the similarity in the structure of their doctrines. They both begin with a discussion of man's good or end and then examine how this can be achieved. However, for Thomas, our ultimate end is God, Who is a necessary timeless being. For Aristotle, on the other hand, our end is a good achievable by action,

8. Giovanni Reale, *The Concept of First Philosophy and the Unity of the Metaphysics of Aristotle*, trans. John R. Catan (Albany, 1980).

thus contingent and embedded in time.[9] Gauthier's indictment continues with such zest that this item, the first, can easily be forgotten in the blur of assertions. But how better test his assessment than to scrutinize this charge closely? If it is true, the radical difference between Aristotle and Thomas will be established beyond the need for any other proof. Of course, disproving this charge does not as such disprove the others, but I will leave that task for another day.[10]

There is at least a prima facie plausibility in what Gauthier has to say about the final end, man's perfect good, happiness. The opposition he suggests between Aristotle and Thomas is powerfully reminiscent of that Aristotle sees between himself and Plato in Book One, Chapter Six. Aristotle is not interested in the Idea of Goodness, a necessary being independent of the human order; he wants to discover a good achievable by action, a contingent quality of acts, and thence a quality of the character of the human agent. Gauthier does not discuss at all this supposed opposition between Aristotle and St. Thomas on ultimate end. Someone unacquainted with Thomas might think that Gauthier is drawing atten-

---

9. "Sans doute, à première vue, la construction thomiste semble-t-elle calquée sur celle de l'*Ethique à Nicomaque*: ici et là, n'est-ce-pas le bonheur qui est mis au principe de la morale? Trompeuse apparence! La construction thomiste a son principe non pas chez Aristote, mais dans le *Beati* du *Sermon sur la montagne*; l'analyse aristotélicienne du bonheur ne fournit que l'instrument conceptuel qui sert à mieux mettre en relief la béatitude évangélique: l'idée que le bonheur est fin et que la fin est le principe de l'ordre moral. Mais, pour pouvoir les utiliser dans sa théologie morale, saint Thomas a dû faire subir à ces idées mêmes une transmutation si profonde qu'il prend le contrepied de ce qui était, au delà des mots, l'essentiel de la pensée d'Aristote. La fin morale, qui est pour Aristote réalité essentiellement contingente puisqu'elle est action de l'homme, est pour saint Thomas la réalité la moins contingente qui soit, car elle est Dieu même, non pas le dieu-objet des philosophes, mais le Dieu-Personne des Chrétiens: la fin de l'homme n'est pas dans une action de l'homme, pas même dans l'action quelle qu'elle soit par laquelle il s'unit à Dieu. . . . Saint Thomas dès lors pourra bien en garder des mots, des formules, jamais l'esprit" (Gauthier, pp. 275–76).

10. I am writing a book called *Aristotle and Aquinas,* which commends a general attitude on Thomas's understanding, dependence on, and use of Aristotle on the basis of a consideration of a half dozen Thomistic commentaries on Aristotle. The commentary on the *Nicomachean Ethics* figures prominently in the discussion.

tion to something that went undiscussed by Thomas himself. It would be incredible if Thomas, in speaking of man's ultimate end, had not adverted to the distinction Gauthier is relying on. But as students of Thomas know, he discusses it quite explicitly, and it is in terms of that explicit treatment that Gauthier's cavalier remark must be assessed. When this is done, it may be asked whether Thomas's claim that there is no conflict is well-founded. Gauthier's remark amounts to the assertion of a conflict between Aristotle and Thomas that Thomas himself explicitly denied. Of course, Thomas may be wrong and Gauthier right, but if that were the case, Gauthier's opposition would have to be rephrased.

The opening five questions of the *Primae secundae* of the *Summa theologiae* provide the focus for the discussion. They begin the moral part of the work with a treatment of man's ultimate end, with explicit reference to Aristotle's treatment of the same matter. Indeed, throughout these five questions, Aristotle is repeatedly cited, though he may seem to be keeping strange and anachronistic company—St. Augustine, St. John Damascene, Holy Scripture. The concern of these questions is:

(1) *De ultimo fine hominis.*
(2) *De his in quibus hominis beatitudo consistit.*
(3) *Quid sit beatitudo?*
(4) *De his quae ad beatitudinem exiguntur.*
(5) *De adeptione beatitudinis.*

After discussing end and ultimate end, and having identified the latter with happiness, Thomas continues the discussion, in Questions 2–5, in terms of happiness. The tone and context are indisputably different from those of the *Nicomachean Ethics*. Thomas, after all, is doing moral theology, and theology is an inquiry that accepts as true a good many claims undecidable by appeal to what everyone knows on the basis of ordinary experience. The word for this acceptance is "faith." Among the things Thomas believes about human action is that it is the means, when informed by grace, whereby in this life we can merit an eternal happiness with God. This destiny is not something owed man on the basis of what he is, his nature, but is the gratuitous complement of the reparation of sin, which is why Augustine spoke of original sin as a *felix culpa*: the last state of the redeemed person is higher than that lost through sin. The short form of this claim is that eternal felicific union with God is man's supernatural end. This means (a) that union with God is not entailed by his nature and is thus undreamt of by philosophy, and (b) that it presupposes and does not destroy man's natural end.

This enables us to express an initial reaction to Gauthier's claim that there is an opposition between Aristotle and Thomas. If he means to say that Thomas speaks of man's supernatural end whereas Aristotle does not, his observation, however true, is banal. Aristotle was not a Christian. In order to have any interest, Gauthier's claimed opposition would have to mean that the supernatural end is in every way an alternative to what Aristotle set down as the good of man. That is, it replaces, destroys or supplants it. But if Thomas's position is as I have described it—and as Gauthier must know it to be—the question becomes: what is the relation between man's natural ultimate end and his supernatural ultimate end in the doctrine of Thomas Aquinas?

Does Gauthier mean that what Thomas says of man's natural end is opposed to what Aristotle says of man's natural end? Clearly, it is only if he does mean this, that the criticism is interesting. Then he must be taken to be saying that whereas for Thomas God is man's natural ultimate end, this is not the case for Aristotle.

Now, as it happens, it can be maintained that, in one sense of the claim, Thomas holds that God is man's ultimate end *sans phrase,* that He is the human good, *no mention being made of the supernatural order.* But, to the extent this is so, a case can be made that Aristotle taught the same thing. In speaking of Aristotle's view of human destiny, we cannot afford to ignore that grand panorama with which the *Metaphysics* begins, where Aristotle traces the perfection of man through a multitude of hierarchical stages culminating in wisdom, that is, such knowledge as man can attain of the divine. Book Ten of the *Nicomachean Ethics* picks up this theme. If Gauthier were making a serious point, he would have to consider such matters.

But enough for the nonce of our adversary. Let us turn to the given questions mentioned to see what light they cast on the points at issue.

Question One, despite the strangeness already alluded to, provides much that is familiar to the student of Aristotle. If nature is teleological, and man is included in nature, man nonetheless is said to act for an end in a way peculiar to himself. The point is made, not simply by the contrasting of human activity with the activities of other kinds of things in article 2, but also by drawing contrasts among the activities ascribable to man. That is, Thomas distinguishes between human acts, those deliberately produced, and acts of a man, a category that includes everything from falling when dropped to digesting. Like Aristotle, Thomas is not content to say that anything that counts as a human act is undertaken for the sake of some end. He also wants to say that there is some end for the sake of which any human act is undertaken. That is, as he says in article 4, there is an ultimate end of human life. "Life" here is a term which covers the sum total of properly human activities (cf. IaIIae, q.3, a.1, ad 1m). That Thomas means this end to be ultimate and comprehensive is clear when he asks in article 5 if one man can have several ultimate ends. Holding that there is but one, in article 6, he asks in article 7 if all men have the same ultimate end and, finally in article 8, if other creatures share in man's ultimate end. What light do these considerations throw on Gauthier's charges?

Thomas cites Augustine to make a distinction in the sense of "end." The end can mean either a ceasing to be, or it can mean that which fulfills or perfects (article 5). It is the second sense of the term that Thomas has in mind here. The first important clarification concerning end in the second sense is found in the discussion of whether an agent wills everything for the sake of the ultimate end. The basis for the affirmative answer is this: whatever man desires, he desires under the note of good (*sub ratione boni*), and if it is not desired as the perfect good, which is the ultimate end, it must be desired as tending to the perfect good, because the beginning of something is always ordered to its consummation.[11]

11. "Primo quidem, quia quidquid homo appetit, appetit sub ratione boni. Quod

Before there can be any discussion of what among various possible candidates can be man's ultimate end, there must first be an understanding of what would count as an ultimate end, what formality would be realized in it. Thomas suggests that in doing whatever we do, we think it to be good for us to do, that is, think it to be perfective or fulfilling of us. Doubtless no single thing we do will exhaust the formality of "perfective of us," since any particular objective is perfective only up to a point and presumably would enter into a complete account of what perfects a human agent.

This distinction is operative in *Nicomachean Ethics* I, though not all have noticed it. Failure to notice it leads to premature identification of some particular goal or activity with the human good. But it is obvious that Aristotle thinks of man's ultimate end as constituted by a variety of activities and their ends. Only if one of these activities, or one of these ends, exhausted the meaning of "perfective of man" could it be identical with the human good. But it is well known that Aristotle does not say that even of contemplative activity. The good for man remains a set, an ordered set, of activities and their ends. The *notion* of the ultimate end, the *ratio boni*, can be distinguished from any one activity and, in a certain sense, identified with a carefully developed ordered set of activities.

The distinction mentioned plays a crucial role in answering the question as to whether all men have the same ultimate end. In article 7 he says: "I answer that it must be said that we can speak of ultimate end in two ways: first, according to the notion of ultimate end; second, according to that in which the notion of ultimate end is found." Men may differ widely in discussing ultimate end in the second sense, but only by being in agreement on it in the first sense. Needless to say, this is a very weak claim for agreement. Any human agent does whatever he does under the aegis of the good; implicit in any choice is the judgment that "X is good

---

quidem si non appetitur ut bonum perfectum, quod est ultimus finis, necesse est ut appetatur ut tendens in bonum perfectum: quia semper inchoatio alicuius ordinatur ad consummationem ipsius . . ." (IaIIae, q.1, a.6.).

for me." The values of X may differ as you like, but the function remains the same.

Of course, no one chooses the *ratio boni,* the notion of the good; a person chooses something as good, because he judges that it saves or embodies the notion "perfective of me." The difference is one between quality and carrier, form and supposit, idea and participant. The Aristotelian will resist the suggestion that the idea of goodness is another item in the world over and above the things that are called good. As one related to many, goodness exists only in the mind. Good, as it exists, is a feature of things, relating them to the appetite of those other things whose perfections they are.

It remains controversial to claim that this explanation of choice entails anything like a dominant goal. One of the most frequent objections to ultimate end is that not every person aims at some one objective to which he subordinates all else. If ultimate end meant only the *ratio boni,* of course, the claim that all men have the same ultimate end, while not without interest, would be less than what it is usually taken to mean. And indeed Thomas, in citing Paul to the Phillipians 3:19 (*Quorum deus venter est*), suggests that there is, at any given time, some dominant thing with which the notion of good is identified. This needs discussion, no doubt, but the appeal to Paul suggests that Thomas, for whom God is that object in whom the *ratio boni* is perfectly realized, sees defective human actions as an attempt to make something other than God into God. This was the point of Chesterton's somewhat lurid remark that the young man knocking on the brothel door is looking for God.

The distinction between the notion of ultimate end and that in which the notion of ultimate end is located does not suggest that just anything can rightly be taken as perfective of the human agent. If there is no one activity whose end is identical with the good for man, there is nonetheless a set of such ends, which variously realize the *ratio boni* and which together can be seen as fully perfective of the kind of agent man is. Given the plurality of constituents of the human good, there seems to be room for much legitimate and desirable diversity in ordering those constituents. In this way, the notion of ultimate end is seen as providing just what traditional objections to it argue that it does not provide.

We may also note here that moral error or sin is understood by Thomas, not as pursuit of something whose nature is evil, but rather as the pursuit of a good in a disorderly way. The glutton pursues a human good in a disordered way; so too the miser, lecher, and thief. Some kinds of action, some ways of pursuing constituents of the human good, are ruled out by what is meant by the *ratio boni* (IaIIae, q.18, aa.5 and 6). When is a good not a good? The distinction Thomas makes when he asks if all creatures share in man's ultimate end is important here.

When Thomas identifies man's ultimate end with happiness (*ultimus finis hominum est beatitudo*), he does so in order to distinguish man's pursuit of the ultimate end from that of irrational creatures. The distinction is this: "the end is said in two ways, namely *cuius* and *quo,* that is, the thing in which the notion of good is found, and the use or attainment of that thing" (art. 8). In the first sense, God is the ultimate end of all creatures. (This is the first statement that God is man's ultimate end, and it is important to notice that it is a cosmic observation: God is the ultimate end of all creatures.) Aristotelian universal teleology is presupposed, and then the question becomes: what is different about the way God is man's ultimate end? The term *beatitudo* expresses that difference: "Man and other rational creatures pursue the ultimate end by knowing and loving God, which is not the case with other creatures" (art. 8). From this point on, *beatitudo* and man's ultimate end are identical in meaning, with *beatitudo* the preferred term.

Gauthier's claim was that Thomas, because he identifies man's ultimate end with God, is in a totally different conceptual universe from Aristotle, for whom the good for man is a quality of action. We are assuming that something more interesting than the distinction between the supernatural and natural end of man is meant—more interesting philosophically, that is. If the supposed difference between Thomas and Aristotle is meant to obtain in the realm of man's natural end, then Gauthier is being willfully obtuse. Aristotle and Thomas hold both of Gauthier's options as elements of their doctrine of ultimate end.

We have thus far drawn attention to three distinctions that Thomas makes with reference to the end: (a) a distinction between end as terminus and end as fulfillment or perfection; (b) the distinction between the *notion* of ultimate end and the *thing(s)* in which the notion is taken to be realized; (c) the distinction between the thing which is the end and the mode of attaining it. The first distinction draws attention to the fact that "when something desires its own perfection, it sees it as an ultimate end which it desires as its perfect and complete good" (art. 5). The second distinction we have discussed sufficiently. The third produces an important assertion: "*beatitudo nominat adeptionem ultimi finis*: happiness means the attainment of the ultimate end" (art. 8). But the *adeptio* or attainment of the ultimate end is accomplished by knowing and loving God, that is, by means of certain human acts. Gauthier's opposition evaporates.

Having identified ultimate end and happiness, Thomas goes on to discuss, in Question 2, what happiness is not and, in Question 3, what it is. The failed candidates for identification with happiness fall into groups: exterior goods, bodily goods, spiritual goods. The denials in article 7 that human happiness can consist of a good of the soul and, in article 8, that it could be any created good, may seem to provide the opposition Père Gauthier has in mind. But do they? Article 7 begins by recalling the distinction between the thing we desire to attain and the attainment of it. "If then we speak of ultimate end with regard to the thing itself we seek as the ultimate end, it is impossible that man's ultimate end should be his soul or any part of it. For the soul, considered in itself, is as it were existing in potency: one becomes an actual knower from being a potential knower and actually virtuous from being potentially virtuous." Thus the very thing Gauthier has in mind as the Aristotelian alternative to God as ultimate end is explicitly rejected by Thomas—*taking ultimate end to stand for that which we seek to possess.* "But if we are speaking of ultimate end with regard to its attainment or possession or whatever use of the thing which is desired as end, then something of man's soul pertains to ultimate end, since man pursues the ultimate end with his soul" (q.2, a.8). Thus it is clear that Thomas sees no opposition of ultimate ends here, but rather two ways of speaking of the ultimate end: *what* we wish to attain and our *attainment* of it.

The denial that any created good can be our ultimate end does two things. First, it provides a crisp reading of what is meant by ultimate end. Second, it shows that only God can be our ultimate end, given the *ratio* or meaning of ultimate end.

St. Thomas gives this account of happiness: "For beatitude is the perfect good which totally quiets desire, since otherwise, if something still remained to desire, it would not be the ultimate end." This is the *ratio boni perfecti,* the notion of ultimate end. The fulfillment of all our potentialities, the completion of our nature, such that nothing more could be desired— that is what Thomas takes happiness to be. It may seem that he has thereby defined happiness out of reach. There seems to be no way in the world that anyone could be happy in that sense. The objection anticipates Thomas's next move. "The object of the will, which is human desire, is the universal good, much as the object of intellect is universal truth. From which it follows that nothing can quiet the will of man except the universal good." We have already suggested that nothing we seek as good is identical with goodness; the objects of appetite have goodness, they share or partake in it. There are many good things. Nor is the class of all things identical with goodness. There is only one value of the variable in "X is good" that exhausts the attribution, such that good is identical with goodness. "Which is not to be found in any created thing, but in God alone, because every creature partakes of goodness."

The use of partaking or participation here suggests that, whatever else might be said of what Thomas is doing here, it seems more Platonic than Aristotelian. That we have here an instance of Thomas's quite considered employment of a Platonic notion, there can be no doubt. Of course what has been called logical participation is present in Aristotle,[12] as the analysis of the predication of substance in Book Zeta of the *Metaphysics* makes clear. While Aristotle denies the Platonic sense of the claim that a thing is not identical with its essence, he provides his own account of the same claim, one that does not entail subsistent essences. The upshot is that while Socrates is not identical with what-it-is-to-be-a-man, and the same is true of any other individual man, there is no Man apart from them which

12. See Cornelio Fabro, *La nozione metafisica di partecipazione* 3d ed. (Turin, 1963).

they are not. We find in Thomas's prologue to his commentary on the *De divinis nominibus*, a sort of treaty with Platonism, a laying down of the conditions of acceptance of certain Platonic themes. If the Platonic Ideas are a misunderstanding of the ontological implications of logical participation, then the position is not only false but contrary to faith. If however the Ideas are taken to be names of God, then the doctrine is most true and in conformity with faith and casts great light on the way things are. Ontological participation is a way of regarding creatures as manifesting some *scintilla divinitatis,* as diminished versions of some aspect of the divine perfection. And just as any given creature falls infinitely short of the complete perfection God is, so does the sum total of creatures, actual and potential. And creature exists to the degree that it does because of God's causality. We have here the ontological difference between God and creatures, which is the point of Thomas's claim that in any creature there is a non-identity of what it is and that it is, whereas in God alone essence and existence are one. He makes the latter point by calling God *Ipsum esse subsistens,* stretching the language and hurting our non-Platonic ears.[13]

Question Three, article 1, begins by recalling the by now familiar distinction, but puts a new twist on it. The distinction is that between the thing that is the ultimate end and our possession of it. "If then man's happiness be considered with regard to its cause or object, it is something uncreated, whereas if it be considered with regard to the very essence of happiness, it is something created." Thus, for Thomas, *pace* Père Gauthier, the *essence* of happiness is a good achievable by action, contingent, embedded in time. In the third question Thomas wishes to speak of the essence of happiness, and he first establishes that it is an activity, citing Aristotle in *Nicomachean Ethics* I. Then in article 4, he excludes certain possibilities and identifies the activity in question as of the intellectual part. Speculative or practical? Speculative rather than practical. It is here that Thomas makes another distinction of maximum importance for the problem raised by Gauthier. If contemplation is the perfection of the speculative

13. See David Burrell, *Knowing the Unknowable God* (Notre Dame, 1986), pp. 19–34.

use of our mind, it is nonetheless in contemplation that human happiness consists. "Therefore the ultimate end perfect happiness, which is expected in the future life, consists wholly in contemplation. Imperfect happiness, however, such as can be had here, consists first and principally in contemplation and secondarily in the operation of the practical intellect ordering human actions and passions, as is said in *Ethics* X" (art. 5).

This distinction between imperfect and perfect happiness, the happiness that can be attained in this life and that for which we hope in another, is clearly not one Aristotle could make. Indeed he is quite mystifying when the question of the alterability of the happiness or unhappiness of the departed comes up in the first book of the *Ethics*. Thomas says things about Aristotle's teaching, then, which can only be said from the vantage point of religious belief—namely that the happiness he defines is a worldly one—although even on that score, he points to Aristotle's insistence that he is speaking of the happiness appropriate to man, that is, as attainable in this world, thus acknowledging that the ideal of happiness is only imperfectly achievable (*Ethics* I, 11, 1101a20). That Thomas sometimes says things about Aristotelian doctrine from a Christian perspective—hardly surprising when he is writing theology—should not, of course, be identified with the claim that he distorts the teaching of Aristotle. Thomas is right to point out that Aristotle himself notes the discrepancy between the concept of happiness and our hope of realizing it. The notes of self-sufficiency and permanence must be modified in terms of the facts of human existence, and it seems fair to say that Aristotle's idea of the ultimate end and our chances of realizing happiness, and the chances of the happiness we attain filling the bill so far as the concept goes, are not identical. In short, Aristotle himself has a measure according to which he could say that the happiness we achieve is an imperfect one. What he does not say of course is that there is a possibility of attaining perfect happiness elsewhere.

Throughout Question 4, St. Thomas continues to contrast the happiness achievable in this life with that hoped for in the next, in such a way that, far from disagreeing with Aristotle, he underscores his agreement with him. The assertion that perfect happiness is not possible in this life is taken to be a reiteration of Aristotle. "And because of this, in our present state of life, perfect happiness cannot be had by man. Hence the Philosopher, in *Ethics* I, speaking of man's happiness in this life, calls it imperfect, concluding, after much consideration, 'happy we mean as men'" (q.3, a.2, ad 4m).

The discussion of the concomitants of happiness in Question 4 glosses much of Aristotle. So too, asking in Question 5 about the achieving of happiness, Thomas sounds almost Pelagian in his optimism about our ability to achieve the imperfect happiness discussed by Aristotle, even while stressing its imperfectness. "For happiness, being 'a perfect and sufficient good,' excludes all evil, but in this life not every evil can be excluded. Our present life is subject to many evils which cannot be avoided" (art. 3). He lists these evils: ignorance, inordinate desire, bodily ills. "So too the desire for good cannot be satisfied in this life." We naturally desire the permanent possession of the good, but in this life goods are transitory and evanescent.

In saying that perfect happiness is impossible in this life, Thomas is underscoring the discrepancy Aristotle saw between his definition of happiness and what we can hope to achieve of it. That Thomas does and Aristotle does not speak of a perfect happiness after this life does not affect their concord on earthly happiness.

Although Thomas locates perfect happiness in the next life, there is an anticipation of it in this life thanks to grace. The acts which can be constitutive of imperfect happiness in this life can also, when informed by grace, merit the perfect happiness of union with God.

The sequel to these opening five questions of the moral part of the *Summa theologiae* is a remarkable theory of human action.[14] But we have seen more than enough to establish that the complete moral thought of St. Thomas Aquinas, as we find it in his theological writings, is not in opposition to the pagan ethics of Aristotle in the way suggested by Père Gauthier. It is unfortunate that a scholar who has devoted so much time

14. See Alan Donagan, "Thomas Aquinas on Human Action," in *The Cambridge History of Later Medieval Philosophy,* ed. Norman Kretzman, Jan Pinborg, Anthony Kenny, and Eleonore Stump (Cambridge, 1982), pp. 642–54.

and energy to the study of Thomas and Aristotle should so thoroughly
misportray the relation between them. The Aristotle subsumed within
the commodious synthesis of Thomas is the historical Aristotle. It is li-
belous to suggest that Thomas simply took words and phrases from Aristotle and turned them to purposes he knew they could not truly serve.
How odd that those who claim to be friends of Thomas should ascribe
such a practice to him. The real test of the relation between Thomas and
Aristotle in moral matters is the commentary on the *Nicomachean Ethics*.
That the editor of the critical edition of that work should be our old friend
Père Gauthier is cause for concern. He has dismissed the commentary as
useless. There is only one way to assess that judgment, and that is by a
careful reading of the commentary. That Gauthier is not a sure guide is
clear from our analysis of one of his misunderstandings.[15]

15. Gauthier's "Saint Thomas et l'Ethique à Nicomaque," appended to vol. 48 of
the *Opera Omnia* does not rectify matters, however irenic it may appear by contrast
to his more polemical statements.

8. Donagan on Thomas on Action

IN HIS essay "Thomas Aquinas on Human Action,"[1] Alan Donagan provides a wonderfully succinct and generally accurate account of the Thomistic analysis of human action that we discussed in Chapter 3 of Part One. The major serious criticism he makes of the doctrine is that Thomas has introduced a superfluous act of will, *usus,* and a corresponding and equally superfluous intellectual act, which are in conflict with his own principles. Donagan alters the analysis accordingly and what we get is this:

With respect to the interior act, we have, first, an act of intellect judging that an attainable end is good, and *voluntas, fruitio,* and *intentio* as elicited acts of will bearing on this end. The mind then deliberates, seeking ways in which the end can be realized by me and judges which means are suitable to the end; the will then consents to them and chooses the most suitable. The external or commanded act then takes place.

Donagan thus holds that the deliberative judgment that a given means is the most suitable should have been identified by Thomas with *imperium.* Furthermore, there is no need for a further act of will after choice, the further act Thomas calls *usus.* Donogan writes:

In a complete human act, a commanded act will be that component which the agent judges is to be made to happen, and which *does* happen as a result of an act of will which he performs in view of that judgment. Taking Aquinas' theory as so far developed, it is natural to identify that act of command (*imperium*) with

1. In *The Cambridge History of Later Medieval Philosophy,* ed. Norman Kretzmann, Anthony Kenny, Jan Pinborg, and Eleanor Stump (Cambridge University Press, 1982), pp. 642–54.

the judgment that terminates deliberation; and to identify the mediating act of will, as a result of which the commanded act happens, with the act of choice. Aquinas, as we shall see, adds a further act of will (namely, *usus*), and provides it with an appropriate generating intellectual act; but that, I shall argue, is muddled. (pp. 649–50)

This criticism is all the more serious coming from one who defends Thomas against the charge that the elicited acts that are said to be components of even the simplest complete human act, e.g., raising one's hand, are too numerous to be credible and correspond to nothing we experience in acting. Donagan replies that the components are not discovered by introspection "but by examining various cases in which an act is begun but not completed" (p. 654). This is indeed a criterion Thomas gives for distinguishing the component acts of will of a complete human act. Presumably, when Donagan rejects *usus,* he does so because it fails to meet this test.

The acts of will Thomas distinguished as bearing on end and bearing on means are *elicited* acts of will as opposed to *commanded* acts. When I lift my hand in response to the command of my will, the motion of my bodily members is a commanded act of will. But there are also acts of mind and of will that are commanded. The will can command us to think but this bears on the exercise and not the specification of thinking—we do not by willing make something true or false. What are we to make of the claim that some acts of will are commanded? Donagan writes:

The article [IaIIae, q.17, a.5] in which Aquinas treats of commanded acts of will is perilously succinct. It will be misunderstood if it is forgotten that, when a certain possible act is commanded in an act of intellect and then chosen in an act of will, what is commanded is the possible act that is chosen, and not the act of choosing or willing it. The crucial premiss in Aquinas's demonstration that acts of will are commanded is that a man "can judge that it is good that [he] will a certain thing" [IaIIae, q.17, a.5c]. He has not forgotten that what is judged in deliberation is that a certain means is most suitable: his point is that sometimes the means judged most suitable for attaining an end may itself be an act of will. And so the act of choice that ensues, if one does, will be an act of willing that act of will. Although Aquinas gives no examples, they are not far to seek. Resolving to act in a certain way in the future, one of the means by which moral virtues are acquired, is one kind of act of will that can be commanded. (p. 651)

The actual doing of the commanded act is the effect of a certain elicited act of will, which is its cause. Donagan then asks what the last act of will in a complete human act is, "the act of will which causes the operation of the executive powers that constitutes the commanded act" (p. 651). He thinks that there is an obvious reason for identifying it with the act of choice and for identifying the intellectual act of command with the act of judgment that terminates deliberation. What is his reason? "That Aquinas himself lays it down that, 'inasmuch as [the power of will] is in the person willing as having a certain proportion or order to that which is willed,' the last act of will with respect to the means is choice (IaIIae, q.16, a.4c)" (ibid.). Donagan's suggestion, then, is that the last judgment of deliberation as to the best means is the *imperium* and the last act of will is choice (*electio*) of which the commanded act is the effect.

Thomas, on the other hand, holds that the last act of will is *usus* and that the commanded act is an effect of it. Why does Donagan reject this? His understanding of Thomas's argument on behalf of *usus* can be schematized thus:

[1] Besides the relation which the power of will can have to the willed inasmuch as it is in the person willing as having a certain proportion or order to the willed, there is a second relation which it can have inasmuch as the willed is in the person willing as an end which he really possesses.

[2] The means, as well as the end, is then declared to be included in this second relation.

[3] Finally, it is argued that, since choice is the last act of will in the first relation, "*Usus* belongs to the second relation of the will to the thing willed by which it tends to its bringing about. From which it is manifest that *usus* follows choice, provided that the word *usus* is adopted inasmuch as the will uses the executive power, by moving it."

Donagan sees this as a blunder. "For if the second relation of the will to the willed in fact obtains—namely, the relation it has when the willed is something already possessed—then the executive power by which the will has been brought about must already have been exercised. Hence if *usus* is an act which belongs to the second relation of the will to the willed, it cannot be directed to the operation of the executive power which *ex hypothesis* has already operated. 'Using' the executive powers can only be an act belonging to the *first* relation of the will to the willed. And Aquinas himself concedes that the last act of will in that first relation is choice. *Usus*, understood as the 'using' of the executive powers, should therefore be identified with choice. And *imperium*, as the act of judgment which gives rise to *usus*, need not be identified with an intellectual act alleged to follow choice (cf. IaIIae, q.17, a.3, ad 1): it should simply be identified with the judgment with which deliberation terminates" (p. 651).

If the complete human act, as Thomas presents it, involves three couples of intellectual and voluntary acts—grasp of end/wish; deliberation/choice and, finally, command/use—Donagan proposes only two: grasp of end/wish and deliberation = command/choice = use. Where has Donagan gone wrong? If he had applied what he rightly saw to be the basis for distinguishing different elicited acts of will, namely, "by examining various cases when an act is begun and not completed," he would surely agree that sometimes the most suitable means is found and chosen, and the act is stopped. To use his example of the final judgment of deliberation, "Socrates' judging that the most suitable means would be his arm going up," the elicited act of will that is consent might be identified with choice if there are no suitable alternatives, but can that judgment be identified with command and choice identified with use? Surely not, if I am prevented from raising my arm. I may have chosen to do so, but I cannot bring it off, cannot use my executive powers, because you are holding my hand down. But if choice were use, only fulfilled acts could be said to involve choice.

But Donagan could reply that, just as consent and choice need not be distinguished when there is not a plurality of means, so choice and use need not be distinguished in the absence of force. To see that this will not do, we must show that Donagan's understanding of IaIIae, q.16, a.4 is flawed.

Thomas distinguishes the will's relation to the good as known, in the order of intention, and the will's relation to the good in the order of execution, the latter being more perfect, since it relates to the good as it exists and not simply as it is known. But it is not only ends which enter into the order of intention, but means as well. The order of intention comes to an end in an act of choice. That order of intention is precisely that series of elicited acts of will which bear on end and then means to the end.

What is use? "But use already pertains to the second relation of the will whereby it tends toward the attainment of the willed thing. Hence it is clear that use follows choice, if we mean by use the will as using the executive power by moving it" (IaIIae, q.16, a.4). Donagan sees a blunder here, because he thinks of the second relation of the will to the thing willed, not as the initiation of a process, but as its completion. The external act having been performed, then of course use has occurred. What Donagan has lost sight of here is the dynamic character of the order of execution. He takes it to be the order of having already been executed. Thomas, on the contrary, sees the process of thinking and elicited acts of will coming to an end in choice, since it is then "that the proportion of the will is completed, such that it completely wills that which is for the sake of the end." We choose the means. Command now comes into play as ordered to the existential as opposed to the intentional realization of the means or series of means that will effect the end willed. What is wanted and chosen must now be done—"Do it!" (Cf. IaIIae, q.17, a.1). Raising one's hand, in Donagan's example, is the use of one's arm to fulfill that command. Use is the will act which is as form to the bodily motion making it voluntary. Use is thus manifest in the bodily motion which achieves the end sought.

For Donagan to explain the commanded act's taking place as "the relevant executive powers having been set in operation by the act of choice" (p. 653), simply does not do justice to the difference Thomas sees between the intentional and executive orders. For him, choice is the term of the internal act, taken as the series of acts of intellect and will which perfectly proportion the thing willed to the will. One has settled on the procedure and is enamored of the first step to be taken. Where Thomas sees the dramatic emergence of the existential, Donagan sees merely the external appearance of the intentional chain.

I conclude that Donagan has not shown that Thomas contradicts his own principles by distinguishing command/use from deliberation/choice and that these two couples could only be identified by construing the constituent acts of intellect and will quite differently from the way that Thomas does. In short, one would have to part company with him on the basis of principles other than Thomas's own.

Dicendum quod non omnis actus voluntatis praecedit hunc actum rationis qui est imperium: sed aliquis praecedit, scilicet electio; et aliquis sequitur, scilicet usus. Quia post determinationem consilii, quae est iudicium rationis, voluntas elegit; et post electionem ratio imperat ei per quod agendum est quod eligitur; et tunc demum voluntas alicuius incipit uti, exequendo imperium rationis . . . (IaIIae, q.17, a.3, ad 1)

It should be said that not every act of will precedes this act of reason which is command: one precedes it, namely choice, and another follows, namely use. For after the determination of counsel, which is a judgment of reason, will chooses, and after choice, reason commands that what is chosen be done; then at last one's will begins to use, executing the command of reason . . .

9. The Primacy of Theoretical Knowledge: Some Remarks on John Finnis

THE WORK of John Finnis taken alone is a production of both range and depth and, when coupled with that of Germain Grisez and Joseph Boyle, with whom Finnis has frequently collaborated, amounts to a massive *oeuvre* indeed. These three have rightly had a great impact on current discussions of natural law and its applications. Here I shall concern myself with two clear and well-defined points found in Finnis's work, first, his dismissal of the Aristotelian appeal to man's function in discussing the human good and, second, his appeal to the way capacities are known from their activities and natures from their capacities as the basis for claiming the autonomy of practical intellect. My interest in these two points is largely in terms of their compatibility with the teaching of Thomas Aquinas. I can never get quite clear whether Finnis thinks he holds views which are fundamentally Thomistic, or whether he is arguing that he has found remarkable adumbrations in the writings of St. Thomas of views developed independently by himself and his friends. However it may be with that question, I shall argue that Finnis's dismissal of the function argument and his claim for the autonomy of practical intellect make his position radically different from that of St. Thomas.

"An Erratic Boulder"

At the outset of *Fundamentals of Ethics,*[1] Finnis is concerned to underscore that ethics is practical knowledge, and he appeals to Aristotle to

1. John Finnis, *Fundamentals of Ethics* (Georgetown University Press, 1983).

explain what he means. This appeal carries problems for Finnis, however, because of "the claim of classical ethics to be founded on *nature* and on a true metaphysics or descriptive knowledge of nature—the claim which to some is the chief merit and to others the all but vitiating fallacy of pre-Enlightenment ethical theories" (p. 10). He proposes, accordingly, to address the "question how practical understanding relates to our knowledge of nature (especially human nature as known in general [metaphysical or other descriptive] anthropology)" (ibid.). What is involved, he adds, is the relation of "is"-judgments to "ought"-judgments.

We are not to think that the distinction between practical and theoretical means that we have two intellects. There is one mind which sometimes operates theoretically, when one is concerned primarily with discerning the truth about some topic, and sometimes practically, when "one is concerned primarily to discover or determine what to do, to get, to have, or to be" (p. 11).

A further point is that "theoretical" and "practical" are analogous terms. "While there are no doubt paradigm cases of purely theoretical or purely practical intellectual activity, most of our actual thinking is *both* theoretical (at least in some qualified sense) *and* practical" (p. 13). As often as not we are interested in the truth because of some practical aim we have. Against the background of these irenic remarks, Finnis lays down his thesis. "What I do assert is that our primary grasp of what is good for us (or: really a fulfillment of our potentialities) is a practical grasp" (p. 12). Finnis feels that both Aristotle and Thomas Aquinas would agree with his thesis. He gives four main reasons why this has not been seen, but it is the last that interests me now. "And finally (iv) Aristotle himself launched at least one argument which uses or presupposes a mistaken view of the way that judgments about nature can contribute to understanding in ethics" (p. 13).

Aristotle set out to identify man's true good, and it is precisely his methodology, rather than its results, that Finnis is concerned with. Aristotle seems to run afoul of the distinction between "is" and "ought" that governs Finnis's thinking. He has in mind Aristotle's appeal to function or *ergon,* and whether it is or is not well performed, on which basis the agent can be called a good or bad so-and-so (as denominated from the function, e.g. a flautist, a golfer, etc.). Aristotle's suggestion is that, if man has a function, we will have a device for determining whether man is good as man; that is, insofar as he performs his specific function well, a human agent will be called a good man. There is, Finnis says, a flaw in the procedure. "The one purely theoretical moment of the argument is where Aristotle says we should be looking not merely for man's function or characteristic activity but, more narrowly, for man's *peculiar* characteristic activity, i.e. the function he does not share with any other being" (p. 15).

What precisely is Finnis's criticism? He is pointing to what he describes as an unequivocally theoretical, nonpractical moment in the proof which, he feels, vitiates it. He would seem to have in mind Aristotle's search for man's function, and Finnis himself suggests a distinction between "man's function or characteristic activity" and "man's *peculiar* activity, the function he does not share with any other being," and it is the latter he objects to. This is of course odd since, in the context, man's function simply means his peculiar and characteristic activity. The distinction Finnis suggests, even if it made sense, has nothing to do with the text. He cites the following Aristotelian passage:

Life seems to belong even to plants, but we are seeking what is peculiar to man. Let us exclude, therefore, the life of nutrition and growth. Next there would be the life of perception, but *it* also seems to be shared even by the horse, the ox, and every animal. There remains then ... (1097b34–1098a3)

Finnis objects by saying that we should not suppose that the most important characteristics of humanity are those which distinguish us from all other kinds of being. Why not? His first point is one he himself seems to see is irrelevant. Aristotle holds that man's good consists chiefly in theoretical contemplation, but contemplation is not peculiar to human beings. To which Aristotle would reply: "It is in the sense I give to 'contemplation.'" In any case, the main thing wrong with Aristotle's argument, according to Finnis, is "that it adduces a bare fact (the alleged fact that we are unique in such and such a respect) and this has no significance for practical understanding," i.e., for an understanding of what is *good* in human life. The argument is a piece of bare "physics," from which nothing of this sort follows for ethics.

But surely Aristotle's point is carried by what he says. His point again is this. I know what I mean by a good golfer: he is one who performs the function of a golfer well. So too with baker and candlestick maker. If man had a function—that is, if some activity pertained to him just insofar as he is a man, *per se*—for him to perform that function well would provide a basis for calling him a good man. Aristotle makes clear what he means, not only by contrasting man with plants and animals, but also by contrasting the function of eye and hand with man as such. Clearly, this is not just a what-if passage; Aristotle thinks man has a function, that is, an activity that can be truly predicated of him and is predicated of no other cosmic thing. He calls it a life lived according to reason.[2]

If Finnis wanted to object that this only enables us to know what is meant by calling someone a good man and does not constitute proximate practical advice, we might be able to follow him. What is difficult to follow is the suggestion that, in the course of asking what man's good is, Aristotle should not have shown us where to look for it. What is Finnis attempting to say?

His point is that, even if it were true that there is some characteristic activity of human beings, this is merely a bare fact about the natural order. Moreover, such "bare facts" do not "usually" play a role in Aristotle's argument. "The 'function' argument is not the deep structure of Aristotle's ethical method; it is an erratic boulder" (p. 17). It is this astounding remark that we must try to understand. It is immediately followed by this passage:

The whole argument of the *Ethics* concludes to a proposition about what is natural to man, in the sense of truly appropriate to and fulfilling of human beings; but

2. The distinction that St. Thomas makes between *actiones humanae* and *actus hominis* in IaIIae, q.1, a.1, is a perfect parallel to the function or exclusivity argument. Thomas is identifying those actions which belong to man as man as opposed to those actions men share with lesser beings. The former he equates with moral actions (ibid., a.3, c).

that is the conclusion, or a way of expressing the conclusion, and the arguments for it are found elsewhere. (P. 17)

Aristotle's true method, he suggests, is to remind us of our own and others' "practical and pre-philosophical grasp of good(s)" (p. 18). He collects passages from the final books of the *Ethics* to illustrate what he means.

What I take Finnis to mean is this. The generalizations about the good that Aristotle makes can be verified or accepted by us, because they echo our own experience in the practical order. This is an important and salutary reminder about Aristotle's *Ethics,* which does indeed presuppose that its reader is already engaged in the moral life. On that assumption, its reflections at a level of generality on that life are meant to provide practical guidance for the future. This advice is of course directed peculiarly to humans and has no relevance to other entities. What the function argument provides is a theoretical basis for distinguishing those among our actions that are human and to which ethical reflection is relevant. Of course Finnis does not want to call that into question.

Finnis, it seems, wishes to maintain that the end, the good, that guides ethical reflection is known in what he earlier called purely practical knowledge. It is not preceded by, is independent of, any and all theoretical knowledge, knowledge, for example, of such brute facts as that man alone speaks and is spoken to. The good(s) are grasped in practical knowledge; this is the beginning point of practical thinking. After that, all kinds of theoretical knowledge can enter into the picture. Practical arguments are often mixtures of practical and theoretical considerations—of "ought" and "is" judgments—but what must be avoided like sin is any suggestion that our first and primary practical knowledge is dependent on theoretical knowledge of nature. That is Finnis's fundamental point. It is on this basis that he takes to task other moral philosophers. It is on this basis that he undertakes to save Aristotle from himself and dismiss the heart of his procedure as an erratic boulder on the landscape. In short, Finnis is scandalized by the function argument.

Existence Precedes Essence

This being clear, Finnis seeks what he takes to be corroboration in the classical account of how nature or essence comes to be known. He makes what he calls the epistemological point that it is by appeal to their objects that we distinguish different activities, e.g., seeing and hearing, and from those activities we come to knowledge of the capacities, and from knowledge of those capacities we have such knowledge of the essence or nature as we do. Ontologically, the order is reversed: capacities depend upon nature and activities on capacities. His point is that we come to knowledge of human nature from knowledge of human action; therefore, we do not come to knowledge of human action or of what we ought to do from nature.

This has come to be Finnis's favorite response to those who have difficulty following his account of practical reason.[3] What began as the insistence that moral philosophy presupposes the experience and practical thinking of its addressee, the former deriving from the latter, is generalized into the view that from *praxis* arises theory even of a nonpractical sort.

Prodded by critics, Finnis has come a long way from the flat assumption that since the first principles of practical reason are *per se nota* they are autonomous, independent of knowledge of any bare facts about ourselves or other things. The stern reminder that "ought" cannot be derived from "is" grounded the rejection of any invocation of "merely brute facts" in understanding our judgments as to what is good for us. But under pressure from Henry Veatch, Finnis now agrees that first principles are derived from experience which includes "not only the stirrings of desire and aversion, but also an awareness of possibilities, likelihoods, *ut in pluribus* outcomes, and so forth" (p. 47). And he even finds adumbrations of this realization in his own earlier writings.

---

3. John Finnis, "Natural Inclinations and Natural Rights: Deriving 'Ought' from 'Is' According to Aquinas," *Lex et Libertas: Freedom and Law According to St. Thomas Aquinas,* ed. Leo Elders and Klaus Hedwig, Studi Tomistici 30 (Rome, 1987), 43–55.

Comments

With respect to what Finnis clearly regards as the *coup de grâce* against his critics, the passage from acts to capacities to nature, it must be said that this has no relevance to his claim that the grasp of action is independent of nature. The string to which he appeals is a sequence of theoretical knowledge: from knowing what action is, I come to knowledge of what capacity is, etc. What leaps out is the fact that knowledge of the *nature* of action is the starting point. We surely would not want to restrict quidditative knowledge to the substantial essence.

What Finnis wants to say is that we must have first acted, have engaged in action, before we can develop an account of action. I think he is absolutely right about this. It is not simply that theoretical accounts depend upon sensory experience. Rather, the point is that the theoretical and practical knowledge with which we begin is not had in the same mode as that formalized in theoretical and practical sciences. Finnis has often said that we do not have to know metaphysics and anthropology before doing ethics, but a similar, obviously true point is made by saying that we do not have to have studied moral philosophy in order to engage in moral activity. The deep structure of Finnis's position is a view of the relationship between the theoretical and practical thinking that all human agents ordinarily engage in prior to, during, and after the study of moral philosophy.

In the matter with which he has been chiefly concerned, natural law, the distinction is that between the formulation of a theory of natural law, as in *Summa theologiae,* the *Prima secundae,* and the knowledge of natural law the theory attempts to formulate, the knowledge which, the theory holds, everyone already has prior to formulating or reading about theories. If Finnis had said that our knowledge of natural law precepts does not depend upon a prior reading of the relevant questions in the *Summa theologiae,* he would have carried the day without question. But that is not his point.

His point is that in the practical thinking in which we all have engaged since the dawn of our moral life, there is embedded a grasp of first indemonstrable self-evident propositions, which St. Thomas calls natural law precepts. One can grasp those precepts without knowing what is meant by "indemonstrable," "self-evident," or any of the other important theoretical terms of the account. But the question Finnis raises for us is this. *Is that pre-philosophical grasp of first practical principles independent of our knowledge of brute facts about the world?* If Finnis intends an affirmative answer to that question, he is simply wrong about what practical reason is and what the grasp of something as good involves. There are reasons for thinking he would answer the question affirmatively; there are some reasons for saying his answer would be negative. Whatever the case, he has directed us to a matter of crucial importance for our understanding of practical reasoning and of moral philosophy.

Knowing Something as Good

Since the speculative and practical intellects are not two faculties, but rather two ways of exercising the same power, and since being is the first thing the mind grasps, knowledge of being is presupposed by all human knowledge, whether speculative or practical. The theoretical use of the mind is primary, presupposed by the practical use. Thus, Thomas approvingly quotes Aristotle's remark that the speculative intellect becomes practical by extension: "Intellectus speculativus per extensionem fit practicus" (*ST,* Ia, q.19, a.11, sed contra). If it is as being that we think of whatever we think, it is as good that we think of things that can become the objects of activities other than thinking. Put most abstractly, this means that it is some being or other that is thought of as good. "Bonum addit rationem appetibilis supra ens, ita et verum comparationem ad intellectum: good adds the note of desirability to being just as true adds [to being] a relation to mind" (*ST,* Ia, q.16, a.3).

These observations are not meant to bear on the theory of the transcendental properties of being, but on the knowledge any human person can be expected to have. Of course, it is quite particular things that we know as being, just as we judge particular kinds of things to be desirable. When something is grasped as good, it is grasped as something and as perfective or fulfilling of us in some way. Such a judgment has embedded in it knowledge of the thing itself and of ourselves. Needless to say, this is not a full-blown and generalized knowledge either of things or self, but it is nonetheless theoretical and presupposed by what may be called the practical judgment that *this* is good for *me*. Such theoretical knowledge is confused, vague, and susceptible to all but endless refinement and addition, but it is for all that theoretical, it is knowledge of nature, a grasp of facts. *The judgment that something is good presupposes and depends upon theoretical knowledge of the thing judged to be good and of the one for whom it is judged to be good.* Far from being a fallacy, an erratic boulder, a vitiating element, the dependence of the judgment that "X is good" on some theoretical knowledge of X, is all but definitionally true. This is the sense of the insistence that evaluative judgments are based upon nature and knowledge of nature. Far from being a theory, this is an inescapable feature of any appraisal of something as good. There has to be some value or interpretation of the variable X in "X is good," for the judgment to say anything. It is difficult to imagine Finnis and friends dissenting from this. It is because, at the least, they seem to dissent from it, that they have been the object of so much criticism.

10. Ethics and Metaphysics

O NE OF the dangers of aggiornamento is that an ancient doctrine can become obscured in the effort to present it anew. Natural law morality is an essential part of our intellectual patrimony and is as relevant to men today as ever it was to men in the past. Nonetheless, our contemporaries have so many misconceptions of and prejudices against natural law that it is no easy thing to win a fair hearing for it. Despite this, there have been several noteworthy recent efforts to make natural law morality a serious contender in philosophical discussions.

The obstacles to the success of such an enterprise are formidable. There is general skepticism about moral absolutes. There is a continuing tendency to think moral judgments are emotive rather than cognitive. And there is the notion, derived from many historical sources, that the practical realm is and must logically be autonomous. This is without doubt the greatest prejudice against natural law morality.

The very term "natural law morality" suggests that in determining what we ought to do, we must take our guide from nature, and it is that suggestion that is anathema to many. The suggested procedure is taken to be an obvious violation of the logical rule that nothing can appear in the conclusion of an argument that is unsupported by its premises. But, Hume objected, moral philosophers seem constantly to be telling us what we ought to do on the basis of a number of observations of what is the case. Such transitions from "is" to "ought" constitute the naturalistic fallacy. Critics of natural law morality have summarized their objections to it with the observation that it commits the naturalistic fallacy.

Now if, in the atmosphere of this criticism, one wished to give a persuasive restatement of natural law morality, it would clearly be impossible to ignore the so-called naturalistic fallacy. But what happens when natural law morality is presented as innocent of the charge of committing the fallacy in question? Despite appearances, the argument would go, St. Thomas does not make the illicit transition from "is" to "ought." From this a number of other surprising claims would follow. We might expect to hear that the practical is pretty much independent of the speculative or theoretical order. Even more oddly, the claim might be made that no appeal to metaphysical theories of human nature are necessary to determine what is the good for man.

Other oddities might follow, but these suffice to show how a theory can get lost or distorted in the effort to commend it to the contemporary world. I do not intend just now to enter into a discussion of these updating efforts. Rather, I want here to recall some features of the dependence of the practical on the theoretical, paying particular attention to texts of St. Thomas which have been, mistakenly as I think, employed to suggest that Thomas himself taught the autonomy of the practical, at least in his more lucid moments.

The Four Orders

A passage that has received a good deal of attention is that found at the very outset of St. Thomas's commentary on the *Nicomachean Ethics*. The commentary begins with a little proem and, as is his wont, St. Thomas swings it around an adage, in this case, Aristotle's remark in the *Metaphysics* that it is the mark of the wise man to order: *sapientis est ordinare*.

The ability to see how things are ordered to one another and not simply to know them one by one is the mark of reason's difference from mere perception. But there is a twofold order in things, first, of parts of a whole or multitude to one another, second, the order of things to an end. The second order is the higher of the two, Thomas continues, because the order of the parts of a whole to one another is for the sake of the order of the whole to its end. (Cf. St. Thomas's commentary on Aristotle's *Nicoma-chean Ethics,* Bk. I, lectio 1 [ed. Spiazzi], n. 1.)

Order, the text continues, relates to reason in a fourfold way.

(1) Est enim quidam ordo quem ratio non facit, sed solum considerat, sicut est ordo rerum naturalium. (2) Alius est ordo, quem ratio considerando facit in proprio actu, puta cum ordinat conceptus suos adinvicem, et signa conceptuum, quia sunt voces significativae. (3) Tertius autem est ordo quem ratio considerando facit in operationibus voluntatis. (4) Quartus autem est ordo quem ratio considerando facit in exterioribus rebus, quarum ipsa est causa, sicut in arca et domo.

(1) There is a certain order that reason does not construct but only considers, such as the order of natural objects. (2) There is another order which reason introduces by considering its own activity, as when it relates concepts among themselves and the signs of concepts which are signifying sounds. (3) Third is the order reason introduces into acts of the will. (4) Fourth is the order reason imposes on external things of which it is the cause, as in a chest or house.

Reason is variously perfected by habits as it considers these different orders, habits which generate different sciences or disciplines. Thus natural philosophy will consider the first kind of order, the order that we discover but do not construct. "Natural philosophy" here stands for the whole range of speculative science, physics, mathematics, and metaphysics, as St. Thomas makes explicit.

Logic or rational philosophy considers the second kind of order, that which reason establishes within its own activity as it considers the order in things; the concern of logic is with the order of parts of discourse among themselves, predicate to subject, conclusion to premises, and so forth.

As for the order of voluntary acts, the third kind of order, that is the concern of moral philosophy.

The fourth kind of order, that constituted by reason in external things, pertains to the mechanical arts.

Now, in the context, all this is meant to clarify the nature of moral philosophy whose proper task it is to consider "human operations insofar as they are ordered to one another and to the end." And what are human operations? Those which issue from will as ordered by reason. "Dico autem *operationes humanas,* quae procedunt a voluntate hominis secundum ordinem rationis: I call human activities those which emanate from man's will under the direction of reason" (ibid., n.3). Many activities or operations which are found in human beings are not subject to reason and will; these are natural rather than properly human activities. For example, "Socrates digests," truly ascribes an activity to Socrates, but it is not one that is subject to his reason and will. As such, it is of no interest to moral philosophy. What then is the subject of moral philosophy? Well, just as either motion or mobile being can be given as the subject of natural philosophy, so the subject of moral philosophy is either human activity ordered to an end or man insofar as he acts voluntarily for an end. "Sicut autem subiectum philosophiae naturalis est motus vel res mobilis, ita subjectum moralis philosophiae est operatio humana ordinata in finem, vel etiam homo prout est voluntarie agens propter finem" (ibid., n.3).

This text is often cited as proof that St. Thomas taught the autonomy of ethics and of practical intellect. The *ordo rerum,* the order of things we discover and do not construct, is fundamentally different from the three other orders which are in their various ways products of man. Whether this text can be used to justify calling ethics autonomous, independent of the *ordo rerum,* is another matter.

Are the second and fourth orders autonomous and independent of the real order, the order of nature? There are indeed those who claim that logic is simply neutral with respect to reality, that it is autonomous and antecedent to what is naturally given. Indeed, so prevalent is the view of the autonomy of logic nowadays that to maintain the opposite can seem quirky and odd. (Cf. Stephen Theron, "Does Realism Make a Difference to Logic?" in *The Monist* 69, no. 2 [April 1986], pp. 281–94). Nonetheless, it would be unwise to cater to the contemporary prejudice in giving an account of the Thomistic doctrine that logic is concerned with second intentions. That second intentions are distinguished from first intentions is true enough, but any attempt to explain the former without reference to the latter will surely fail. Thus, in the case of the logical order, its distinction from the real order does not seem a basis for asserting its autonomy or independence.

As for the fourth order, the order imposed on natural things by the artisan, nothing is more familiar than the Thomistic (and Aristotelian) distinction between the natural and the artificial. But this distinction, whether we are thinking of the mechanical arts or the fine arts, is consistent with the maxim that art imitates nature. The artisan must know the nature of the materials with which he works if he is to succeed at his craft. It would be odd indeed to portray Thomas's views of the artistic order as autonomous and wholly independent of the real order.

This being so, the text suggests a similar caution with regard to the implications of the distinction between the order introduced by reason into our voluntary acts, on the one hand, and the *ordo rerum*, on the other. Indeed, in the moral order, the end is given by nature, St. Thomas will say, and the moral task is to find appropriate means to achieving that end.

This text from the commentary on the *Ethics*, then, can scarcely be read as providing an unequivocal basis for maintaining the autonomy and independence of the ethical. Rather, the third order, like the second and fourth, is distinguished without being separated from the first.

A Precision

If someone were to understand the claim that the moral order reposes on the natural order, that ethics presupposes natural philosophy (in the broad sense that includes metaphysics as well), as meaning that anyone, in order to know what he ought to do or be, must first become a metaphysician, he would be right to dismiss the claim as fantastic.

So let us be precise. Moral knowledge does not presuppose knowledge of metaphysics or indeed of any theoretical science. Insofar as moral philosophy is a theory about moral knowledge, a theory which presupposes that the learner already knows a thing or two about what he ought to do, moral philosophy is not presupposed to moral knowledge.

This is a particular instance of a wider point. For St. Thomas and

Aristotle, knowledge does not begin with the study of philosophy. The study of philosophy presupposes that we already know some things for sure. Obvious, of course, but sometimes the obvious bears stating.

No more should the "theory" of natural law, the kind of account we find in the *Prima secundae* of the *Summa theologiae,* be taken to be what anyone is said already to know about what he ought to do. If we have in mind the content of natural law, the truths which constitute it, then not only is knowledge of it possible without metaphysics, knowledge of it is possible without ethics or moral philosophy.

This is not tantamount to saying, however, that moral knowledge is independent of knowledge of the way things are. When any human agent, independently of moral theory or philosophical reflection, knows what is good for him, this knowledge entails knowledge of the sort of agent he is. Practical knowledge is always an extension of theoretical knowledge.

An Imagined Riposte

One who champions the autonomy and independence of ethics from theoretical knowledge may welcome what I have said and suggest that it actually establishes the point he wants to make. His point, remember, is the Humean one that "ought" cannot be derived from "is." Whatever else may be said of the relation of the logical order to the *ordo rerum,* he will say, it cannot be said that the former is deduced from the latter. Logical principles are not conclusions of arguments whose premises are truths about the natural world.

To this retort, two things should be said. In the first place, the desire to show that natural law does not commit the naturalistic fallacy has led some to speak quite generally and broadly about the independence and autonomy of the ethical. When this claim for autonomy is questioned, there is retreat to the narrower claim and the talk turns again to deduction. The "ought" cannot be *deduced* from the "is." But who prior to Hume spoke in terms of deduction? Perhaps the original mistake was to assume that Hume's criticism had a target in traditional moral philosophy. The appropriate response to the charge of naturalistic fallacy is to take a close look at the nature of the supposed fallacy as well as at the claim that it is widely committed in traditional moral philosophy.

The second thing is to examine the nature of the dependence of the logical order on the natural order. An obvious place to begin is at the beginning. Consider the following:

a. It is impossible for a thing to be and not to be at the same time and in the same respect.

b. It is impossible to affirm and deny the same thing at the same time.

c. It is impossible for a judgment to be both true and false at the same time.

These are three different expressions of the so-called principle of contradiction. We can call (a) a metaphysical or ontological expression of the principle, (b) the logical expression of it, and (c) the epistemological expression. All three can be said to be *per se nota* in the sense of nongainsayable. But is there no order among them, no prior and posterior?

"Evidently then such a principle is the most certain of all: which principle this is, let us proceed to say. It is, that the same attribute cannot at the same time belong and not belong to the same subject and in the same respect; we must presuppose, to guard against dialectical objections, any further qualifications which might be added. This, then, is the most certain of all principles, since it answers to the definition given above. For it is impossible for any one to believe the same thing to be and not to be, as some think Heraclitus says. For what a man says, he does not necessarily believe; and if it is impossible that contrary attributes should belong at the same time to the same subject (the usual qualifications must be presupposed in this premiss too), and if an opinion which contradicts another is contrary to it, obviously it is impossible for the same man at the same time to believe the same thing to be and not to be; for if a man were mistaken on this point, he would have contrary opinions at the same time. It is for this reason that all who are carrying out a demonstration reduce it to this as an ultimate belief; for this is naturally the starting point even for all the other axioms" (*Metaphysics,* IV.3 1005b17ff.). Note, parenthetically, the very last remark. Axioms, that is, *per se nota principia,* have this principle for their starting point. For their principle?

But notice the text itself. There are three different principles or three different expressions of the same principle:

(1) The same attribute cannot at the same time belong and not belong to the same subject in the same respect.

(2) It is impossible for anyone to believe the same thing to be and not to be.

(3) It is impossible for the same thing to be and not to be.

In Chapter 4 of Book Four, the principle at issue is stated as "it is not possible for anything at the same time to be and not to be." And the *reductio* offered on its behalf suggests:

(4) "Man" cannot mean the same thing as "Not man."

(5) Contradictory statements cannot be simultaneously true.

Is the principle of contradiction an ontological principle or a logical principle? "p.v.~p" and "~(p.~p)" are commonly called logical truths. By this is meant that they are true in virtue of their logical form, as opposed to "p.v.q," which will be true or false depending on the truth or falsity of the values of its variables—truth tables being constructed to determine that only when both p and q are false is the disjunction false.

What does "true" mean here? Is it not derivative of such uses as "It is true to say that snow is white, because snow is white"?

The logical principle of contradiction presupposes and in a way is a special instance of the ontological principle of contradiction. How should we express the dependence involved in (a), (b), and (c) above? It is because the states of affairs expressed by contradictory judgments cannot simultaneously obtain or exist that contradictories cannot be simultaneously true, and we cannot think them to be simultaneously true.

In the light of such considerations, it can be appreciated that any claim that logic is an autonomous realm, independent of the *ordo rerum,* a claim analogous to that relating to the autonomy and independence of ethics, must be viewed as very strange indeed.

The Primacy of the Practical

In commenting on this text of the *Metaphysics,* St. Thomas casts light on the relation between the various expressions of the first principle. In *lectio* 6 of his commentary on Book Four, he dwells on the three characteristics of the starting point of knowledge, namely, that no one can be mistaken about it, that it not be conditional, and that it not be acquired through demonstration. He goes on, "sed adveniat quasi per naturam habenti ipsum, quasi ut naturaliter cognoscatur, et non per acquisitionem: but it comes to the one having it as if by nature and not by learning" (*lectio* 6, n. 599). He has adverted, in the previous lesson, to Boethius's distinction between propositions self-evident to all and propositions self-evident only to the wise, and notes that the first principles of demonstration must be of the former kind. Thus, they will involve words and concepts no one can fail to know, and their truth will be seen straight off as a consequence of the meaning of their constituent terms. "Determinat autem ea philosophus non demonstrando, sed rationes terminorum tradendo, ut quid totum et quid pars et sic de aliis. Hoc autem cognito, veritas praedictorum principiorum manifesta relinquitur: The philosopher establishes these, not by demonstrating them, but by discussing the meaning of their terms, as what is a whole, a part, and the like. These being known, the truth of the foregoing principles is manifest" (n. 595). In *lectio* 6, he describes the process whereby the meanings are grasped. "Quod quidem fit per hoc, quod a sensibilibus accipitur memoria et a memoria experiment[or]um et ab experimento illorum terminorum cognitio, quibus cognitis cognoscuntur huiusmodi propositiones communes, quae sunt artium et scientiarum principia: It comes about like this: from sensible things memory arises, and from memory experience, and from experience the knowledge of those terms, which [terms] being known, common propositions of the kind in question, which are the principles of the arts and sciences, are known" (n. 599).

Then, still discussing the fact that such principles are not acquired or proved, St. Thomas proceeds in a way reminiscent of *ST* IaIIae, q.94, a.2.

Ad huius autem evidentiam sciendum est quod, cum duplex sit operatio intellectus: una, qua cognoscit quod quid est, quae vocatur indivisibilium intelligentia: alia, qua componit et dividit: in utroque est aliquod primum: in prima quidem operatione est aliquod primum, quod cadit in conceptione intellectus, scilicet hoc quod dico ens; nec aliquid hac operatione potest mente concipi, nisi intelligatur ens. Et quia hoc principium, impossibile est esse et non esse simul, dependent ex intellectu entis, sicut hoc principium, omne totus est maius sua parte, ex intellectu totius et partis: ideo hoc etiam principium est naturaliter primum in secunda operatione intellectus, scilicet componentis et dividentis. (n. 605)

To grasp this we need to know that there is a twofold operation of the intellect, one whereby it knows what is, which is called the understanding of simple things, another whereby it composes and divides. In both of these there is something primary, for in the first operation there is something first that occurs in the intellect's conception, namely, what I call being; nor can anything be grasped by the mind in this activity without being's being understood. Since the principle, "it is impossible for something to be and not to be simultaneously," presupposes the understanding of being, much as "every whole is greater than its part," presuppose an understanding of whole and part, this principle is naturally first in the second operation of the mind, namely, composing and dividing.

Now, it is interesting that Thomas should illustrate the first principle by appealing to "Every whole is greater than its part," but he is not through with the comparison. If "It is impossible for something to be and not to be simultaneously" is the very first principle, it is presupposed by such self-evident principles as "Every whole is greater than its part." To understand the latter, is to understand the former. "Sicut enim totum et partes non intelliguntur nisi intellecto ente, ita nec hoc principium omne totum est maius sua parte, nisi intellecto praedicto principio firmissimo: Just as whole and parts are not understood without being's being understood, so the principle that every whole is greater than its part [is not understood] unless the foregoing most firm principle is understood" (n.

605). The sense is clear. Even the grasp of other self-evident principles depends on a grasp of the very first principle. Self-evidence, then, is not equivalent to total independence, lack of presupposition, etc.

But what of the relation between the propositions we enumerated earlier? St. Thomas gives us this remarkable statement of it.

Ex hoc enim quod impossibile est esse et non esse, sequitur quod impossibile sit contraria simul inesse eidem. . . . Et ex hoc quod contraria non possunt simul inesse, sequitur quod homo non possit habere contrarias opiniones, et per consequens quod non possit opinari contradictoria esse vera . . . (n. 606)	From the fact that it is impossible for a thing to be and not to be, it follows that it is impossible for contraries to be in the same subject simultaneously . . . and from the fact that contraries cannot simultaneously inhere in the same subject, it follows that a man cannot hold contrary opinions, and consequently that contradictories cannot be thought to be true . . .

Sequitur occurs twice and *per consequens* once in this brief passage. But what sort of "following" or "consequence" is meant? In the very next paragraph, St. Thomas takes up Aristotle's remark that it is an error to try to demonstrate the first principle.

There is, however, a way to defend the first principle and in a certain way to demonstrate it, and that is by an elenchus, by showing that a rejection of it is self-refuting. Aristotle will concentrate on the statement itself that purports to reject the first principle and point out that in order to be intelligible, the words in it cannot mean both a thing and its opposite.

But of course the point of the last quoted passage is not to show that the first principle follows from something or other, but rather to say that other things follow from it:

i. Impossibile est esse et non esse simul.
ii. Impossibile sit contraria simul inesse eidem.
iii. Homo non possit habere contrarias opiniones.
iv. Non possit opinari contradictoria esse vera.

[iv] is said to follow from [iii], which follows from [ii], which in its turn follows from [i].

Such considerations lead to a single conclusion. For St. Thomas, the logical order is not independent of the *ordo rerum*. For all that, one would not expect the rule of the syllogism to be demonstrated from truths about the natural order. Does this leave the position we are criticizing untouched? Hardly. The so-called naturalistic fallacy was used as the reason for asserting the autonomy of the precepts of natural law. How could they be derived from anything else if they are self-evident principles, it was asked. But the kind of "following" involved, although it is not that of demonstration, is far more immediate.

Good and Being

"Sicut autem ens est primum quod cadit in apprehensione simplicter, ita bonum est primum quod cadit in apprehensione practicae rationis: Just as being is the first thing that occurs to intellect as such, so the good is the first thing grasped by practical reason" (IaIIae, q.94, a.2). If the theoretical and practical orders were as unrelated as is sometimes suggested, and if *ens* stands at the head of the one order, and *bonum* at the head of the other, there should be a corresponding lack of relation between being and good. Is this what St. Thomas teaches?

In the *Q.D. de veritate,* q.1, a.1, after recalling the familiar doctrine that being is the first thing the mind grasps, St. Thomas goes on: "Unde oportet quod omnes aliae conceptiones intellectus accipiantur ex additione ad ens: Hence all other conceptions of the intellect must be taken as adding to being." The concept of good is among those others, so good must presuppose yet add to being in some way. He goes on to discuss the various ways in which other notions add to the notion of being; a similar discussion is to be found in *Q.D. de veritate,* q.21. In the first question, he is chiefly concerned with the way in which "true" adds to "being"; in the later discussion, his concern is the way in which "good" adds to "being."

There is a threefold way, we are told, in which such additions can come about: (a) an accident adds to substance something not contained in its essence or definition; (b) a species adds to its genus by contracting and determining it, so that the genus becomes a part of its definition; (c) a privation adds to our understanding of a thing without adding to the reality of the thing. For example, when we add blind to man, we are drawing attention to a lack, not an addition, in the real order. The addition, then, is in the order of understanding, not in the order of being.

It is this third kind of addition that Thomas employs to speak of the way good and true add to being. Nothing can be added to universal being as an accident, since the accident too would fall under being. Universal being can be subject to the second sort of addition, however, as when it is divided into substance and accidents. But good is not a category or type of being; rather it seems to have the range of being itself. This should not be taken to mean that "good" and "being" are synonymous; it is not pointless to say that being is good. "Et sic oportet quod bonum, ex quo non contrahit ens, addat aliquid super ens, quod sit rationis tantum: So it must be that the good, in that it contracts being, adds something to being which is of reason alone" (*Q.D. de veritate,* q.21, a.1). "One" adds to being the negation of division, but "true" and "good" signify positively, and both add a relation to the understanding of being. "Illa autem relatio, secundum Philosophum in V Meta, dicitur esse rationis tantum, secundum quam dicitur referri id quod non dependet ad id ad quod refertur, sed e converso, cum ipsa relatio quaedam dependentia sit, sicut patet scientia et scibili, sensi et senisibili; scientia enim dependet a scibili, sed non e converso: unde relatio qua scientia refertur ad scibile est realis; relatiom vero qua scibile refertur ad scientiam est rationis tantum: That relation, according to Aristotle in *Metaphysics* V, is said to be of reason alone, insofar as something is said to be relative to something on which it does not depend, but rather the reverse, since relation itself is a kind of dependence, as is clear from knowledge and knowable, sense and sensible, for knowledge depends on the knowable, but not conversely, hence the relation whereby knowledge is related to the knowable is real, whereas the relation whereby the knowable is related to knowledge is of reason alone" (ibid.). Something is called true because it is conformed or conformable to mind, but this relation to mind is not a real relation.

Alio modo ens est perfectivum alterius non solum secundum rationem
speciei, sed etiam secundum esse
quod habet in rerum natura: et per
hunc modum est perfectivum bonum;
bonum enim in rebus est. . . . In
quantum autem unum ens est secundum esse suum perfectivum alterius
et conservativum, habet rationem finis
respectu illius quod ab eo perficitur
. . . (ibid.)

Secondly being is perfective of another not only with respect to the
grasp of its species, but also with respect to real existence, and in this way
good is perfective, for the good is in
things. . . . Insofar as one being is perfective and conservative of the existence of another, it has the notion of
end with respect to what it perfects . . .

The upshot of all this, put concisely, is that "bonum rationem entis includat: good includes the understanding of being" (ibid., a.2, c.). Furthermore, any *per se notum* principle other than the first presupposes the first. Thus it is that the practical order depends upon and presupposes the theoretical order.

Concluding

So, too, a discussion of the nature of art would exhibit the analogous way in which the artificial presupposes the natural and is inconceivable apart from it. *Ars imitatur naturam.* The conclusion seems obvious. The text in St. Thomas's commentary on the *Ethics* to which appeal has been made to show the autonomy and independence of the moral order, actually makes a far different point.

11. Natural Law and Natural Rights

ALTHOUGH historically the theory of natural rights was elaborated as a conscious alternative to the metaphysical presuppositions of natural law theory, there have been attempts from the side of natural lawyers to effect a marriage between the two.

Maritain on Human Rights

One of the most striking chapters of Jacques Maritain's *Man and the State* is the fourth, entitled "The Rights of Man." Here Maritain, writing in 1949, in the wake of the 1948 International Declaration of Human Rights, puts forward what may seem to be a version of the conversation I described at the end of my first chapter. Section one of Maritain's chapter four is headed by a thesis: "Men mutually opposed in their theoretical conceptions can come to a merely practical agreement regarding a list of human rights."[1] It is Maritain's view that the historical development of mankind has reached a point where moral conscience and reflection have become aware, more fully than before "though still imperfectly, of a number of practical truths regarding their life in common upon which they can agree." Proof of this is found in the 1948 Declaration of Human Rights, about which Maritain says (1) that the rights stated amount to *practical conclusions* and (2) that they are derived from ideologies, philosophical or religious traditions, theoretical conceptions which are "ex-

1. Jacques Maritain, *Man and the State* (Chicago: University of Chicago Press, 1951), p. 76.

tremely different or even basically opposed." Looking over all the human rights declared in the 1948 document, Maritain observes:

> It would be quite futile to look for a common *rational justification* of these practical conclusions and these rights. If we did so, we would run the risk of arbitrary dogmatism or of being stopped short by irreconcilable differences. The question raised at this point is that of the practical agreement among men who are theoretically opposed to one another. (p. 76)

It may occur to us to think that the diversity and opposition Maritain saw in international terms could now be verified within the boundaries of our own country. Despite the seemingly irreconcilable philosophical or theoretical differences among Americans, there is a general tendency to make lists of rights, and not infrequently such lists overlap. Group A will justify rights claims in one way, Group B in another, but both agree that certain rights have to be recognized. Maritain sees here the paradox that "rational justifications are *indispensable* and at the same time *powerless* to create agreement among men" (p. 77). Paradox indeed.

> They are indispensable, because each of us believes instinctively in truth and only wishes to give his consent to what he has recognized as true and rationally valid. Yet rational justifications are powerless to create agreement among men, because they are basically different, even opposed to each other; and is this surprising? The problems raised by rational justifications are difficult, and the philosophical traditions in which those justifications originate have been in opposition for a long time.[2]

Where agreement on their rational justification is practically impossible, it is still possible to agree on a list of rights which are practical conclusions from the theories, justifications, and ideologies whose diversity is simply acknowledged.

2. Ibid., p. 77. I am going to interpret the *powerlessness* to be merely accidental, not a feature of rational justification as such. Maritain can recognize the *de facto* pluralism of philosophical accounts without for all that relativizing the search for truth. I take him to mean that the conversation that could issue in agreement of rational justification will be so prolonged and arduous that the practical order cannot await its outcome.

Maritain was a member of the French delegation to UNESCO that produced the universal declaration. He quotes a fellow delegate as saying that they will be able to agree on a list of rights, *provided we are not asked why*. With the raising of the question why, disputes begin.

The interest of Maritain's discussion of the thesis with which his fourth chapter begins lies in what is clearly his attempt to provide, from his own philosophical outlook, a rational justification not only of the list of human rights, but also of the possibility of agreement on them by signatories who would give radically different rational justifications. If he is successful, he will have accounted, from within his own theory, for a practical agreement on human rights even with those who reject his theory. When he describes the agreement as constituting "*grosso modo* a sort of common residue, a sort of unwritten common law, at the point of practical convergence of extremely different theoretical ideologies and spiritual traditions" (p. 78), he would seem to be offering a rational justification of the *de facto* agreement about the list of human rights on the part of those whose theories would not let them accept his justification of the rights or of their agreement to them.

This seems to be a version of what I was suggesting in my first chapter. If we distinguish, as we must, between the theory of natural law and that of which it is the theory, then we see that natural law can be held before the theory and independently of the theory, even the Thomistic theory. But, if the Thomistic theory is true, natural law will be held even by those who reject all theories of natural law, who reject any and all kinds of moral realism and embrace emotivism. Maritain can be taken to be saying, then, that the Declaration of Human Rights is a proof of this: embedded in everyone's practical knowledge are certain truths, and they have bubbled to the surface in the declaration, despite the wild and various theoretical constructs that might be brought forward to justify them.

Despite this apparent similarity, it must be noticed that Maritain is speaking of a list of rights. Whether we have in mind the 1948 declaration or the more modest one of 1789, the rhetoric is distinctly different from that of any list of natural law precepts.

Man is free to do anything that does not harm others, and he can only be restrained in the exercise of this right to the degree that he prevents others from exercising the same right.

Man has a right to the free expression of his opinions.

The Bill of Rights—the first ten amendments to the Constitution—are clearly claims a citizen can make against the encroachment of the state.

The 1948 list is positively luxuriant by comparison to the eighteenth-century list. Moreover, if it were to be read now, I think it would be seen to be highly controversial, because of its adoption of what might nowadays be dismissed as "traditional understanding of gender roles" and of the nature of the family.[3]

Of course Maritain was aware that talk of natural rights is not at all identical to talk of natural law. How are they related? "The philosophical foundation of Rights of man is Natural Law" (p. 80). He invokes Heinrich Rommen in support of the view that the history of the rights of man is bound to the history of natural law, so much so that when natural law was discredited, human rights suffered.[4] Nonetheless, Maritain suggests that Natural Rights arose from a very rationalist conception of natural law.[5] He notices that natural law came to be identified with the autonomy of the human will, and the rights of the human person were to be subject to no law other than that of his own will and freedom. For Kant, a person is subject to no other laws than those which, alone or jointly with others, he gives to himself.

3. E.g., Article 16.3: The family is the natural and fundamental element of society and has a right to protection by society and the state. See, too, 25.2 and 26.3 on maternity rights and parents' rights to the education of children. Of course no right to an abortion is present even in the penumbra of these 29 articles or their many subsections.

4. H. A. Rommen, *Natural Law* (St. Louis: Herder, 1947).

5. Maritain, *Man and the State*, p. 82. "Wait a little more than a century [after Pascal], and you will hear Condorcet promulgate this dogma, which at first glance seems self-evident, yet which means nothing: 'A good law should be good for everyone'—say, for man of the age of cave dwellers as well as for man of the age of the steam engine, for nomadic tribes as well as for agricultural peoples—'a good law should be good for everyone, just as a true proposition is true for everyone.'"

Thus, at one and the same time, Maritain sees lists of natural rights as practical conclusions with which he as a Thomist can be in agreement, while at the same time criticizing the theories out of which modern talk of natural rights came. Despite this suspect provenance, Maritain sets out to ground a true doctrine or philosophy of the rights of the human person in a true idea of natural law. But the actual historical relation is somewhat dubious.

I have said that natural law is unwritten law: it is unwritten law in the deepest sense of that expression, because our knowledge of it is no work of free conceptualization, but results from a conceptualization *bound* to the essential inclinations of being, of living nature, and of reason, which are at work in man, and because it develops in proportion to the degree of moral experience and self-reflection, and of social experience also, of which man is capable in the various ages of history. Thus it is that in ancient and mediaeval times attention was paid, in natural law, to the *obligations* of man more than to his *rights*. The proper achievement—a great achievement indeed—of the XVIIIth Century has been to bring out in full light the *rights* of man as also required by natural law. That discovery was essentially due to a progress in moral and social experience, through which the root *inclinations* of human nature as regards the rights of the human person were set free, and consequently, *knowledge through inclination* with regard to them developed. But according to a sad law of human knowledge, that great achievement was paid for by the ideological errors, in the theoretical field, that I have stressed at the beginning. Attention even shifted from the obligations of man to his rights only. A genuine and comprehensive view would pay attention *both* to the obligations and the rights involved in the requirements of natural law.[6]

The short form of the relation Maritain sees is simply this: the same natural law that lays down our obligations assigns us our fundamental rights. Perhaps this could be taken to mean that we have a right to whatever is necessary to do what we are obliged to do. If the human agent must pursue

6. Ibid., p. 94. I do not at all agree with Maritain that Thomas's teaching that the goods constitutive of man's integral good, since they are grasped as the ends of natural inclinations, are known *per inclinationem* in the sense Maritain associates with the phrase, the sense of knowledge through affective connaturality. He proposes this on p. 91.

goods personally, that is freely, he must have a right to freedom. Or: rights are correlatives of obligations.

Ius naturale vs. Lex naturalis

Maritain discusses the relationship between natural law and natural rights by considering the former to be historically antecedent to the latter. Thus the problem is one of comparing modernity with medieval and classical conceptions. This does not take into account the fact that we find in St. Thomas a discussion of *ius naturale,* which is not simply reducible to his discussion of *lex naturalis.* Scholars such as Michel Villey have argued that Thomas's *ius naturale* derives from a notion in Roman law and that both differ from later and modern conceptions of natural right.[7] To say that Villey is skeptical of modern human rights would be an understatement. This skepticism is shared by Alasdair MacIntyre.

A barefoot statement of the basis for such skepticism would use one of Maritain's remarks that the theory at least of human rights so exalts the individual that he becomes a law unto himself, such that the only obedience required is obedience to himself. Now if we consider the view of the human agent that seems in play in human rights talk, say in contractarian schemes, namely, of ontological atoms who enter into political covenants to make claims on the state and on their fellow citizens, such that law is largely the orchestration of these rights claims by autonomous individuals— skepticism begins with the observation that there are no individuals of the kind required for rights theories.

Human rights repose on a view of human nature abstracted from all genetic and social links and subsisting in atomic units. But moral agents live in communities and have no moral language independent of communities or moral traditions. So, if natural human rights require for their underpinning a false conception of man, then there are no natural human rights. Something like that is the MacIntyre and/or communitarian cri-

---

7. Most recently in Michel Villey, *Le Droit et Les Droits de l'Homme* (Presses Universitaires de France, 1983), and *Questions de Saint Thomas sur le Droit et la Politique* (PUF, 1987).

tique of human rights. The upshot is that rights and all other moral language are bound to traditions or communities, there are many traditions or communities, there are no universally common human rights.

Presumably the classical conception of *ius naturale* does not repose on such a false view of man. What I want to do in the remainder of this chapter is: sketch the classical conception of *ius naturale,* as we find it in Thomas; ask how *ius naturale* in this sense relates to Thomas's conception of *lex naturalis*; return briefly to the question of the relation between classical *ius naturale* and modern natural right.

Ius naturale

The treatise on law, which includes the discussion of natural law, is found in the *Prima secundae* of the *Summa theologiae.* In the *Secunda secundae,* we find the treatise on justice, and it begins with Question 57, *De iure*: Concerning the right. The Latin word is *ius, iurem, iure,* and its nominative form indicates its link with justice—*ius/ iustitia.* What does Thomas talk about in Question 57? The question is articulated into four subquestions:

1. *utrum ius sit obiectum iustitiae*: whether the right is the object of justice.

2. *utrum ius convenienter dividatur in ius naturale et positivum*: whether the right is properly distinguished into natural and positive right.

3. *utrum ius gentium sit ius naturale*: whether the right of nations is natural right.

4. *utrum ius dominativum et paternum debeat specialiter distingui*: whether the ruling and paternal right should be recognized as distinct types.

The first article asks whether the concern of justice is the right, and the modern reader could easily take this to mean that it is the role of justice to preserve human or natural rights. But would that be a reading or a misreading?

The virtue of justice perfects those acts in which one person is related to others, and it connotes equality. When we speak of justified margins in a printout we mean that the right and left margins are equal, or that each end of the line is equal with the margin. Justice seeks to bring about equality between persons. If justice perfects our acts as they relate to others, the other virtues perfect the person only in what refers to himself.

Sic igitur illud quod est rectum in operibus aliarum virtutum, ad quod tendit intentio virtutis quasi in proprium obiectum, non accipitur nisi per comparationem ad agentem. Rectum vero quod est in opere iustitiae, etiam praeter comparationem ad agentem, constituitur per comparationem ad alium: illud enim in opere nostro dicitur esse iustum quod respondet secundum aliquam aequalitatem alteri, puta recompensatio mercedis debitae pro servitio impenso. (IIaIIae, q.57, a.1, c)	That is why correctness in the works of the other virtues, the correctness to which the virtue tends as to its proper object, is read with reference to the agent. But the correct in the work of justice, besides reference to the agent, is constituted by reference to the other: that is called right in what we do, which answers to some equality with the other, for example, the payment of money owed for service rendered.

Michel Villey insists that we cannot understand Thomas here unless we see that he is taking the Roman jurists as his guide. The right or *ius* is a relation or proportion among things, equalizing them, and it is the task of justice to establish this. The *ius* is the correct proportion between work and payment for it. This is what Aristotle calls *to dikaion,* the just—the neuter noun refers to an object, the just thing, not to the agent (*dikaios*), not to the just action: agent and action are just derivitively from the just object, the right proportion between things.

In Aristotle, and in Roman law, Villey observes, the *ius* to be established had to do with an adjustment among things—work/pay, a property boundary, an injury and a recompense. By and large, it had to do with material things or things that could be adjusted and compared as material things can be compared.

Ius, sive iustum, est aliquod opus adaequatum alteri secundum aliquem aequalitatis modum. Dupliciter autem	The right (*ius*) or the just is a certain work adequated to another in some manner of equality. But there are two

potest alicui homini aliquid esse adaequatum. Uno quidem modo, ex ipsa
natura rei: puta cum aliquis tantum
dat ut tantundem recipiat. Et hoc vocatur ius naturale. —Alio modo aliquid est adaequatum vel
commensuratum alteri ex condicto,
sive ex communi placito: quando scilicet aliquis reputat se contentum si
tantum accipiat. Quod quidem potest
fieri dupliciter. Uno modo, per aliquod privatum condictum: sicut quod
firmatur aliquo pacto inter privatas
personas. Alio modo, ex condicto
publico: puta cum totus populus con-
sentit quod aliquid habeatur quasi
adaequatum et commensuratam alteri; vel cum hoc ordinat princeps,
qui curam populum habet et eius
personam gerit. Et hoc dicitur ius
positivum. (IIaIIae, q.57, a.2, c)

ways in which something can be adequated to some man. In one way, by
the very nature of the thing: for example when someone gives so much
in order to receive such and such.
This is called the natural right (*ius
naturale*). In another way, something
is adequated or commensurated to
another by agreement or by common
consent, as when a person thinks
himself satisfied if he receives so
much. This is subdivided into two.
First, when the agreement is private,
as based on an agreement between
private persons. Second, when the
agreement is public, for example,
when the whole people agree that a
thing is held to be adequated and
commensurated with another, or
when the prince, who has care of the
people and acts in its person, orders
this. This is called positive right (*ius
positivum*).

What one notices about this discussion of the right (*ius*) with which
Thomas's treatise on justice begins is its objective as opposed to subjective
reality. Justice will look to establish an objective relation between persons
based on trade, commerce, and services. Harm to another calls for a redressing of balance, and a capital crime is one such that redressing, ad-
equation, right, can only be established by the execution of the offending
agent.

Ius naturale et lex naturalis

Law is a product of thought, of reason: it is the expression of a judgment
as to what ought to be done, what ought to be avoided, or what may be
permitted in the overt activities of members of a civil society. This is clearly
the case with "law" in the obvious sense of the term: the bills that are

written, debated, and voted on in Washington, in state capitols, in city councils, and the like. They do not just happen; they emerge, for better or worse, from the deliberations of men. Natural law involves the extension of that term "law" to some few judgments we make to guide our actions— that we should seek good and avoid evil, feed and clothe ourselves in ways fitting to our nature, reproduce ourselves responsibly, with an eye to the raising and nurturing of children, and so forth. These are the judgments that are not so much abstractly formulated as embedded in the conscious acts human agents perform; they are implicitly recognized. As inescapable assumptions of particular moral judgments, they are said to be hit upon naturally (*naturaliter*), to be consequent upon or in accordance with our nature (*secundum naturam*), and to constitute a natural law (*lex naturalis*).

What is the relation between *ius naturale* and *lex naturalis*? Are they the same thing? Law as something of reason may be an expression of *ius naturale*, and when it is, the law can be called *lex naturalis*, but the judgment can also be expressed in positive law. That the male is correlative to the female, their genders finding their meaning in coition which insures the continuation of the species, involves adequations and commensurations that will be called *iura naturalia*. The effort of the judge to insure that this natural proportion obtains is the work of justice. He is aided in his task by the fact that the natural proportion is encoded in positive law.

So natural law can be an expression of natural right. This is not to say that all natural law precepts bear on *iura naturalia* as we are discussing them here. And it is not simply that I have in mind the distinction between *ius gentium* and *ius naturale* (IaIIae, q.57, a.3). Natural law precepts can bear on what we ought to do in matters of temperance, say, and this is a virtue numbered among those which *perficiunt hominem solum in his quae ei conveniunt secundum seipsum* and are thus distinguished from justice.

In the classical tradition, as it comes to a head in Thomas Aquinas, then, we can relate *ius naturale* and *lex naturale* without equating the two.

Ius naturale and Human Rights

Perhaps the simplest way of contrasting *ius naturale* as it came out of Aristotle and Roman law, on the one hand, and modern conceptions of human rights is in terms of the contrast of objective/subjective. In the classical sense, the right was an external relation to be established between persons on the basis of things. As the object of justice, right did not exhaust the field of morality or of law, and its establishment was the result of painstaking judicial procedures. In its modern sense, right has become subjective, it attaches to the individual taken singly as an instantiation of human nature and amounts to a claim that he can make on the state or on others. We have already mentioned the proliferation of such claims. Indeed, there seems to be a good deal more than mere development. Some rights now claimed conflict with rights that show up on earlier lists. Both claim to follow with pellucid self-evidence from the most cursory reflection on human nature.

This suggests a further contrast: concrete/abstract. Which suggests another: realizable/unrealizable.

Michel Villey on Human Rights

I have already mentioned Villey, the great historian of Roman law, as skeptical concerning modern talk of human rights. In an article of 1972[8] Villey remarks that in an era of juridical positivism, the individual has no recourse against the state, and the rights of man seem our only defense. While positivism is productive of stagnation, the rights of man set forth an ideal. "Voilà pourquoi les Droits de l'Homme sont aujourd'hui necesssaires" (p. 10).

Faint praise, you will detect. Villey goes on to associate himself with Edmund Burke's criticism of the 1789 declaration of the rights of man. The critique is threefold:

First, they are *metaphysical,* by which is meant abstract, a priori, unrelated to experience. All one has to do is think of man, and rights begin to unroll. (Just as an aside, Villey sees the seeds of this in Iberian scholasticism—Francisco de Vitoria and Suárez—whereas Brian Tierney sees

---

8. Michel Villey, "Critique des Droits de l'Homme," *Anales de la catedra Francisco Suárez* no. 12, fasc. 2 (1972), pp. 9–16.

its historical roots in the adjudication of the disputes among the Franciscans.)

Next, they are not adapted to the real world, where judicial activities take place. Being inapplicable, they become illusory. Villey agrees with Burke on this too. Burke pointed out that while the declaration was being formulated, outside the decapitated heads of those condemned and put to death without due process were paraded around on the ends of pikestaffs—due process being of course a natural right. While the assembly was waxing poetic about property rights, it was appropriating the property of the rich. How can popular sovereignty and democratic government be right, when they are not everywhere applicable? Villey notes that now we speak of rights—to a job, a home, health care, on and on—that can be asserted, but that cannot be had simply on the basis of the claim. If a claim cannot be vindicated, it is empty, words, soap bubbles.

Last, they are impostures—they pretend to be universal, belonging to all. But Marx showed that the declaration of 1789 was used by the bourgeoisie to triumph over the nobles and the poor. Rights claims conflict— the rights of women collide with the rights of men, those of parents with children, on and on. Far from being universal, they are regional, quite specific.[9]

So much for the critique. Villey goes on to suggest that the classical doctrine of *ius naturale* is superior to our talk of human rights.

He reminds us that the setting in which *ius naturale* flourished recognized at least as much as we do the dignity of the person and even on a certain scale the equality of persons. Aristotle is called anti-feminist, but Villey argues that his anthropology, psychology, and morality are as applicable to women as to men. Morality was common to all human agents.

9. "Voilà pourquoi je ne suis pas un admirateur passionné du *langage* des Droits de l'Homme. Je donnerais raison à Burke, qui (entre parentheses) a *plus fait* que les revolutionnaires français de 1789, contre ces victimes de l'injustice—qu'étaient à l'époque les Americains—ou les Indiens victimes des grandes compagnies coloniales. Il avait même pris la defense des homosexuels, du moins il les a defendu contre les torturées raffinées que leur infligeait le droit penal d'alors il n'a pas fait l'apologie des 'droits' naturels des homosexuels à l'égalité avec tous."

Villey's strongest praise for classical rights talk is that it emerges from and is consonant with experience. The aim *suum ius cuique tribuere* takes us immediately into the realm of persons in the plural, not humanity or human nature. To find the proper proportion in a matter under dispute is painstaking, and it must take into account differences of circumstance, of people, of place, and so on. Things cannot be settled simply by appeal to some abstract claim that can be made indiscriminately by all as instances of humanity. In short, Villey speaks as a lawyer, and you can, perhaps, understand his impatience with windy human rights claims that do more to stir up discontent and rage than to establish justice. Nonetheless, not unlike Maritain, having said much that is critical of the theoretical context of human rights talk, he acknowledges that in what he calls an era of juridical positivism, human rights must seem necessary as claims to be made against the state.

12. The Right Deed for the Wrong Reason: Comments on Theo Belmans

THE THEORY that denies the possibility of moral absolutes based upon the nature of the deed done and instead seeks the source of all morality solely in the end for the sake of which the agent acts, the *finis operantis*, is manifestly different from the Church's moral teaching as well as from the teaching of St. Thomas Aquinas.[1] This revisionist theory, variously called proportionalism and moderate teleology, has found one of its most determined foes in Father Theo Belmans.[2] Belmans has put us all in his debt for the way in which he has brought his own broad and deep understanding of St. Thomas Aquinas to the appraisal of proportionalists as well as of the work of other Thomists. By and large, his reminders of the true meaning of the texts and his questioning of other interpretations of them have served as salutary occasions for correction or clarification. No student of St. Thomas would wish to take lightly what Father Belmans has to say about the doctrine of their common master. Nonetheless, *etiam Belmans dormitat,* and in a recent article, in the course of making an important point, our colleague gives two interpretations of Thomas which seem manifestly wrong to me. The first has to do with

1. See Brian Thomas Mullady, O.P., *The Meaning of the Term 'Moral' in St. Thomas Aquinas,* Studi Tomistici 27, Pontificia Accademia di S. Tommaso (Citta Vaticana, 1986).
2. See T. G. Belmans, *Le Sens Objectif de l'Agir Humain,* Studi Tomistici 8 (Vatican, 1980), and its German version, which includes a number of changes and improvements, *Der objektive Sinn menschlichen Handelns,* Patris Verlag Vallendar (Schönstatt, 1984).

his interpretation of the word *iudicium* in the phrase *iudicium electionis* or *iudicium liberi arbitrii* which occurs in *Q.D. de veritate,* q.17; the second has to do with attributing to Thomas the startling claim that ethical reason is autonomous. In what follows, I will examine each of these claims, but before doing so, I want to lay before the reader the overall objective Belmans has in the article in which these claims occur.[3] I could not be in greater agreement with Belmans as to the questionableness of the theory he attacks. My ultimate point will be that, in this case, some of his means of showing the position wrong are themselves faulty.

Belmans's Target

Since the appearance of his *chef-d'oeuvre,* Theo Belmans has been presenting the moral doctrine of St. Thomas Aquinas as an antidote to the reigning moral subjectivism, and nothing attracts his critical attention more surely than any suggestion that such subjectivism finds support in the teaching of Thomas. This is why his contribution to *"un authentique renouveau de la morale"*[4] has always been accompanied by severe criticisms of those whose interpretations of Thomas contribute, however remotely, to what he sees as the continuing deleterious influences of existentialism and situation ethics on Catholic moral theology. Presented schematically, here is the target of Belmans's critique. Very early on, in his analysis of the human act, Thomas asks if an act is the kind of act it is because of its end. In the course of the discussion, he mentions that a human act may be classified as natural as well as moral. This is not, as the context may invite us to expect, a distinction between the human act and the act of a man.[5] Rather, Thomas is distinguishing the act as abstracted from its

3. The two claims mentioned are to be found in T. Belmans, "Au croisement des chemins en morale fondamentale," *Revue thomiste* 89, 2 (April–June 1989), pp. 246–78. For convenience I will in future cite this article as: Belmans, *Croisement.*

4. Cf. Belmans, *Croisement,* p. 276.

5. "Illae ergo actiones proprie humanae dicuntur, quae ex voluntate deliberata procedunt. Si quae autem aliae actiones homini conveniant, possunt dici quidem *hominis* actiones, sed non proprie humanae, cum non sint hominis inquantum est homo" (IaIIae, q.1, a.1, c).

moral quality and the act as either morally good or bad. Both the murderer and the public executioner kill a man, and killing a man can be described in abstraction from that which makes the former an act of injustice and the latter an act of justice. What is added to the *species naturae* that enables us to assign a moral character to it is the end of the agent.[6]

This text, taken by itself, invites misinterpretation, since it will be some pages before Thomas returns to the discussion of the sources of the moral qualities of the human act. The misinterpretation Theo Belmans has in mind is this: acts taken just as such have no moral quality; whatever moral quality they have derives from the purpose for which they are done. Isn't that what the text says? Killing a man is morally good or bad depending on the end. The text does indeed say this, but its meaning will be missed if "end" is understood as the purpose of the agent (*finis operantis*). Thomas guards against this interpretation by distinguishing, at the beginning of the passage, proximate and remote ends. The proximate end is also called the object of the act, that which is deliberately done, whatever further purpose one may have in mind.[7]

6. "Ad tertium dicendum quod idem actus numero, secundum quod semel egreditur ab agente, non ordinatur nisi ad unum finem proximum, a quo habet speciem: sed potest ordinari ad plures fines remotos, quorum unus est finis alterius. Possibile tamen est quod unus actus secundum speciem naturae, ordinetur ad diversos fines voluntatis: sicut hoc ipsum quod est occidere hominem, quod est idem secundum speciem naturae, potest ordinari sicut in finem ad conservationem iustitiae, et ad satisfaciendum irae. Et ex hoc erunt diversi actus secundum speciem moris: quia uno modo erit actus virtutis, alio modo erit actus vitii. Non enim motus recipit speciem ab eo quod est terminus per accidens, sed solum ab eo quod est terminus per se. Fines autem morales accidunt rei naturali; et e converso ratio naturalis finis accidit morali. Et ideo nihil prohibet actus qui sunt iidem secundum speciem naturae, esse diversos secundum speciem moris, et e converso" (IaIIae, q.1, a.3, ad 3m). Just as murder and just punishment are accomplished by killing a man, so just punishment can be achieved through killing a man or imprisoning him and murder by revolver or knife.

7. "Actus aliquis habet duplicem finem: scilicet proximum finem qui est objectum ejus, et remotum quem agens intendit" *In II Sent.,* d.36, q.1, a.5, ad 5m: "Duplex est finis, proximus et remotus. Finis proximus actus idem est quod objectum est ab hoc

Nonetheless, many have suggested that the thing done, the object of the act, is identical with the act as naturally characterized (the *species naturae*), and that its moral specification comes from the end in the sense of the remote end. That the act as naturally considered may involve good or evil is true enough, it is allowed, but this is ontic or premoral evil, which is accidental to the moral specification of the act. For example, sexual intercourse may go well or badly from the point of view of being a reproductive act: it may or may not achieve that natural goal. But good or evil on that level carries no moral weight. The morally good and the morally bad act may involve either ontic good or ontic evil, but the moral appraisal appeals to the end the agents have in mind when they act. So goes the interpretation. Everything depends, of course, on what is meant by "end" and, when it means the subjective purpose of the agents, we have the misinterpretation against which Theo Belmans has been arguing throughout his career.

There are more and less crude versions of this misinterpretation. The crudest would have it that all acts are morally indifferent and receive moral goodness or evil from the purpose for which the agent performs them. Since Thomas explicitly denies that all acts are morally indifferent in kind—though when they are, they are good or bad when performed because of the agent's purpose[8]—this crude view cannot be foisted on him. A less crude form of the misinterpretation would have it that while, as a kind of act, a deed receives an initial moral appraisal, nonetheless the crucial and definitive source of morality is the purpose of the agent (*finis operantis*).[9] In this version of it, moral judgments of the object of the act, indeed universal norms for such acts, are granted a role in moral decisions, but this role is provisory and prima facie and must give way to the purely

---

recipit speciem. Ex fine autem remoto non habet speciem sed ordo ad talem finem est circumstantia actus" (*Q.D. de malo*, q.2, a.4, ad 9m).

8. Cf. IaIIae, q.18, aa.8 and 9.

9. A merit of Mullady's book, already referred to, is to see in Karl Rahner's "On the Question of a Formal Existential Ethics," *Theological Investigations* Volume 2 (London, 1963), pp. 217–34 one of the sources of later dissenting moral theology. See Mullady, op. cit., pp. 11–16.

personal and individual judgment in which the agent is influenced by the Holy Spirit. In short, supposed moral absolutes can be overridden by the judgment of conscience.

Dissident moral theology has made us all too familiar with such claims, particularly in the realm of sexual ethics. Even when the ban on contraceptive sex is accorded objective status, it is rejected as an absolute which overrides the singular peculiarities of this contraceptive act as such. Karl Rahner acknowledges that "this kind of situation ethics comes in the last analysis to the same thing as a massive nominalism; it basically denies the possibility of any universal knowledge which has objective significance and truly applies to concrete reality."[10] His own kind of situation ethics accords at least provisional objective signification and applicability, but leaves the door open to exceptions to the moral absolute.

In the article I have chiefly in mind here, this tendency to assign to the subjective intent of the individual agent the source of the morality of action is tracked by Belmans to what he regards as a faulty reading of a distinction Thomas drew between *iudicium conscientiae* and *iudicium liberi arbitrii,* the latter sometimes being called *iudicium electionis,* which is taken to mean that there are two competing judgments as to the rightness or wrongness of a proposed course of action. His target can be succinctly seen in this remark of Joseph Fuchs's about an instruction from the Holy Office in situation ethics.

La question dont il s'agit dans l'Instruction et dans ce système condamné est celle de *la moralité objective de "l'acte a executer,"* non celle de *la moralite de "l'execution de l'acte."* La conscience en effet se forme un double jugement: d'abord sur la moralité de "l'acte à accomplir" consideré en soi, jugement où la conscience peut se tromper; ensuite sur la moralité de "l'execution de l'acte," jugement où la conscience ne se trompe jamais puisqu'elle y oblige la volonté à se decider selon le bien *tel qu'il est connu.*[11]

10. Karl Rahner, loc. cit., p. 219.

11. Joseph Fuchs, "Ethique objective et éthique de situation," *Nouvelle revue de theologie* 78 (1956), p. 799. See Belmans, *Croisement,* pp. 265–68.

While he does not, of course, attribute this view to Dom O. Lottin, it is Belmans's contention that the great Benedictine scholar's writings sowed the seeds that grew into the later position. He has most particularly in mind Lottin's understanding of Thomas's distinction between the judgment of conscience and the judgment of choice.[12]

This supposed mistake of Lottin's is linked with another, concerning the nature of practical or ethical reason. Lottin's remark that the moral goodness of human action is a special case of the goodness natural to every being ends thus: *la morale est un corollaire de la metaphysique*.[13] Belmans finds similar confusions in Etienne Gilson, Josef Pieper, Jacques Maritain, and Thomas Gilby. Far from reducing moral good to the ontological good, which is a transcendental property of being, Belmans asserts, Thomas sees an abyss separating the two.[14]

In what follows, I will argue that Belmans himself misinterprets the sense of the distinction between *iudicium conscientiae* and *iudicium electionis*. I will then show that his portrayal of ethical reason as autonomous, separated by an abyss from the objects of speculative reason, cannot be attributed to St. Thomas Aquinas. Finally, I will argue that Belmans can still make his points against dissident moral theologians by understanding Thomas correctly.

Is the Judgment of Choice a Judgment?

In the *Quaestio disputata de veritate*, q. 17, Thomas gives us a treatise on conscience in which he first asks whether conscience is a power, a habit, or an act. Among the arguments holding that conscience is a power to which Thomas will respond after his resolution of the question is this one:

12. Belmans refers explicitly to O. Lottin, *Morale fondamentale* (Tournai, 1954), pp. 24 and 226. See *Croisement*, pp. 252–53.

13. O. Lottin, "Le problème des fins en morale," *Annales de l'Institut superieur de philosophie* 3 (Louvain, 1914), p. 397. This is cited by Belmans, *Croisement*, p. 254.

14. "Tout d'abord, loin de reduire le bien moral à la notion transcendantale de bien ontologique (*quod convertitur cum ente*), saint Thomas tient à marquer l'abîme qui sépare les deux notions" (*Croisement*, p. 255).

Praeterea, conscientia dicitur esse rationis dictamen, quod quidem dictamen nihil est aliud quam rationis iudicium. Sed iudicium ad liberum arbitrium pertinet, a quo nominatur. Ergo videtur quod liberum arbitrium et conscientia sint idem. Sed liberum arbitrium est potentia Ergo et conscientia. (Obj. 4)

Moreover, conscience is said to be a dictate of reason which is nothing other than reason's judgment. But judgment pertains to free will (*liberum arbitrium*) from which it is named. Thus it seems that free will and conscience are the same. But free will is a power, so conscience must be as well.

In his resolution of the question in the body of the article, Thomas concludes that conscience is the act of applying general knowledge to the particular in order to assess an act to be done—or that has been done—as morally right. As to the general knowledge applied, he identifies three instances of it (and it is because there are many such general knowledges that "conscience" could not have been used to name one habit), synderesis, wisdom, and knowledge. His answer to the fourth objection quoted above has long been recognized as of special importance and, since Belmans's critical point turns on what the text means, let us have it before us.

Ad quartum dicendum, quod judicium conscientiae et liberi arbitrii quantum ad aliquid differunt, et quantum ad aliquid conveniunt.

Conveniunt enim quantum ad hoc quod utrumque est de hoc particulari actu—competit autem judicium conscientiae in via qua est examinans—et in hoc differt judicium utriusque a judicio synderesis. *Differunt* autem judicium conscientiae et liberi arbitrii quia judicium conscientiae consistit in pura cognitione, judicium autem liberi arbitrii in applicatione cognitionis ad affectionem, quod quidem judicium est *judicium electionis.*

Et ideo contingit quandoque quod judicium liberi arbitrii pervertitur

In reply to the fourth it should be said that the judgments of conscience and of free will are in some ways alike and in other ways different.

They are *alike* in this, that both concern a particular action—the judgment of conscience in the way of examining—and in this both differ from the judgment of synderesis. The judgments of conscience and of free will are *unlike* in that the judgment of conscience is purely cognitive, but the judgment of free will consists in the application of knowledge to affection: this is the *judgment of choice.*

Thus it happens that the judgment of free will is sometimes perverted, but not the judgment of conscience,

non autem judicium conscientiae: sicut cum aliquis examinat aliquid
quod imminet faciendum et judicat
quasi adhuc speculando per principia
hoc esse malum, utpote fornicari cum
hac muliere; sed quando incipit appli-
care ad agendum, occurunt undique
multae circumstantiae circa ipsum actum ut puta fornicationis delectatio,
ex cujus concupiscentia *ligatur ratio*
ne ejus dictamen in electionem pro-
rumpat. Et sic aliquis errat in eli-
gendo et non in conscientiae, sed
contra conscientiam facit; et dicitur
hoc mala conscientia facere inquantum factum judicio scientiae non con-
cordat. Et sic non oportet
conscientiam esse idem quod liberum
arbitrium. (Ibid. ad 4m)

as when someone examines something
that ought imminently to be done and
judges as still speculating through
principles that something is bad, for
example, to fornicate with this
woman. But when he begins to apply
it to action there spring up from all
sides many circumstances of this act,
such as the delight of fornication,
from desire of which *reason is bound*
such that its dictate does not issue in
choice. And so it is that one errs in
choosing, not in conscience, but acts
against his conscience. This is called
acting in bad conscience insofar as the
deed does not agree with the judgment of knowledge. So it cannot be
that conscience and free will are the
same.

This seems clear enough. There are two judgments, one of conscience, the other of free choice. The former is purely cognitive and judges whether a particular act is right as an application of synderesis, wisdom, or knowledge; the latter is an affective judgment. The judgment of conscience is like an instance of speculative reasoning, whereas the judgment of choice is quintessentially practical knowledge.

Father Belmans asks us to read this passage, not as a contrast between two kinds of judgment, but rather as a contrast between knowledge and choice: ". . . loins de constituer un nouvel acte *cognitif,* il s'agit ici du *choix* concluant en dernière instance le processus de la raison ou conscience" (art. cit., p. 247). What Thomas is distinguishing here is *"le niveau cognitif de la conscience"* from *"le niveau affectif (ou appetitif, si l'on veut) du choix"* (p. 248). Actual choice is called a *conclusio affectiva* and is opposed to the *conclusio cognitiva* of conscience. Thomas makes clear that the difference between these two is manifest when choice does not follow the *dictamen conscientiae* but is influenced by concupiscence to do otherwise. Belmans rightly quotes with approval Leo Elders: "Il semble, en effet, que ce qu'on appelle souvent 'suivre sa conscience,' comme une excuse pour ne pas obéir a la loi, ne soit, dans de nombreux cas, autre chose qu'une refoulement du jugement de la conscience. Alors on se laisse conduire par le désir, par l'ambition, etc."[15]

How would Belmans have us understand the passage? Among the points he makes are the following. The judgment of conscience precisely as the judgment of what is right is fully synonymous with the judgment of prudence (p. 249). How then understand Thomas's description of the judgment of conscience (*consistit in pura cognitione*)? This does not mean speculative reason. We should understand it as the "purely cognitive stage" of the reasoning that will issue in a choice. What characterizes Belmans's interpretation is his suggestion that Thomas is not speaking of two judgments in the proper sense of the term judgment. Like a number of other terms (conclusion, error, ignorance), judgment is used by Thomas to speak both of the cognitive and the volitional: *il s'emploie soit au sens propre pour designer une acte cognitive, soit au sens dérivé quand il s'agit d'une volition* (p. 250). When choice is described in terms of a judgment distinguished from the judgment of conscience, Belmans tells us this is a case of metonymy. There is no other judgment in the proper sense—*dictamen rationis*—than the judgment of conscience, which in turn, Belmans says, is fully synonymous with the judgment of prudence.

None of the texts he adduces in support of this extraordinary reading makes his case.

Practicae inquisitionis est duplex conclusio: una quae est in ratione, scilicet sententia quae est judicium de consiliatis, alia vero quae est in voluntate, et hujusmodi est electio et dicitur conclusio per quamdam similitudinem, quia sicut in speculativis ultimo	Practical inquiry has two kinds of conclusion: one which is in reason, namely the opinion which is a judgment on things about which one has taken counsel, another which is in the will. Choice is the latter and is called a conclusion because of a certain si-

15. Leo Elders, "Le doctrine de la conscience de saint Thomas d'Aquin," *Revue thomiste* 83 (1983), p. 545.

statur in conclusione, ita in operativis ultimo statur in operatione.[16]

militude: for just as in theoretical matters the conclusion comes last, so in matters of behavior the operation is what comes last.

This can support the denial of two judgments, that is, two *dictamina rationis,* that of conscience and that of choice, only on condition of imagining a choice which is unspecified by reason. What is happening in the situation mentioned by Thomas in our key text is that a person, because of concupiscence, does not choose in conformity with the judgment of conscience. If not, there must be some *dictamen rationis* that specifies the choice. Since, *ex hypothesi,* it is not the judgment of conscience, it must be some other judgment. St. Thomas makes the point in such texts as the following.

Ad quartum dicendum quod ille qui habet scientiam in universali, propter passionem impeditur ne possit sub illa universali sumere, et ad conclusionem pervenire: sed assumit sub alia universali, quam suggerit inclinatio passionis, et sub ea concludit. Unde Philosophus dicit in VII Ethic., quod syllogismus incontinentis habet quattuor propositiones, duas universales: quarum una est rationis, puta 'nullam fornicationem esse commitendum,' alia est passionis, puta 'delectationem esse sectandum.' Passio igitur ligat rationem ne assumat et concludat sub prima: undem ea durante, assumit et concludit sub secunda.[17]

In reply to the fourth objection it should be said that one who has universal knowledge is impeded by passion from bringing matters under the universal and thus coming to a conclusion; rather he brings them under another universal suggested by the inclination of passion and concludes from it. Thus Aristotle says in *Ethics* VII that the syllogism of the incontinent man has four propositions, two universal, one of which is of reason, for example, "no fornication is to be committed," another of passion, for example, "pleasure is to be pursued." Passion therefore binds reason and prevents it from assuming and concluding under the first; hence, while

16. *Q.D. de veritate,* q.22, a.15, ad 2m.

17. IaIIae, q.77, a.2, ad 4m. The *locus classicus* in Aristotle is *Nicomachean Ethics,* Book 7, 1147a24ff. This is treated in *lectio 3* of St. Thomas's commentary, lines 221ff.

it endures, it assumes and concludes
under the second.

Belmans's suggested reading of our key text would have us oppose the
cognitive act which is the judgment of reason to an act of pure will, unspecified by any *dictamen rationis*. Clearly this is not what St. Thomas
means by a choice. Choice is guided by a judgment, which is the conclusion
of the practical syllogism.[18] If choice does not follow the *dictamen rationis*
that is the judgment of conscience, then it must follow some other conclusion, some other *dictamen rationis,* which is concluded from premises
other than those involved in the judgment of conscience.

Can we, as Belmans suggests, identify the judgment of conscience and
the judgment of prudence? I think not. The former *consistit in pura cognitione,* the latter *consistit in applicatione cognitionis ad affectionem.* To be
sure, in the case of the virtuous, the judgment of conscience all but elides
into the judgment of choice, but the case Thomas puts before us, the case
of the intemperate man, tells us this identification is illusory. The judgment of conscience is *per modum cognitionis,* the judgment of prudence—
and of imprudence—is *per modum inclinationis.*[19] It is because the virtuous
man has affective connaturality with the good expressed in the major
premise that as soon as he judges a certain means to be in the circumstances the best to achieve the end, he acts straightaway.

I conclude that, when in *Q.D. de veritate,* q.17, a.1, ad 4m, St. Thomas
speaks of two judgments, that of conscience and that of choice, he means
what he says, and he illustrates what he means by taking the case of a
man who does not follow the judgment of conscience but rather, because

---

18. ". . . electio consequitur sententiam vel iudicium, quod est sicut conclusio syllogismi operativi. Unde illud cadit sub electione, quod se habet ut conclusio in syllogismo operabilium" (IaIIae, q.13, a.3).

19. Cf. *Ia,* q.1, a.6, ad 3m. "Dicendum quod, cum iudicium ad sapientem pertineat,
secundum duplicem modum iudicandi, dupliciter sapientia accipitur. Contingit enim
aliquem iudicare, uno modo, per modum inclinationis, sicut qui habet habitum virtutis, recte iudicat de his quae sunt secundum virtutem agenda, inquantum ad illa
inclinatur. . . . Alio modo, per modum cognitionis, sicut aliquis instructus in scientia
morali, posset iudicare de actibus virtutis, etiam si virtutem non haberet."

of concupiscence, chooses to follow another judgment, one that is a conclusion from quite different premises than those which entered in the discourse of conscience.

Why This Misreading?

One has a sense of unreality in bringing to the attention of Theo Belmans matters as basic as these in the thought of St. Thomas. Why has so sure an interpreter of our common master proposed this untenable reading of a text? Why does he resist reading it in the obvious way, the only way consonant with the moral doctrine of St. Thomas? "De fait, ceux qui croit devoir entendre par là un authentique 'jugement' se sont vus forcés d'admettre l'existence d'un double jugement de conscience et d'enserrer à cet effet nombre d'enonces de saint Thomas dans le lit de Procruste de leur parti pris" (p. 263). In short, unless the text is twisted as Belmans has twisted it, we will end up claiming that there are rival judgments of conscience in the same individual, one of which is peculiar to him and permits him to overturn moral absolutes. Belmans here alludes to a view of which every Thomist must be the resolute foe. It is because proponents of that view have invoked the *De veritate* text in which we read of two judgments to bolster their case that Father Belmans has sought to deprive them of a specious thomisticity by saying the text does not really mean two cognitive judgments at all. Surely the view he opposes can be countered without misreading the text. Let us see how the correct reading of the text deprives dissident moral theologians of support in St. Thomas and thus enables Father Belmans to accomplish his laudable objective.

I mentioned earlier that Belmans sees the seeds of the noxious weed he would root out in texts of great Thomistic interpreters of the past, in Sertillanges, in Lottin, in Deman.[20] But his real target is more recent

---

20. Cf. art. cit, p. 263. From Lottin's *Morale fondamentale,* he quotes this, "Le jugement de conscience qui par définition est personnel, est précedé d'un autre jugement qui s'attache sans doute au cas concrete, mais reste objectif et impersonnel." Admittedly this sounds odd, as if it is the judgment of conscience that is affective, *per modum inclinationis,* and some other concrete judgment that is impersonal. How an impersonal

offenders. Here he mentions Philippe Delhaye, A. Capone, and Joseph Fuchs. Delhaye is quoted as holding a distinction between two phases of the judgment of conscience, the first of which is a "judgment of licitness," e.g., "I may act thus," followed by a "judgment of free choice," namely, "Do it," described as the mature fruit of the virtue of prudence. One wants to know more than this citation, but on the face of it, there seems nothing sinister in what Delhaye is saying (p. 264). Capone and Fuchs are something entirely different.

Capone is portrayed as distinguishing two moral judgments, one pertaining to moral science, the other to the prudence of the acting subject. The distinction is grounded in another, that between *operatum* and *operatio*. The moralist judges the truth of the *operatio* of the *operatum* and "la science ne saurait évidemment avoir le dernier mot; celui-ci reviendrait au 'jugement prudentiel' qui n'est pas necessairement conformé avec le dictamen de la science, pour la bonne raison qui'il trait à un 'objet' different, à savoir la 'position de l'acte' dans toute sa concrétude. Capone va même jusqu'à proclamer la certitude absolue, voire, en tant qu'acte de la prudence, *l'infallibilité* du jugement cité en dernier lieu" (p. 264). As for Fuchs, Belmans has quoted his startling interpretation of the Instruction of the Holy Office on Situation Ethics.[21] By contrasting a judgment of the object of the act with a judgment of the execution of the act and tailoring the latter to the individual, it becomes possible to see the judgment of conscience (or the second and final judgment of conscience) as capable of overriding the principles of morality and setting aside the teachings of the Magisterium. Belmans is all the more intent on opposing this view, because it pretends to find its basis in St. Thomas. Here is the text from the commentary on the *Ethics* that is taken to warrant Fuchs's position.

---

judgment could be concrete in the requisite sense is difficult to see, unless Lottin is thinking of a general judgment, e.g., "*One* ought not . . ." and the judgment of conscience as, "So *I* ought not. . . ." The judgment of conscience is concrete, personal, but, for all that, *consistit in pura cognitione*. And it can be said to follow on another judgment that is objective and impersonal.

21. Art. cit., p. 265. Fuchs was writing in 1956.

Illa enim dicimus *per se* facere et non per accidens quae intendimus facere. Nihil autem specificatur per illud quod est per accidens, sed solum per illud quod est per se; et ideo justificatio et dicaeopragma (id est operatio justa), et similiter injustificatio, determinatur per voluntarium et involuntarium, ita scilicet quod cum aliquid sit voluntarium laudatur quis vel vituperatur. Unde manifestum est quod erit *ex parte ipsius operati* quid injustum sed non erit injustificatio *quantum ad species operationis*, si non sit voluntarium ex parte operantis.[22]

We say that we do *per se* and not accidentally those things we intend to do. Nothing is specified by the accidental but only through the per se; therefore justification and *dicaeopragma* (that is, just operation), and similarly its opposite, are determined by the voluntary and involuntary, such that when something is voluntary the agent is praised or blamed. Hence it is clear that there will be *on the side of the thing done itself* something unjust, but there will not be injustice *with respect to the species of deed*, if it is not voluntary on the part of the agent.

This text is taken to support the view that a judgment about what is done, the object of the act, is premoral, related only *per accidens* to the moral act as such, which is voluntary and assessed as good or bad on the basis of the end for which it is done, the *finis operantis*. Belmans is rightly incensed that such nonsense should be attributed to St. Thomas. He has observed again and again that it bears more kinship to Abelard than Aquinas. The text argues that if an objectively unjust act is not knowingly, intentionally, voluntarily done, the act is not judged immoral. But of course if one does such a thing knowingly, that is the very essence of immorality. To read the passage as denying that the voluntary act is specified by the kind of act performed is preposterous. Belmans's critique is magisterial and gathers a cumulative force from what he has written since *Le Sens Objectif de l'Agir Humain*. Nonetheless, what amazes, for reasons given earlier, is that he should have seen the correct reading of *Q.D. de veritate*, q.17, a.1, ad 4m, as a version of this reprehensible moral doctrine. Nothing in the distinction between the judgment of conscience and the judgment of choice gives the least support to the position of Capone and Fuchs. The virtuous man makes a purely cognitive judgment as to what he ought or ought not

22. *In V Ethicorum* lect. 13, n. 1036. (Leonine, lines 27–37).

do here and now, given the principles of synderesis, moral science, or other general moral knowledge, and he goes on to apply this judgment in the affective order so that his choice is specified by a judgment *per modum inclinationis.* The only time a judgment of the second sort conflicts with the judgment of conscience is when one acts immorally. The dissident moral theologian would have to read this text as supporting a conflict between St. Thomas's correct, purely cognitive judgment as to what he ought to do and the judgment he makes as to what he ought to do under the influence of moral virtue. Such a view introduces a fissure into moral knowledge that is in itself absurd and of course has no basis whatsoever in St. Thomas. It is unfortunate that Belmans felt constrained to introduce a cognitively unspecified choice as his interpretation of the *judicium electionis,* lest he seem to lend credence to the Fuchs view.

The Autonomy of Practical Reason

In the same article [*Le Croisement*] that has been occupying us throughout, Belmans adopts a position on the nature of moral or practical reason in its relation to theoretical reason that seems questionable. Given the foregoing, it is not perhaps surprising that he takes issue with the description of choice he finds in Sertillanges: "L'acte de choix (*electio*) est un jugement en même temps qu'un vouloir, une synthèse spirituelle impliquant lumière et force, détermination rationelle et motion effective."[23] Why should this invocation by Sertillanges of an Aristotelian commonplace, embraced by St. Thomas,[24] bother Belmans? He fears that Sertillanges is guilty of an extreme form of reductionism.

23. A. D. Sertillanges, *La philosophie morale de saint Thomas d'Aquin* (Paris, 1942), p. 27.

24. "Hence choice is either desiderative reason or ratiocinative desire, and such an origin of action is a man" (*Nicomachean Ethics,* VI, 3,1139b4). "Dicendum quod in nomine electionis importatur aliquid pertinens ad rationem sive intellectum, et aliquid pertinens ad voluntatem: dicit enim Philosophus in VI Ethic. quod electio est *appetitivus intellectus, vel appetitus intellectivus*" (*Summa theologiae,* IaIIae, q.13, a.1). Thomas's own more elaborate statement of this same truth is found toward the end of

Son tort consiste en effet a reduire non seulement la raison pratique à la raison theorique, mais toute activité de la raison à la raison *ut ratio* ainsi que toute volition à la volonté *ut voluntas*, ce qui ne rend justice ni à la raison *ut natura* ni à la volonté *ut natura*, telles que saint Thomas les concoit. (p. 254)

He finds dangerous as well Lottin's remark that "La bonté morale de l'activité humaine n'est q'une application de la bonté naturelle de tout être; la morale est un corrollaire de la métaphysique." Moreover he chides Josef Pieper for asserting the primacy of the speculative reason over practical reason.[25] What Theo Belmans calls into question is precisely the primacy of the theoretical over the practical. This is a serious deviation from the thought of Thomas Aquinas, and I find it difficult to believe that Belmans read seriously the marvelous second chapter of the book of Pieper, which he cites. Pieper does little more than present the texts of St. Thomas himself, and the one that was his guide was the well-known *intellectus speculativus per extensionem fit practicus.*[26] Does Belmans wish to assert that the practical intellect is independent of the theoretical? Pieper attributes this view to Kant and draws out the implications of it. "Kant makes the practical reason entirely independent of the theoretical and of all that can be the object of theoretical activity, that means, *independent of all knowledge of reality.*"[27]

---

this same article: "Manifestum est autem quod ratio quodammodo voluntatem praecedit, et ordinat actum eius: inquantum scilicet voluntas in suum obiectum tendit secundum ordinem rationis, eo quod vis apprehensiva appetitivae suum obiectum repraesentat. Sic igitur ille actus quo voluntas tendit in aliquid quod proponitur ut bonum, ex eo quod per rationem est ordinatum ad finem, materialiter quidem est voluntatis, formaliter autem rationis."

25. Josef Pieper, *Die Wirklicheit und das Gute* (Munich, 1965), p. 45ff. Translated into English as *Reality and the Good* (Henry Regnery, 1967), it has been reissued in a composite Pieper volume called *Living the Truth* (Ignatius Press, 1989).

26. *Summa theologiae,* Ia, q.79, a.11, sed contra. In the body of the article, Thomas writes, "Accidit autem alicui apprehenso per intellectum, quod ordinetur ad opus, vel non ordinetur. Secundum hoc autem differunt intellectus speculativus et practicus."

27. Pieper, op. cit., p. 48. It is I who have italicized. Germain Grisez and John Finnis have made a similar denial, motivated by fear of committing what G. E. Moore called the naturalistic fallacy. Finnis invokes the maxim that the essence is known via

All practical knowledge embodies and presupposes theoretical knowl edge. Our mind is not first of all the measure of reality; it is a measured measure. The very first principles of practical reason embody a grasp of being, the proper object and measure of the intellect as such. It makes no sense to say that practical reason judges food and sex as goods to be rationally pursued, unless the agent has some knowledge of what food and sex are. This is not of course to say that one must first have *scientific* knowledge of the world before making practical judgments. The theoretical knowledge that is presupposed by and embedded in practical judgments is the kind of knowledge that is presupposed by scientific knowledge and in its occurrence no doubt looks no more like scientific knowledge than the actual living grasp of the first principles of practical reason looks like a theory of natural law. I cannot believe that Theo Belmans would really contest such fundamentals of Thomistic thought, yet his criticisms of Gilson, Maritain, even John of St. Thomas, suggest that he is embracing the primacy of practical reason. To do this, however, as Pieper points out, is to make man the unmeasured measure of his doings and makings.

Why Belmans Went Wrong

Earlier we argued that Theo Belmans refused to find two judgments in St. Thomas's *iudicium conscientiae* and *iudicium electionis* because he mistakenly thought that to do so would give aid and comfort to those who maintain there is a second personal judgment that enables the agent to override moral absolutes. But no misreading of the *De veritate* is needed in order to make that refutation. In the present case, Belmans is adopting an extraordinary view of practical reason, because he thinks that acknowledging the primacy of theoretical reason leads to aberrations he would oppose. But these aberrations can be dealt with without doing violence to the tradition he would defend.

Belmans takes to task those who, as he puts it, wish to maintain that

---

its powers, and powers are known by their operations as basis for the claim that praxis precedes speculative knowledge.

all human knowledge begins with a theoretical phase or, to put it differently, that every imperative is rooted in an indicative. His reference is to Josef Pieper.

> Or ce n'est pas l'Aquinate qui parle ainsi. Selon lui, non seulement le processus intellectuel conduisant au choix part d'un premier principe nettement distinct de celui qui nourrit le savoir théorique, si bien que toute tentative de reduire le principe en cause (*bonum est faciendum, maulum vitandum*) au principe speculatif de non-contradiction se trouve d'avance condamnée à échouer, mais l'analyse dudit processus révèle déjà le caractère pratique des diverse phases alleguées par lui. (p. 257–58)

Surely Father Belmans would not care to deny that the first principle of practical reason presupposes the principle of contradiction. That is, the precept, "Do good and do not do good, avoid evil and do not avoid evil" presumably self-destructs because it gives contradictory advice. No more could Father Belmans wish to deny that *bonum addit rationem appetibilis supra ens.*[28] His excellent account of the phases of practical reasoning—*consilium, judicium, praeceptum*—loses nothing by acknowledging the fundamental Thomistic teaching that theoretical reason becomes practical *extensione.*[29]

What has driven him to such extremes is his desire to preserve the character of practical reason. It is his view that others read Thomas as if he taught that practical reason were simply theoretical reason plus will,

---

28. *Summa theologiae,* Ia, q.16, a.3, c.

29. Cf. Theo Belmans, "Le 'Volontarisme' de Saint Thomas d'Aquin," *Revue Thomiste* 85, 2 (1985), pp. 181–96, esp. 183. In the article we are chiefly concerned with ("Au croisement des chemins en morale fondamentale"), in note 39, Father Belmans notes that in IaIIae, q.153, a.5, St. Thomas places *apprehensio* or *simplex intelligentia* before the triad *consilium, judicium, praeceptum,* and remarks, "Etant donné que le Maître parle à ce propos d'une fin saisie *ut bonum,* il n'y a aucun doute que c'est déjà la raison pratique (*in agendis*) qui est en cause—quoi qu'en ait écrit J. M. Ramirez, *De actibus humanis,* Madrid, 1972." But again, the grasp of something *ut bonum* presupposes the grasp of it *ut ens.* Furthermore, "good" must be a descriptive term in order to be used prescriptively. Statements like "Guinness is good for you" are either true or false, and it is from that truth that the prescriptive takes its force. Practical reason depends upon theoretical knowledge of the world and of ourselves.

and that thus it is the human will that is formal to practical reasoning.[30] Such an interpretation clearly runs counter to what Thomas says, but recognizing this should not lead to dismissing Gilson, for example, when he says that it is will that supplies the motor to practical reasoning. It is appetite specified by the end, taking delight in it and intending it, that prompts reason to go into those other phases Father Belmans has so magisterially described. What Father Belmans thinks he finds in a number of writers is the suggestion that it is because one wills it that something is a good. But his point is obscured, I think, when he berates Gilson and others for noting the role that will plays in the phases of practical reasoning, as if Gilson were making the absurd claim that something is or is not perfective of me simply because I will it or not. The will is a cause in the order of exercise, not of specification; its specification always comes from intellect.

Conclusion

It is not as an empty formality that I end by emphasizing the debt I believe we are all under to Father Theo Belmans for the penetrating work that he has done in moral theology. He has rightly never shrunk from criticizing his fellow Thomists when he felt they were in error. Indeed, that fact has made me less reluctant to draw attention to what I take to be the flaws in the article that has occupied me here. If on the points discussed here he has erred in the way alleged, this scarcely calls into question the value and solidity of his *oeuvre* taken as a whole. Who among us has been so diligent in addressing a theory of moral decision that erodes the very foundation of Christian morality? "Une théorie de plus en plus répandue voudrait nous faire croire, en effet, que ce qui décide en dernière instance de la moralité d'un agir serait tout simplement la conscience ou bonne foi de chacun—et que ceux qui s'obstineraient à nous 'inculquer des norme objectives' auraient manqué le train de l'évolution" (p. 276). Theo Belmans's critique of that theory has been in the main decisive and

---

30. "Coniunctio intellectus ad voluntatem non facit intellectum practicum, sed *ordinatio eius ad opus.*"—*In III Sent.,* d.23, q.2, a.3, sol.2, ad 3m.

telling. It is because I would not want the strength of his critique weak-
ened that I have, in a spirit of fellowship, brought forward the matters
discussed in this essay. Belmans has insisted over and over again on the
centrality of the *finis operis* in the analysis of the moral act, rejecting the
view that it is simply the *finis operantis* that decides. My chapter title is
taken from some lines of T. S. Eliot's *Murder in the Cathedral*, the drama
about St. Thomas Becket.

> The last temptation is the greatest treason,
> To do the right deed for the wrong reason.

Without the *sens objectif de l'agir humain*, on which Theo Belmans has
insisted, Eliot's lines would be devoid of meaning.

Index

Aquinas on Human Action
was composed in 11.5/14 Granjon
by Brevis Press, Bethany, Connecticut;
printed and bound by Braun-Brumfield,
Inc., Ann Arbor, Michigan; and designed
and produced by Kachergis Book Design,
Pittsboro, North Carolina.